AN ASTONISHING FELLOW

AN ASTONISHING FELLOW

The Life of General Sir Robert Wilson,
K.M.T., M.P.

Ian Samuel

British Library Cataloguing in Publication Data.

Samuel, Ian
   An astonishing fellow.
   1. Wilson, *Sir* Robert, *1777–1849*
I. Title
   355.3'32'0924   DC146.W7

   ISBN 0-946041-35-0

Published by The Kensal Press
Kensal House, Abbotsbrook, Bourne End, Bucks.

Typeset by Sprint, Beckenham.

Printed and bound in Great Britain by
Hollen Street Press, Slough, Berkshire.

Acknowledgements

I could not have written this book without Miles Izzard's help in going through the thousands of Wilson's papers in the British Library, many of them barely legible, and I am duly grateful to him; also to my grand-daughter Emma Samuel for drawing the maps.

I have received good advice and, most important of all, encouragement from many friends.

Contents

Preface

This book is for the general reader who is interested in the by-ways of history and the odd characters who lurk there. General Sir Robert Wilson was certainly one of them. He favoured the Light Cavalry approach to life and politics as well as war – draw your sword, shout 'huzzah' and charge. This got him into serious trouble – and out again. He saw all the world as a stage and played his parts in Brazil and Flanders, Egypt and South Africa, Portugal and Spain, Germany, Russia, Italy and France. For years he was the star of the Southwark hustings and had a supporting role at Westminster. As in an adventure story in which we wonder what will happen next, Wilson's career hurries us along the high roads and by-roads of British and European history at a vital formative period, that of the Napoleonic Wars and the Reform Bill.

He deserves a biography. But he has already had two: one, published over fifty years ago by Professor Costigan of the University of Wisconsin, and another published in 1978 by the distinguished military historian, Michael Glover. The former calls Wilson a 'Soldier of Fortune,' which does not seem to me to be either accurate or fair; and the latter is entitled 'A Very Slippery Fellow'. Neither of these biographers appears to like his subject and I do not think that they have done him justice. Slippery Wilson certainly could be (the epithet was Wellington's) and he could behave irresponsibly and shabbily at times. But he was a lot of other things too – brave, patriotic, humane, charming, good company and so on – and I think that it was from among his better qualities that his inconsistencies mainly sprang, and not only from his undoubted compulsion to win what he called 'consideration.'

My narrative concentrates on the active parts of Wilson's military and political life, covering the intervals only briefly. After his astonishing performance over the Reform Bill, his life was uneventful and his last twenty years are covered in half as many pages. I have given short and simple accounts of the political and military events which led to the various situations and predicaments in which Wilson found himself, and I have described the battles in which he distinguished himself without overburdening the general reader with tactical detail. I have, however, included such small, everyday, humdrum, personal details as are available, in order to get behind the medals and the warts, the slipperiness and the astonishment of the public figure. Unfortunately no private, personal papers survive, which means that we know little of Wilson's life with the beautiful Jemima and their thirteen children.

For all his faults, I should have liked to have known Wilson: and if I had known him, I am sure that I should have liked him.

CHAPTER ONE

An Exceeding Fine Boy

In 1862 a clergyman named Herbert Randolph published the first part of a Life of his uncle and father-in-law, General Sir Robert Wilson, beginning the work with the General's Last Will and Testament. This unusual chronology was in keeping with the strangeness and contradictions of Wilson's eventful career. He was twice married, once at Gretna Green and once at St George's, Hanover Square, but to the same woman. He cultivated the friendship of imperial and royal despots and yet supported liberal causes all over Europe and South America. He ended his life a full general in the British Army, but was once summarily dismissed from it. He was present at many of the greatest battles of the Napoleonic era, but as a general he never commanded more than a few thousand Portuguese and Spaniards. He held, and frequently wore, the Orders of Maria Theresa, St George of Russia, St Anne of Russia, the Tower and Sword of Portugal, the Red Eagle of Prussia, the Crescent of Turkey and the Saxon Order of Merit, but he never received a decoration of any kind from his own country, and even his knighthood was conferred by the Holy Roman Emperor. He combined love of war, a fascination with battle, with a deep humanity which got him into trouble, indeed into gaol, and in his first campaign nearly cost him his life. He was an early and ardent opponent of flogging in the army and yet a firm disciplinarian. His judgement could be very wrong, but it was sometimes prophetic and sound. He was as courageous, and as unpredictable, in politics as he was in battle. He was a competent military historian and, by all accounts, a charming and attractive man. In spite of his oddities and his immoderation, he neither bore nor excited malice. Even Napoleon forgave him in the end, as he forgave Napoleon. On two or three occasions he played a key role in the events of his time and his name occurs frequently in historical books, though often only in footnotes.

Stendhal and Tolstoy mention him. For all his abilities, he never quite reached the heights. Not only was he erratic and partisan, but there was something in his temperament which held him back from final achievement. When the summit was only a few feet away he turned aside. But in his death his country gave him his due, for he is buried, beside his wife Jemima, in Westminster Abbey. He is probably the only one there who ever had water-fights with the Tsar of Russia.

Wilson was born on 17th August 1777 in London. His father, Benjamin Wilson, was a distinguished man, in some ways as improbable as his son, who achieved fame both as a portrait painter and an electrician. His family came originally from Leeds where they were substantial merchants. Benjamin's father lost most of his money, though fortunately not before a painter employed to decorate his house with murals had given young Benjamin his first lessons in painting. Having decided to try his fortune in London, the young man got there by wagon and on foot and was given shelter by friends of the family. He had only two guineas in the world and he claims that by living on bread and milk he made this last for twelve months. It is also suspected that he lived a good deal on his friends. He worked as a clerk for three half-crowns a week and saved two of them. He painted assiduously and was noticed by Hogarth and others. But he felt uneasy in such company because of his lack of education. So he began systematically to put this right. The list of authors that he set himself to read is formidable and tends notbly towards the scientific. In pursuing his scientific interests Wilson made the acquaintance of a Mr Watson who conducted experiments in electricity, one of which, we are told, was a method of demonstrating "the velocity of the fluid" by passing it through a length of lark-spit. Young Wilson thought this silly and suggested using wire.

Before long he was a considerable figure in the worlds of art and science, reading papers before the Royal Society, disputing with Benjamin Franklin over the best shape for the end of a lightning-conductor, and painting the portraits of his eminent friends, including Lord Chesterfield and David Garrick. At the age of fifty he married a Miss Heatherington, who is described as being of good birth but with no dowry except her rare beauty and her many virtues. They had seven children, of whom Robert Thomas was the fourth. Benjamin's professional and social success mounted steadily, so that before long he was to be seen at Court, chatting to George III and his Queen about painting. Several learned societies in Europe recognised his scientific work. He also had a reputation for candour, and despite his delight in the society of the great, he did not hesitate to contradict them if he thought they were wrong.

At the age of three young Robert acquired the first of his many royal friends. As the family were passing the Queen's apartments at Windsor, the King greeted Benjamin from a window and asked whether the children were his. He then called the Queen to see "Bob" who, it is recorded, declined to remove his hat. A few days later the King introduced Bob to his suite as "an exceeding fine boy". These compliments are admittedly taken from family sources, but there seems no doubt that from his early days Robert Wilson was a fine and attractive figure, physically powerful and spirited. To these attributes he added more than a dash of knight-errancy; at Westminster School he found that his elder brother was being bullied, so in his defence he fought thirty-one boys, one after the other. It would be reasonable to dismiss this sort of thing as the indulgent reminiscences of an admiring family, were it not for the fact that the rest of his life affords many instances of what must have been a genuine revulsion against seeing anyone beaten down, even Napoleon himself. He was combative to a fault at the outset, but he could not sustain hatred for long.

Benjamin Wilson died in 1788 when Robert was eleven years old. He must have left his son a reasonable inheritance and he certainly left him some advice: the boy should not go into the army; he should not marry before he was thirty-five; he should make the law his profession; and he should make Parliament 'the object of a patriotic ambition.' In the event only one of these injunctions was obeyed. Benjamin had predicted that his wife would not survive him two years and had told her so. This evidently made an impression on her mind and she duly died within the prescribed time. On his father's death Robert was removed from Westminster to Winchester where one of his school fellows was the future Sir Sidney Smith. Attracted to English literature he wrote a tragedy called *Alonzo* which his brothers and sisters acted. Alonzo was a tyrant whom the author 'had the pleasure of slaying as such'. The knight-errant was already in evidence, and so was the combativeness, for at about this time he had a quarrel with his guardian about his allowance. That gentleman 'sternly withheld those pecuniary supplies which custom rendered indispensable' and he did so 'in consequence of his unreasonable resistance to the habits of time'. Most schoolboys sooner or later detect these symptoms in their elders but few would bother to record them thirty years later. Wilson did so in a fragment of autobiography which gives an account of his life until towards the end of his first campaign in 1794.

From Winchester he went to be the pupil of the Reverend Mr Thompson of Tottenham Court Chapel, but he does not say what he was supposed to be learning. He helped Mr Thompson with his burial services and through the good offices of an apothecary and surgeon he was able to witness several dissections. But his real higher education was taking place in the house of Mr Bosville, a former army officer who had resigned his commission rather than fight against American independence. He had travelled a great deal in Europe and met many of the most eminent men of his time. At this period he had established something of a salon, partly at his own table in the Piazza coffee-house, and partly in his house in Welbeck Street. Here the Opposition and Radical leaders were welcome – Fox, Grey, Sheridan, Burdett, even Tom Paine and Parson East, whom Wilson described as the most instructive and wit-exciting companion he ever knew. Young Wilson was appointed reader of the *Courier*, an evening paper which during the early part of the French Revolution carried a great deal of news about what was going on in Paris and on the battle-fronts. Wilson leaves no doubt that his outlook on the world was formed by this society. 'It was impossible', he wrote, 'in a circle so gifted with intelligence and intellectually communicative not to acquire knowledge, habits of thinking and manly tendencies. It was a hot-bed for a young mind.'

After being rebuked by Mr Thompson for his carelessness in setting his night-cap on fire, Wilson decided he had had enough of 'pedagogue government', and his thoughts turned towards the army, not, he says rather cryptically, in spite of his father's advice, but because of it. The attractions of a military career were further increased for this independent young mind by the advice of Colonel Bosville of the

Coldstream Guards, who was Mr Bosville's brother and had recently married Wilson's sister Fanny. The colonel not only advised against the army as being 'a bad profession for profit, unfavourable for the intellect and destructive of an independent spirit', but proved his point by being killed in action at Landrecies only a few months after his marriage. This, and the cheers of the crowd as the Guards marched by, decided the matter and the boy told Mr Bosville that he should consider him as one of those glory-hunters who, in Bosville's phrase, were 'the derision of philosophy and the plague of humanity.'

As he was a ward in chancery there would have been difficulty in getting money released for the purchase of a commission, so strings had to be pulled. He obtained an introduction to the acting Commander-in-chief, Lord Amherst, and asked to be given a commission in one of the regiments then in Flanders. However, the gift of commissions was reserved for the Duke of York, so Amherst advised Wilson to petition the King. Wilson himself drafted a memorial which recalled his father's friendship with His Majesty and presented it in person as the King was entering the Chapel at Windsor. He was later told that the King had suggested that he should go to Flanders and that 'Frederick would look after him.' This was enough for Wilson. He brushed aside those who warned him not to put his trust in princes, borrowed £160 from his sister Fanny, and acquired, on tick, an English mare and a 'serviceable horse' together with the groom who had looked after them ('a civil brave fellow but with his head too weak for his love of strong liquor.') Thus equipped and accompanied by his two scotch terriers, he set off for the wars. He did not, for this was 1794, acquire any military training.

On the Dover-Ostend packet young Wilson exercised his gift for easy friendship on two colonels who agreed to take him to the Duke of York's headquarters. Everyone there from the Duke downwards was kind and indeed there was even some competition for his services. This is not as surprising as it may sound, for not only was Wilson a spirited and engaging young fellow, but the cavalry was desperately short of officers. This was because the army was expanding and because the hopelessly inadequate pay and allowances made it almost impossible to find purchasers of commissions. In a very short time, at the beginning of April 1794, Wilson found himself a cornet in the 15th Light Dragoons. He was sixteen.

The army that he had joined was, in the words of its Chief of Staff, General Sir Henry Bunbury 'the most undisciplined, the most ignorant, the worst provided army that ever took the field'. The system of granting senior rank to anyone who either himself or through rich relatives could raise a certain number of troops had produced an incredible state of affairs. The same writer notes that, "out of fifteen regiments of cavalry and twenty-six of infantry – which we have here, twenty-one are literally commanded by boys or idiots – I have had the curiosity to count them over . . . We have no discipline, we don't know how to post a picquet or instruct a sentinel in his duty, and as to moving, God forbid that we should attempt it within three miles of the enemy. Plundering is beyond everything that I believe ever disgraced an army.' Fortescue, the historian of the British army, described the men as 'the off-scouring of the nation, who could be purchased at a cheap rate by the crimps – criminals, decrepit old men, raw boys, the half-witted, the feeble-minded, even the downright lunatics.' Another young officer who joined the army five years after Wilson, wrote of lax discipline, total lack of system and weakness in numbers. Fortescue attributes most of the trouble to drink and notes that the officers were as bad as the men.

Supply was as deficient as discipline and training. Men were without food for long periods; their boots, if they had any, soon fell to pieces. They were badly clothed at the best of times and there were occasions when drafts were sent overseas half-naked on the theory that they could pick up the rest of what they needed from the bodies of those who fell in action or died of sickness. It was widely believed in the Army that you might as well kill a man as send him to hospital, such was the state of military medicine.

How such men, so organised, so led and so supplied, ever won a battle, let alone a war, is one of those puzzles to which anyone may suggest a solution. Wellington's answer was that the army was officered by gentlemen; an unnamed Frenchman is supposed to have put it down to the insufferable conceit of the British soldier which prevented him from admitting that he was beaten; others have attributed British military success to pride in the regiment, the refusal to abandon comrades, a national capacity for dogged endurance and a sense of humour.

Whatever virtues he had, the British soldier needed them all in the Low Countries in 1794. The revolutionary government of France had conquered the Austrian Netherlands, roughly modern Belgium, in 1792 and had declared war on Great Britain and Holland early in the following year. Dutch military efficiency at the time was even lower than British, and in any case not all the people wanted to resist the armies of the Revolution. However, the French were checked by the Austrians, and a small British force totalling about 17,000 men was sent to help. The Duke of York, George III's second son, was in command. He has been much ridiculed as a military commander, and it must be admitted that he was no Napoleon. But he was personally brave and above average as a military adminstrator, who did much to improve the discipline and training of the British army – that is, to play a part in remedying those appalling defects which caused the early British efforts in the war against Napoleon to end so disastrously. He deserves to be remembered for more than the ten thousand men he supposedly led to the top of the hill and down again.

In the campaign of 1793 there was never a hope of a successful outcome because the Austrian government, under the guidance of Baron Thugut, secretly wished to abandon the Netherlands and compensate themselves for the loss by filching territory in Eastern Germany and Poland.

Indeed there were times when it seemed that the British and Hanovarian forces would be completely destroyed. In the autumn of 1794 they retreated with some skill towards the line of the Waal which they intended to hold until the French went into winter quarters. But the French were a revolutionary army which did not play, perhaps did not know, the accepted rules. They did not go into winter quarters. Instead they used the exceptionally bad weather to further their advance. Rivers and canals which in summer formed lines of defence, now served the advancing French as high roads. The half-hearted Dutch were bundled aside and the British and Hanovarians forced back in misery until they reached the line of the Weser early in 1795, their passage marked by the frozen bodies of men and horses lying in heaps along the road. Such was Wilson's first campaign. Among others who went through this terrible retreat was Lieutenant-colonel Wesley of the 33rd, also on his first campaign. He saw so clearly what not to do, that neither Sir Arthur Wellesley's troops in India nor the Duke of Wellington's in the Peninsula, hard though the campaigning was, were ever exposed to such horrors.

Cornet Wilson too had lessons to learn. The first was the need to accept discipline, though he never completely mastered this lesson. He tells us that although cheerful and good-tempered by nature, he was self-willed and liable to resist discipline, particularly in the Mess. This apparently meant that he objected to some of the duties and obligations of a very young officer. He admits that he was 'deservedly checked' and that it took heavy fines to bring him to his senses. But he seems to have been lucky in his unit and to have fallen among competent officers and trained men who took some pains to teach him his business. He needed to learn fast, for within three weeks of joining the army he was in action. He also had his first taste of the horrors of war and was deeply affected. Writing thirty years after his first battle, he vividly recalls the misery of the children, the burning homes and the plight of ordinary people: 'In all the campaigns I have witnessed,' he wrote, 'the inhabitants were made the prey of friends as well as foes.' He is contemptuous of soldiers decking themselves with silks and quilted petticoats looted from the villages and of the wholesale and senseless destruction of the houses. 'The inhabitants had all fled or been murdered; but here and there a cat was seen on the roofs, squatting in fearful contemplation.'

His next battle started him on the road to fame. On 24th April, 1794, two squadrons of the 15th Light Dragoons and two of the Austrian Leopold Hussars supported, as they supposed, by ten more squadrons of British and Austrian cavalry, advanced to dislodge a large French force from the village of Villers-en-Cauchies. The first French troops they met were a body of horse two or three times their own strength, whom they flung back with great dash. As the French retired on their main body, the Allied Commander, General Otto, an Austrian, seventy years old, whom Wilson describes as a 'savage', pressed them closely and looked round for the supporting squadrons. The usual muddle had occurred and they were not there. Otto's squadrons were too closely committed to turn back, and in any case it was essential for the French to be thrown back as they were in a position to cut off the Emperor of Austria who was in the field. The British and Austrian officers crossed their swords and swore to charge home. As they set off at a brisk trot, Otto's parting words were: 'Gentlemen, remember your numbers do not permit prisoners.' The French tried to check the advance by throwing forward their Chasseurs-à-Cheval to harass and disrupt the oncoming lines, and Wilson, riding on the flank, had the silver edging of his helmet removed by a shot from one of these horsemen. But the attackers kept their ranks and the French did not await the full shock. They wheeled outwards, right and left, and unmasked a line of artillery and six battalions of infantry, some three thousand men, formed into squares. The Fifteenth and Leopold mustered about three hundred sabres in all. Grapeshot from the guns momentarily checked the charge, but 'with repeated huzzas' the advance swept forward through the battery and the guns were taken. The infantry was in three ranks, the front rank kneeling with their musket butts pressed into the ground and the bayonets bristling towards the cavalry. They stood till the last moment but the charge had become irresistible and the French line gave way. Even then the Fifteenth were not clear, for the French cavalry had regrouped behind their infantry and tried to stop them. The Leopold took them in the flank and they joined the fleeing infantry. For four miles the British and Austrian sabres cut down the fugitives in what Wilson describes as a dreadful massacre. But when three hundred men are pursuing six thousand, it is difficult to take prisoners, as Otto had told them. Wilson actually tried. He wounded a French N.C.O. who begged for quarter and asked to be handed over to a body of British cavalry which was coming up. Fortunately for Wilson a British N.C.O. who had seen what was happening, rode up, shot the Frenchman through the head and hurried Wilson away from the cavalry, who were in fact French. The Fifteenth continued their advance and dispersed a line of guns and ammunition wagons, before coming up against more artillery in position. At this they checked and turned back, only to find that they were cut off. Before they could reach safety they had to ride through more infantry and guns, but they achieved this with little further loss.

It was an astonishing action. The Fifteenth lost thirty-five men out of about one hundred and fifty engaged, and the Leopold about

the same. The French loss was eight hundred killed, four hundred
wounded and three guns taken. Had Otto been supported by the other
ten squadrons, he would have won one of the most brilliant cavalry
victories. Writing at the end of his active military career Wilson
described the action as "the most daring in conception, the most
resolute in execution and the most unaccountable in its success that
ever fell under my notice." The Emperor of Austria believed that the
charge had ensured his safety and made the surviving officers of the
Fifteenth, Knights of the Order of Maria Theresa, an honour which
carried with it the dignity of Baron of the Holy Roman Empire. It
was this which in due course entitled Wilson to call himself "Sir
Robert."

Meanwhile Cornet Wilson was finding that it was not all cavalry
charges and glory. Owing to the shortage of young cavalry officers,
he was on outpost duty four nights out of five; but he was fortunate
in receiving instruction in this work from a veteran Hungarian Hussar.
Like front-line soldiers before him and ever since, he claimed that the
rest of the army was living a life of ease and debauchery behind the
line. 'While we were keeping night after night our watch with our
horses in hand, or patrolling from post to post, that no enemy might
glide between, the officers of the line were enjoying uninterrupted
repose or carousing without anxiety.' He was right about the carousing
and notes that the fashionable drink was 'strong port wine.' He claims
that drunkenness was not so bad among the light troops and that his
own officers set a good example of sobriety. What shocked him most
was 'to see courts martial adjudging men to be punished for an offence
of which the members themselves had often been guilty at the same
time, and from which they had frequently not recovered when passing
sentence'.

But there were compensations. In his campaigns Wilson never
fails to comment on the women, for whom he undoubtedly had an
eye and who presumably had an eye for him. 'By preserving good
discipline in our camp', he writes, 'the peasant girls from far and near
flocked daily into it, bringing in baskets of butter, cream, fruit, eggs,
flowers etc., and in this time I never saw so much youth, beauty and
fascination combined in any society'. Those girls came first for trade
but 'more generous symptoms soon were kindled and glowed not

merely to passion but to the most ardent affections'. There were also the usual camp-followers from England and Wilson particularly mentions Sally of the 14th Foot who was so beautiful that she almost stopped a grand review by the Emperor of Austria: he and his suite kept inspecting Sally when they should have been inspecting the troops. Wilson met Sally again in the rout at Roubaix and later in Asia Minor.

He was again involved in serious fighting on 10th May and his English mare was wounded in the neck. He records with disgust how quarter was refused to a French force of whom several hundred were massacred in 'cold-blooded butchery;' and with admiration of the courage of the French soldiers who died shouting 'Vive la République' at their attackers. Some days later the Fifteenth and some troops of the Guards were cut off in the village of Roubaix which was itself under enemy fire. Wilson was left to command the rearguard, but a Colonel Blunt 'very generously' stayed with him and gave him advice and help. He needed all the support, moral and military, that he could get. The retreating column was slaughtering the French prisoners taken in previous fighting, even the wounded in their wagons, they themselves being wanted for barricades. 'A disgusting and sorrowful scene.' In Roubaix itself even the Guards were beginning to abandon their ammunition carts as they retired down the long main street commanded by the enemy's cannon and musketry. Wilson and his rearguard were so pressed back upon the main body that the infantry were leaving the street at one end as he and his horsemen entered at the other. But a narrow street with cannon-balls flying down it with dreadful whirr' is no place for cavalry, and Wilson's men broke at full speed down a road leading off to the right, riding through the French infantry posted in the hedges and gardens. Wilson's mare received a bayonet wound in the croup and a musket ball through the crest of her neck. Two more lodged in the cloak-case behind the saddle and another carried away part of his sash. Suddenly the whole column of horsemen was checked and thrown into confusion. Three-quarters of the horses were brought down and the scene was such that for a few moments the French were too astonished to fire into the struggling mass of men and horses. Wilson was up and down several times, but his mare always regained her feet and carried him on. 'It was not till I got over the ditch,' Wilson wrote,

> that I saw the cause of our calamity . . . Fifty-six pieces of cannon, with their tumbrils etc., stood immovable in the road; the drivers having cut away the traces and escaped with the horses when they found the enemy's fire surrounding them. Such was the consequence of sending out as drivers the refuse of our gaols – for that was the practice at that day. It was there also that I saw a soldier's wife take a baby from her breast and giving it a kiss fling it into the stream or ditch, when she frantically rushed forward, and before she had got ten yards was rent in pieces by a discharge of grape that entered her back, sounding like a sack of coals being emptied.
>
> More fortunate was pretty Sally, the pride of the British fair; for when I was assisting in rallying the fugitives that we might at least show some countenance and thus obtain the only chance of safety, she came up to me and gallantly promised to give me one of her best kisses for my exertions. She showed me how three shots had penetrated her petticoats. I soon afterwards procured her a seat upon the limber of a gun, for which she was always most grateful. In my zeal, however, to form something like a rearguard, I very nearly had a serious quarrel; for I addressed myself in a strong German term of reproof to an Austrian officer passing me at full speed, mistaking him for a private galloping away from a post of duty and danger. Our swords clashed, when an old Austrian sergeant who had been several times on outpost duty with me passed his sword between ours and explained to the officer that I did not understand German enough to know the force of certain expressions; saying that I was far from likely to offend intentionally, as I was a 'very good-natured boy.' The officer then addressed me in French and we came to an immediate good understanding; he explained to me that it was not a proper place to form the cavalry; that the infantry should cover the retreat through the enclosed grounds; and that he was going to endeavour to re-assemble the Hussars on the other side where there was offered more open ground.

I felt properly humbled for having been so ignorant and accompanied him to the spot where the surviving cavalry reunited and formed into squadrons; the far greater part of them were in a wounded state, and the escapes had been remarkable. One man had received twelve shots in his cloak, and the saddle-bags of many were riddled with bullets, numbers of which were found lodged in them.

A great deal of Robert Wilson was displayed on this grim day when he was still not seventeen: the personal courage under fire; the knack of attracting friendship and help when he most needed it; the quick temper and impetuous judgement; the encounter with Sally; and the compassion that his love of battle never dulled. His admiration for the French, which may well have been first aroused in Mr Bosville's circle, was stimulated by the readiness of the men of the Revolutionary armies to die for their principles. He resolved the problem that this might have set for him by regarding his fight as being against the tyranny of first Robespierre and then Napoleon. But the solution was not permanent.

Wilson's own account of this campaign breaks off soon after the action at Roubaix, but he remained with his regiment for the next year and a half, skirmishing and fighting from the Waal in Holland back to the Weser in Germany. In July 1794 he and another officer with a small patrol penetrated an enemy headquarters and interrupted the preparation of the General's dinner. But it needed more than light cavalry raids to restore the fortunes of the Allies. The British infantry or what was left of it after the terrible winter retreat, embarked for home in the Spring of 1795. The cavalry spent the summer in camp at Bremen and the Fifteenth did not return until February 1796 to their depot at Croydon. Meanwhile Wilson purchased first his lieutenancy and soon after his captaincy.

CHAPTER TWO

The Beauty and The Captain

In the summer of 1796 the 15th Light Dragoons went to camp near Weymouth, at that time a favourite summer resort of the King, George III, and he duly reviewed them. It was also the resort, in that year at least, of Jemima Belford. Her father was a colonel and her grandfather a general, and on her mother's side she was connected, though distantly, with the Dukes of Newcastle. She was beautiful and fashionable. Wilson met her and fell in love. Randolph says that no narrative of this period has been found among Wilson's papers, adding that the feelings of husband and wife are sacred and that the history of their courtship and their faithful affection is preserved only in the memory of their family. There is therefore nothing to prevent posterity imagining a pure Jane Austen situation – Weymouth, the dashing cavalry officer fresh from the wars, the young beauty, well connected but not very, and the essential twist to the plot provided by the fact that they were both under age and both wards of court. This meant that there must be some delay before they could marry. But the war still raged and at any moment the young man might be sent overseas for what could in those days be a very long time. In any case Wilson did not normally wait for anything if he could help it. Fortunately all concerned approved of the match and a solution was available in the form of a marriage according to the laws of Scotland at Gretna Green. The couple therefore set off from Jemima's uncle's London house in Dover Street and were married on 7th July 1797. On 8th March of the following year – presumably after the necessary formalities had been completed – they were married once again in St George's, Hanover Square. Crowds gathered in the church and in the street, drawn by the bearing and reputation of the bridegroom and the beauty of the bride. Nearly thirty years later one of those who had stopped to stare, wrote to Wilson of the 'day when the bravest of the brave won the fairest of the fair.' Jemima was in fact four months pregnant on her second wedding day and her daughter was born in August at their home in Windsor. All three godparents were royal – the Queen, the Duke of York and the Princess Mary.

Before the ceremony in St George's, Wilson had been appointed to the staff of General St John in Ireland where rebellion had broken out. He did not take up his duties until May 1798, when he served as Brigade-Major and Aide-de-camp. He has left no account of his service in Ireland, which is unfortunate as his humanity seems to have got him into trouble with the authorities. All he tells us is that he 'opposed the tyranny and tortures of the High Sherriff of Tipperary and rescued several victims, among whom was Fox, the miller, from his flagellation horrors.' For this he was reported by the High Sheriff as a protector of rebels. Twenty-five years later he told the House of Commons with indignation and obvious sincerity that he should 'never forget the tears and howling of women and children, lamenting the fate of their husbands and fathers, who were sent either as felons to New South Wales, or as conscripts to swell the armies of the King of Prussia.'

In 1799 he heard that another expedition was going to Holland and he rejoined his regiment. A treaty had been signed whereby Britain agreed to send thirty thousand men to recapture Holland and to pay Russia to send eighteen thousand more. As there were only ten thousand serviceable British troops available, arrangements were made to attract men to the regular army from the militia by offering a bounty of ten pounds to every man who transferred. As a result of thousands of drunken militiamen reeled into the ranks. Many of them were stout fellows who knew some drill and when sober were promising military material. Unfortunately before they could be further trained they were hurried aboard the transports and dumped higgeldy-piggeldy on the coast of Holland to face the veteran troops of France.

The object of the expedition was to re-conquer Holland north of the Waal and restore its independance under the Prince of Orange. But the campaigning season was already nearly over and the Russian contingent had not arrived. The government in London, the naval authorities and the generals were at sixes and sevens over where a landing should, or even could, be made, for intelligence was entirely inadequate. So, for that matter were the forces available, even with the doubtful addition of the militiamen. The command of the British troops was given to one of the better generals in the service, Sir Ralph Abercromby, while the overall command of the allied forces was entrusted to the Duke of York. That might have been tolerable had not the ministry stated that the Duke, whose capacity in the field they had some reason to doubt, was to be guided at all times by a Council of War consisting of four British generals and one Russian.

The disaster for which all this was a recipe did not occur at once. Abercromby's troops, after fourteen days at sea and two gales, disembarked on the sand-dunes south of Den Helder in no sort of order because the navy did not understand that troops needed to be in their proper formations before they could fight. However, dogged determination and the supporting fire of the ships' guns enabled them to gain and keep a foothold. Two days later they entered Den Helder and a large part of the Dutch fleet surrendered to them. Abercromby then turned his army southward towards Amsterdam, took up a good defensive position and waited for the Russians. The French promptly attacked him in force, but were thrown back with heavy losses. Then both the Russians and the Duke of York arrived and things began to go wrong. The Allies decided to advance but their attack was begun by twelve battalions of Russians several hours too soon, simply because they were impatient to go and their officers could not stop them. They pushed forward in one solid mass, yelling like savages and scattering all before them. A good many fell out to loot the villages through which they passed, but the rest rolled on relentlessly, gradually losing cohesion and suffering heavy casualties from their own fire. Soon they were out of control, the French had rallied and brought up their reserves, and the Russians were thrown back whence they had come. The British in the centre were unable to continue their advance when the rout of the Russians exposed their flank, and the British on the left, who were to deliver what in a later war and on another sandy coast became famous as a 'left hook', failed to get their timing right. The battle was lost, and so were fifty British officers and a thousand men, and 2,500 Russians. Lost too was any confidence between the allies, even before the Duke of York took to making disparaging remarks about the Russians over his port. The weather deteriorated as well.

At this point Captain Wilson and the 15th Light Dragoons joined the army. On 2nd October the allies again attacked southward with the Fifteenth on the British right. At dusk, after a long and bloody day's fighting, Abercromby's men had made an impressive advance, but had halted from exhaustion. His troop of Horse Artillery was pushed well forward, its escort of dragoons standing dismounted in its rear and hidden from the French by a sand-hill. The French commander thought the guns were unprotected and sent forward a squadron of hussars to take them. The hussars dashed in, making such good use of the cover of the sand-dunes that they were among the guns before the British realised the danger. But a few British officers, ten or twelve in all, were chatting together close by, and they, closely followed by half a dozen sergeants and a few troopers who happened to be still on horseback, dashed straight at the French. Among them were Wilson, his colonel, Erskine, and Lord Paget who, as Lord Uxbridge, commanded the British cavalry at Waterloo. This gallant action stopped the French and gave the rest of the dragoons time to mount and join in. Every man of the French squadron was cut down or taken.

Wilson was in action again on 4th, 5th and 6th October, and on 10th the Fifteenth captured two French guns that were sweeping the beach. But although the affair of 2nd October could be claimed as a victory, the allies' losses had been heavy and their position was becoming untenable. The weather was appalling, with incessant rain, food was short, and there were not even enough troops to hold a defensive line. Evacuation became essential and Abercromby expected to lose half his army and all his horses in achieving it. Fortunately the French did not realise how desperate the allies' position was. They agreed to a capitulation under which the allied troops were allowed to leave Holland unmolested and to retain the Dutch men-o'-war that they had captured. With great difficulty, because of the weather, the bedraggled British and Russians were embarked within the stipulated time limit. The Russians went first to Yarmouth where they refreshed themselves by drinking the oil from the street lamps, and then to the Channel Islands. By the end of November 1799, the Fifteenth were in Canterbury barracks, not far from Jemima's family home at Harbledown.

But Wilson was at home for less than a year. The sodden dunes of North Holland and the ignominious return had not damped his enthusiasm for soldiering. Indeed they probably intensified his thirst for military glory or, as he usually put it, for opportunities to render distinguished service. Jemima was expecting a child at any moment, but she was the daughter and grand-daughter of soldiers, and she lived at a time when wives were expected to put up with their lot and not to seek to thwart their husband's ambitions or sense of duty. So when Wilson bought the majority in Hompesch's Hussars as a means, according to his own account, of joining the army that Abercromby was to lead against the French in Egypt, she presumably did not complain. At any rate her feelings are not recorded. When the time came to leave his wife and child, Wilson wrote in his journal that he 'set sail with a heavy heart, having left my wife expecting her confinement shortly; grateful, however, for a very happy additional day with her and my little daughter, Charlotte, who happened to be more amusing than I had ever seen her, as if she were to leave a compensatory impression on my mind'.

Abercromby and his men were in the Mediterranean, and Wilson was to go overland to Venice and thence to Malta to join them, acting as a diplomatic and military courier on the way. He sailed from Yarmouth on 21st September 1800 and travelled via Hamburg, Berlin, Prague and Vienna. Two of his characteristics showed themselves immediately – his extraordinary gift for easy friendship with almost anyone and everyone, and his refusal, perhaps inability, to rest once he had set out on a journey. It was clearly difficult not to respond to his enthusiastic interest in people and places and to his instinctive generosity. One of his travelling companions, a bookseller from Hamburg, anxious not to infringe the law against taking money out of the country, had miscalculated his expenses and arrived at Yarmouth without enough money to pay his passage to Cuxhaven. Wilson promptly lent him five guineas, a considerable sum in those days. It was duly repaid. Another companion was the Portuguese Chargé d'Affaires in Sweden, who claimed to be the greatest poet and tragedian since Shakespeare. He too found himself lending money on the pier at Yarmouth, but in his case it was only sixpence to 'a poor Bohemian' who could not afford to pay the boatmen to take him out to the packet: the Portuguese had his reward a few minutes later when he lost his footing boarding the packet in the heavy swell and was saved by the Bohemian from falling into the sea. There was also a Frenchman in this assorted party and he too was 'wretchedly poor'. People nowadays do not normally describe the financial circumstances of their travelling companions unless they are rich: in Wilson's case it was the other way round. Poor though the Frenchman was, he was a man of spirit, after Wilson's own heart, who 'was always gay, even when vomiting,' Wilson noted.

He stayed two days in Hamburg during which he made a survey of the town's defences, as he so often did during his active military career when he found himself in new and important places. Though a dashing leader of light cavalry, he did not lack professionalism.

Travelling by barouche over roads which caused him to break down seventeen times between Hamburg and Trieste, he reached Berlin in three days and found it a handsome city with many fine buildings, but very gloomy. He pressed on to Dresden and Prague, no doubt delivering and taking on despatches. In Bohemia the roads were even worse than before as they had been deliberately left unrepaired as a means of defence. In Prague Wilson paid his respects to 'The Archduke' – presumably Charles – whom he would have known in the Netherlands in 1794, and pressed on to Vienna in his usual manner, that is, non-stop. In Vienna he put up at Wolfe's Hotel where the roast beef was excellent, having been included on the menu at the insistence of Nelson when he stayed there. After eleven nights in his barouche and, of course, the beef, Wilson slept soundly.

The next day he delivered his despatches to the British Ambassador, Lord Minto, and set about achieving what was evidently the real object of his going to the Mediterranean overland. Of course he was acting as a courier, but it seems likely that he had applied for this tiresome job with another idea in mind which, judging by his own record of his call on Lord Minto, was not official. 'The next day,' he wrote in his diary, 'I went to Lord Minto, who received me very kindly and warmly promised his support in the business of my mission.' He does not say what the mission was, but as he spent his weeks in Vienna trying to obtain the crosses of the Order of Maria Theresa awarded to him and his brother officers six years before, it is fair to assume that this was what mattered to him most. Indeed he probably did not know exactly what the award amounted to, for he reports that he was urged by Austrian friends not to think of 'accepting anything but the cross, pension and privileges.' With his usual ease he obtained an audience with the Emperor Francis who 'behaved most graciously' and the Empress who 'was very civil.' He records various details of court etiquette such as – and this reads like the dutiful husband remembering what interests his wife – that the ladies did not wear hoops. He particularly praised the custom whereby once a week the poorest individual had the right to speak privately to the Emperor.

He enjoyed himself enormously in Vienna. Through the ambassador and other well-placed friends the great houses were open to him, and he came in for his share of admiration. Still only twenty-three, he was a major of hussars, with a magnificent uniform, a fine bearing and a well-deserved reputation for dash and courage on the battlefield in an age when gallantry, in both senses of the word, was much admired. He noted proudly how delighted he was to hear people saying that he was married to one of the most beautiful women in England. He also noted that Baron Arnstein's daughter, who had a fortune of at least £300,000, heard with no small regret that he was married. If he was vain for himself, he was vain for his country too. 'An Englishman found universal admittance and respect. Our national character stands highest in the estimation of the Germans, although the ladies find more amusement in the society of other foreigners, from their greater freedom of conversation and ease of manners.'

But his crosses were not handed over and news arrived that Abercromby was on his way to Malta, where Wilson would have to join him. He made final enquiries and was told that all would be settled in a few days. He had heard this before and he decided to go. He went to take leave of old Baron Thugut, of whom he had become very fond in spite of the fact – if indeed Wilson knew it – that it was Thugut who had been responsible for Austria's disastrous policy during the Netherlands campaign in 1794. The old man embraced him and both wept, Wilson regarding this as 'the greatest honour that I ever gained, the most flattering food for my vanity.' He evidently had some awareness of his vanity, but he was as immoderate with his superlatives as with so many other things. 'Having obtained the esteem and friendship of many valuable men,' he set off for Trieste without his crosses. He was again carrying despatches and this time was crossing territory in which the French were active. With communications slow and uncertain, it was difficult to know what roads were safe and what towns were in friendly hands. For the next few weeks he made a series of hazardous dashes in north-eastern Italy, trying to find the recipients of his despatches, to avoid capture by the French and to work his way south towards Malta. Unfortunately his skill as a diarist was not up to the task of giving coherent accounts of where he went or even why: indeed so frantic were his trips and so reckless – as if the land were not dangerous enough, he did not hesitate to put to sea in storms – that it is clear that he regarded travel, particularly if he carried despatches, as a form of battle which a man of honour never stopped fighting, day or night. He wrote that though he detested the sea, his fears disappeared when duty made it necessary for him to embark and an 'irresistable impulse' urged him on. His first voyage was from Trieste to Venice on a stormy night in a cattle boat containing forty-one oxen and thirty Jews, Turks and Christians. At the Customs he used his courier's privilege to smuggle in two pounds of tobacco 'for a poor Turk' who said that it would be his food during Ramadan. Wilson easily believed what he was told by the inhabitants of the eastern Mediterranean; he had the same propensity in Egypt.

After delivering his despatches in Verona, he returned to Venice and was gratified to find a letter from Lord Minto saying that he had at last received the crosses and enclosing Wilson's own. Travelling again he put up at a house in Ferrara which he said was the only clean one he saw in Italy. But the family had a private rule that they would solicit some favour from every officer who dined with them. Wilson was asked to obtain for the father the job of consul and British Resident, a 'post of honour' from the courts of either Tuscany or Naples, the continuance of his job as president of the lottery of Ferrara (a Papal office, this) and a dispensation from requisitioning. What is more, Wilson actually got him the last.

He pressed on southwards through Ancona and thence across the Appenines, suffering much discomfort through having to keep his poodle on his lap the whole time because the dog had been shorn in Vienna and was cold. He was evidently fond of dogs and regarded them as suitable companions for a soldier on active service: when he first set out for the wars he had taken two Scotch terriers; now he had a poodle; and on his next campaign he was accompanied by 'Pacha', breed unspecified. One spot on a hilly and wooded road was so obviously suitable for a hold-up that he warned his servant and ostentatiously primed his pistols. The postillion promptly gave several whistles which were answered from the woods. Wilson then got out, pistol in hand, and walked by the postillion's side, to the latter's dismay. It was notorious that postillions and bandits were often in collusion. Nothing happened on this occasion and the party reached Terni where Wilson was anxious to visit the waterfall because Jemima had sketched it. But his compulsion drove him on and he dined in his carriage off bread and figs. At the bottom of a hill they were confronted by five men with 'long guns.' He and his servant jumped out with their pistols and the men let them pass. He afterwards reflected that his conduct 'was rashness: had there been a contest, five long guns must have beat our two pistols – but then these fellows were Italians.'

So he came to Rome. It did not impress him. 'The city of Rome,' he wrote,

> is a very bad one; nothing but its antiquities can claim any person's regard. The houses are wretched, the streets unlighted, the people miserable and there is a universal want of cleanliness and comfort. I was much disappointed with St Peter's. The building does not look so vast, so grand, or so lofty as St Paul's. Its front I think paltry. The colonnade, however, is very fine: but it has this fault, that it diminishes perspectively in the distance, so that the eye does not recognise the true dimensions of the columns; and the church, which forms the centre, partakes of this apparent diminution. The building looks as if sunk by the cause below the standing level of the spectator. In comparing St Peter's with St Paul's, I speak, of course, only with reference to the vision; the facts of the comparative dimensions are greatly in favour of the Roman Cathedral. The Pope's palace itself – the famous Vatican – is but a poor building.

From Rome he went on south to Naples, entering Neapolitan territory on 10th November 1800, and was stopped on the border because his passport did not include his servant. 'I explained that in England and in Germany it was taken for granted that a gentleman took his servant with him if he chose; that as an officer I insisted on passing him through, and as an Englishman I bade them stop him at their peril. My menaces had their effect.'

From Naples he went to Messina in the corvette *Aurora* in whose cabin he found, as he wrote in his diary,

the prints of 'War' and 'Peace' as copied by Jemima, represented by a soldier leaving and returning to his family . . . They call up many feelings: hope inspires me and ambition keeps me towering. On quitting the continent of Europe I feel as it were a strain on the chain which binds me to England, and which seems reluctantly to allow of extension; but no distance, although the drag may be heavy, can break it. God grant that I may be able to wind myself up again by it, to the hearts by which I am attached to life, fame and virtue.

Ambition might keep him towering, but curiosity and compassion were never far away. In Messina, Dolomieu, one of the band of savants whom Bonaparte had taken with him to Egypt, was being kept in prison by the Neapolitan authorities, having had the misfortune to be shipwrecked on their coast. His treatment had been disgraceful at first, but the intervention of an English Quaker merchant had brought some improvement. Wilson reasoned 'the more countenance and protection he received from individuals, the greater would be the check upon the tyranny of an unjust and unscrupulous government.' He also thought that his standing and rank as a British officer would help. So he obtained permission to call on the unfortunate scientist and told him of the efforts that were being made to secure his release. He offered to do whatever was in his power, adding that his father, who had been a scientist and a member of many learned societies in Europe, would be gratified to see him help a man to whom science was so much indebted. Dolomieu seems to have been comforted by this visit and before leaving Messina, Wilson sent him his pencil-case, having learnt, he says, that he had been obliged to write his *Essay on Minerology* with a piece of sharpened bone using lamp-black as ink.

Three days before Christmas 1800, Wilson left Messina for Malta, well supplied with 'very fine figs', but after five terrible days at sea, the ship was driven back to Syracuse. He described the shift of wind which saved the ship from a lee shore as 'destiny.' He wrote his customary account of the defences of Syracuse and thought the catacombs the greatest curiosity he had yet seen. At last on 30th December, his ship arrived off Malta in time to see the troop-ships sail out on their way to Egypt. The compulsive traveller went to work.

> My anxiety of course was great. I got a boat, rowed to shore, and ran up to the top of the hill of La Valetta where the Governor's house, the ci-devant palace, is. I there saw Governor Pigot and Captain Ball, who instantly gave me an order to embark on any ship of war or transport I could reach. I hastened back nearly breaking my neck in running down, for the streets are a slippery pavement, got my baggage from the *Anne,* and rowed to join the fleet, but could only reach a brig. Mounting her sides I presented my order to the Master. Some officers of the 12th Regiment of Light Dragoons were on board who did not seem well pleased at my coming; but to that I was indifferent; and in answer to their representations that there were already three in a small cabin and that I should be ill-accommodated, I told them that the exigency of the service did not admit of etiquette, and that I was too old a soldier to regard my comfort as essential. I afterwards found them very kind indeed; it was with difficulty that I could prevail with them to retain their own bed-places and allow me to lie upon the floor, but upon this I insisted. I was obliged to live at their table for I had literally not an article of my own: my figs I gave to the mate of the *Anna,* being rather ashamed to carry them about with me – a modesty which I and my comrades since regret.

After another difficult voyage – Wilson was something of a Jonah – the fleet reached the Bay of Marmoris in Turkey. There the expedition was to collect itself before the descent on Egypt and to pick up horses and supplies that had been promised by the Turks.

Wilson lost no time on calling on Sir Ralph Abercromby and was soon dining with Lord Keith, the Naval Commander. He also made the acquaintance of his own detachment of Hompesch's Hussars who received him, he says, with great marks of attention and hearty welcome. They were not, it must be said, a very smart regiment, but were one of a number of foreign, mostly German, units raised at this period for service with the British Army. Although known as hussars and wearing hussar uniforms, they figure in the Army Lists of the time as 'A Regiment of Mounted Riflemen.' Their colonel was a Baron Friedrich Hompesch and apart from Wilson's the list of officers does not contain a single English name, unless one may count Bryan O'Toole. The first thing that Wilson records of them is that they found tortoises in the woods which they ate after boiling them, he regrets to say, like lobsters. But the real difficulty was that the horses provided by the Turks were so wretched that out of about a thousand, only two hundred could be kept for the cavalry and another fifty for the artillery: the rest were either shot or sold for a dollar apiece. Wilson had seen nothing like them except the turf-carriers in Ireland; his detachment received only seventy and even they were unfit for a charge. Attempts were made to obtain more horses from the interior of the country and Wilson was a member of one such horse-buying expedition to the Aga of Cujas, a local chieftain with no respect for any authority but his own. He received the visitors somewhat cavalierly, excusing himself from seeing them first on the ground that it was Ramadan and he had to say his prayers, and then because he had a fever which he was curing by eating ice. Eventually he did receive them, though they had to take their boots off before entering his audience chamber. They retired to their sleeping quarters confident that their mission would be successful, but then 'events occurred which compelled us to keep watch all night with our swords drawn,' for the Aga's attendants 'wished to take liberties which, though not unnatural to them, were highly repugnant to British ideas'. The next day the horses were brought, and fine animals they were; the trouble was that the price asked was a thousand dollars each, though the most that the British were empowered to pay was two hundred. Anxious lest their hosts should be incensed by their refusal to buy, no less than by their reserve the night before, Wilson and his companions determined to leave at the first opportunity. The outward journey to Cujas had been bad enough, involving a night in a caravanserai where a room about 24 feet by 16 contained fourteen people sitting on the ground,

> Greeks, Turks, Negroes and others, travelling to sell fowls etc., at Marmoris. The room was filth itself: a mat full of vermin covered the floor. Here were four English gentlemen obliged to seek shelter. Strange destiny! We emptied our basket of provisions and then entered into a kind of monkey conversation with our wretched companions. I pass over the incidents which shocked us, for we were not then accustomed to the depravity of these barbarians nor had any conception of its existence. They saw our expression of aversion and horror, but treated them with derision.

This was no doubt why at the Aga's they drew their swords.

Because of their hasty departure the return journey threatened to be worse, as they had virtually no food for themselves or their horses. They managed to reach the caravanserai late at night, but the keeper refused to admit them. This was too much for four English gentlemen and their men: they forced their way in and took up positions round the fire, with their backs to it – a reasonable precaution in the circumstances – and kept everyone else away. Wilson thought the four days of this expedition the most miserable of his life: he was, he said 'in the power of barbarians; separated by impassable barriers from the humanised part of the world; exposed to insults abominable and mortifying; in cold, hunger and the most nauseating filth.' Sir Sidney Smith, who knew the region and the Aga, was surprised that they got back alive.

Soon after their return the camp was hit by a terrible storm. Wind and hail damaged the ships and lightning 'played experiments.' Rain flooded the tents and Sally, now the wife of a trooper in the 7th Dragoons, miscarried when the torrent of water rushed over her as she lay in her tent. 'I mention this,' Wilson adds, apologetically, 'as an instance of the suffering which these poor creatures endure.'

At last, on 21st February 1801, the expedition sailed for Aboukir, east of Alexandria, fifteen thousand strong, on board one hundred and seventy-five vessels.

CHAPTER THREE

Egypt and France

Bonoparte, after occupying Egypt in 1798, had tried to add Syria to his dominions in the following year, despite being partially cut off from France as a result of Nelson's victory at the Nile. Thanks to the successful defence of Acre by Sir Sidney Smith and the Turks under Djezzar Pasha, he was forced back into Egypt, and in the summer of 1799 he left his army and returned to France. The French troops still in Egypt were a powerful force which constituted a threat both to India and the Ottoman Empire. They were known from captured correspondence to be homesick and low in morale: so in a sense they were ripe for taking. Strategically the British plan was sensible and a great improvement on previous thinking. But no attempt was made to find out how strong the French really were nor, until the expedition was committed, how effective the Turkish allies would be. As usual, the means provided were inadequate: to assault a veteran army in possession of all the harbours and fortified places in an unknown but certainly inhospitable country, Abercromby had only fifteen thousand troops, while the French, it was learnt later, had twenty-eight thousand. However, if the authorities at home had not learnt from previous fiascos, the commanders on the spot had. Abercromby and Keith worked together at Marmoris to train both soldiers and sailors in landing operations, and the muddle that was nearly disastrous at Den Helder was not repeated at Aboukir. There the men reached the shore in battle order and in their correct formations. The naval support was available at the right time and place, proper reconnaissance having been made beforehand.

The issue of the campaign was virtually decided in the early days. After landing his men against strong opposition, Abercromby advanced along a narrow sand-spit towards Alexandra. If the French had sat tight behind their defences, Abercromby would have been in serious trouble; in the nature of things he had to attack, but he now realised that the French were more numerous than he was and ready to fight hard; they could almost certainly have beaten him off and it would have been North Holland all over again. However, not for the last time in French military history, their belief in *élan* came to the help of their enemies and they attacked first. The British repulsed them with severe losses, particularly of senior officers. This seems to have accelerated the decline in French morale; looking about them they saw the Royal Navy between them and France, and a steady, victorious European army in front of them. British morale was correspondingly boosted, though the victory of Alexandria had cost the life of the gallant Abercromby. His successor, General Hutchinson, was not popular, partly because of his unmilitary appearance, but there was more to this judgement than the British army's traditional obsession with shiny buttons. Bunbury describes the new commander thus:

> John Hely Hutchinson, brother of Lord Donoughmore, was at that time about forty-four years of age, but appeared to be much older . . . Harsh features, jaundiced by ill-health, extreme short-sightedness, a stooping body, a slouching gait, and an utter neglect of his dress, presented in him a figure at variance with every idea that one forms of a soldier. Shunning general society, abstracted, reserved, slovenly and indolent, with ungracious manners and a violent temper, the general was little calculated to gain the confidence or win the affection of those who had fallen suddenly under his command. Yet was Hutchinson a man of no ordinary mark. He was a good scholar; he had read much and profitably; his understanding was strong, his information extensive. Nor had he neglected to study the theory of his profession. On military subjects his views were large; and his personal bravery was unquestioned.

Non-conformity on this scale had disadvantages in military circles. When Hutchinson decided on sound military grounds to mask Alexandria and press on to Cairo, there was, in Bunbury's words, 'a storm of opposition, swelling almost to a mutinous cabal,' the officers concerned being motivated by 'their personal dislike and want of confidence' in Hutchinson. They tried to secure the support of General Moore, later of Corunna fame, but his reply was stern and uncompromising and the movement collapsed.

Curiously enough, Hutchinson's opponent, General Menou, was also unmilitary in appearance, being described by Mr Herold as 'looking every inch the proprietor or headwaiter of a rustic bistro . . . with his balding and greying hair, his undistinguished features, his pot belly and unmartial stance, it is difficult to visualise him commanding an army.' He too was unpopular with his officers, one of whom on being ordered home wrote to him saying, 'Personally, I should be pleased to be removed from the disgusting spectacle of your operations and from the necessity of communication with a man whom I sincerely despise.' At least Hutchinson was spared that. General Abdullah Menou had embraced Islam, though it is generally assumed that he did so in order the more easily to embrace Zubeida, the daughter of a bath attendant in Rosetta, whom he married. Hutchinson was spared that too.

Hutchinson, the slovenly, unmilitary, unsociable, ungracious introvert later became a close friend of the handsome, brilliantly uniformed, gay, charming, extrovert Wilson. But the two men also had a great deal in common: they were both ardent Whigs, both well read, both serious soldiers of proven courage and both, in their different ways, non-conformists. This was not their last campaign together.

In the march from Alexandria to Cairo, Wilson was everywhere, as usual, but not for long at the head of the Hompesch Hussars. He records that in front of Rosetta, before the advance on Cairo began, three of his hussars deserted and 'the corps was withdrawn from the outposts.' Though he describes the campaign in detail, he never again mentions his own men as having been in action. Indeed when he was outside the walls of Cairo his men were still at Aboukir, suffering from plague. It seems that with cavalry horses so short, those of the Hompesch were taken away and given to regiments whose men were less likely to desert. Before the end of the campaign he asked that if his men could not be remounted, and the service did not need them, they – though not himself – might be sent home, and his request was granted.

'By removal of my people first,' he wrote, I have performed to them my most sacred duty; yet I trust that it will be the last that will be exacted of me as Major of the Hompesch. The detachment had been an unfortunate one indeed: but individually, apart from the loss of my command and my feelings on this account, the service had been most favourable to me in every other point of view. Nothing could be more flattering than the attention and consideration shown me by the highest in rank everywhere, and more particularly by the recommendation which the Commander-in-Chief has sent home.

The activities which won him this attention and consideration were those which he was later to display on the greatest battlefields that the world had yet seen. It is not necessary to believe every word of his always high-flown accounts to accept that he must often have been the eyes and ears of his general, carrying out dashing reconnaissances right up to the enemy's lines and ready at all times to carry orders and intelligence to and from the thick of the fighting. He had a way with difficult subordinates or allies, and he was always on the alert for a wavering battalion to rally or a weak spot to cannonade. His greatest exploit in Egypt was diplomatic and bloodless – an indication, no doubt, of the low morale of the French after the battle of Alexandria. At El Gam, about half-way to Cairo, the Arabs reported a body of French cavalry crossing the desert about seven miles away. Although he had just returned from one of his non-stop journeys with despatches, Wilson at once went out with Colonel Abercromby to reconnoitre. Two hundred dragoons under General Doyle were ordered to follow them and the infantry were to be ready in support if needed. In his Journal Wilson described what happened.

I was the first who got up tolerably close. It was my wish to make the Arabs fire on the front and flank of the enemy's column, but they would not venture within musket-shot. I was, however, compelled to ascertain the strength of the column and got very close, when two or three tirailleurs gave me the benefit of their shots; one of which was nearer to me than I wish another to be in Egypt: the man who fired it afterwards told me that he was glad he did his duty in endeavouring to hit me, but equally glad that destiny had averted the direction, for at the same distance he would engage to hit an apple. I perceived some confusion among the enemy, but saw a very formidable force indeed. I knew that our cavalry alone could get up, and that for the infantry it was impossible. I thought of Sir William Erskine who with a very few men took two battalions by only asking them to surrender; and I took my resolution knowing that at all events delay was a considerable object. I therefore galloped to Colonel Abercromby and begged permission to go with a flag of truce and ask the French to surrender. He approved much of the idea. For some time I could get no white pocket-handkerchief. At last a Major of the 12th lent me one. The cavalry, 240 in number, were by this time come up; also two pieces of cannon. I stuck the handkerchief on my sword but when I got near the French it blew off. However, I galloped on and asked for the Commandant, observing everything at the same time most carefully. The commandant, Cavalier, chef de brigade and of the dromedary corps, advanced. I said: 'I am come, sir, to propose that you should surrender to the English. Our columns are advancing against you and it is humanity to offer you permission to go to France after laying down your arms.' Cavalier replied: 'You must, retire from our columns. It is our duty to fight.' I answered: 'Then, sir, the responsibility rests on your head; and remember that it is a dreadful one. You sacrifice your people.' I turned my horse to go away. I heard the soldiers ask whether I had not said the words 'return to France.' I was presently called back but pretended not to hear. An aide-de-camp galloped after me, and said that the commandant wished to hear my proposals again. I repeated them. He said that he must consult with his officers. There was a visible sensation in the corps. I saw the termination of this affair. In a moment Cavalier came up to me and said that he would consent to give up the camels and baggage, but demanded that the troops should go to Cairo unmolested. My reply was: 'You, sir, must have a poor opinion of our judgment or yourselves if you suppose that we will allow the army at Cairo to be increased by a force of five or six hundred men. At length it was settled that they should lay down their arms at headquarters; that all private property should be respected; and that in conformity with the King's direction to the commander-in-chief, all men taken by his army should be sent free to France and not considered prisoners after their arrival.

In his usual fashion Wilson at once made a friend of his beaten enemy and before he left Egypt, Cavalier gave him his dromedary and wrote of his deep and sincere feeling of esteem and affection: he also said that he had met very few people like Wilson. Another officer presented him with 'a costly marquee' and all the French said very flattering things. This gave Wilson 'the pleasure of reflecting that I have certainly obtained or increased their esteem for the English character.'

His Journal was intended for his family only and it was perhaps in order to edify his children that he so harped on the esteem in which he claimed that the English were held from St. Petersburg to Cairo, though he was convinced of it himself. In Egypt he was continually being told how much the Turks, the Mamelukes and the Arabs preferred the English to the French, and he claims to have been overwhelmed with hospitality and marks of esteem. The French had not made themselves loved in Egypt, but Wilson gives no indication that he was aware of the tendency not only of the inhabitants of the Levant, but of down-trodden people everywhere, to back the stronger side and say what they think the armed stranger wants to hear. His own capacity for friendliness would have strengthened the chances that he would be welcomed with a wide smile, whatever might lie behind it. 'The joy at seeing a British officer,' he noted, "was universal and most sincere;' and again, 'the people everywhere fed me with bread and milk.' However, he was not the last European recipient of Arab hospitality who did not entirely appreciate the service. They used only their hands to divide their meat and take up their rice. I have seen seventeen hands at once, black, brown and tawny, in a large dish. This formed a horrid contrast with the rice. My diet was milk and bread. My friend Mahomet Aga one evening indeed took up a bone from which he tore a bit of meat and thrust it into my mouth; but I spit it out again, nauseated beyond endurance.' His endurance improved with the rank of the feeder, for when he dined with the Turkish Capitan Pasha, he 'pulled my meat to pieces with his fingers and I was under the necessity of playing the courtier's part and appearing much pleased with the attention. He, however, very nearly made me forget my courtesy by asking whether I could write.'

Despite this, Wilson got on well with both the Capitan Pasha and the Grand Vizier, the chief Turkish naval and military commanders respectively, and they asked him to stay with their forces. The Grand Vizier gave him a fine Mamaluke sabre and embroidered silks. 'I told him I was a married man and mentioned the number of my family, saying that his silks were therefore of higher value to me. He laughed much at my having so many children; and was much pleased when I answered to his observation that I had 'married too young', that this was impossible as I had only known real happiness from that moment.' Wilson admired the Mamelukes for their horsemanship, though not for their social system. The plight of some Frenchmen who had been captured by them aroused his compassion and he exerted himself on their behalf.

> There are about a hundred French among them who had been taken, and who, averse to being exposed to the shame of returning among their comrades after their *humiliation*, preferred remaining in the service of their Mameluke masters. Yet country is an overpowering sentiment: one told me that he would prefer death in France to the honours of a Bey in Egypt. I am endeavouring to rescue them, and am intriguing at the pride and interest of those who have the power to release them. Last night I represented to the Capitan Pasha the impolicy of allowing Frenchmen to be Mamelukes: urging that among the number there were some clever men who might aspire to and probably gain the dignity of Bey, when of course they would be influenced by French politics. This day I shall use much the same language to General Hutchinson, whose humanity and generosity will induce him to do all in his power.

There were other local customs that displeased him. Like all the British, he was shocked at the Turks' habit of cutting off the heads of their French prisoners, though he reported without comment the Capitan Pasha's wish to present the wife of the French General commanding in Cairo, Zubeida from the baths presumably, to the Sultan of Turkey. The Grand Vizier's camp he found 'a scene of universal confusion – horsemen galloping about in all directions; Pashas and Agas moving with vast suites to show parade rather than inspect their troops; others in their tents smoking, and surrounded by their numerous slaves; firing of pistols, neighing of stallions, dead carcasses, pestilential air, clouds of dust.' The contrast with the British troops, still steady, if somewhat shabby, struck the Grand Vizier. Wilson reported that he 'was delighted at the appearance of the English troops, who, notwithstanding their rags, formed a very martial parade. The Scotch regiments, from being *sans culottes*, particularly excited his wonder.' Inured to military looting as he must have been by his experience of the British and Russians in the Low Countries, Wilson evidently found the Turks in a class by themselves at this.

> The villages through which we marched, and their inhabitants, were wretched in the extreme; yet the Turks plundered all they could even from these miserable beings. The exertions of the English officers saved much cruelty . . . Nothing can exceed the high character of the British, or the love which the inhabitants and the Arabs show to us; but the Turks do the cause much harm. Their thirst for plunder is so great that this morning they even entered and rifled the pest-houses, or straw huts, where the infected people are abandoned to death.

By September both Cairo and Alexandria had fallen to the British and Turkish forces without further heavy fighting, though General Hutchinson was obliged to invest Alexandria and begin the assault before the French agreed to capitulate. On 3rd September, 'at 11.0 a.m. the grenadiers, with drums beating, colours flying, and firing of cannon, marched to take possession of the enemy's lines; the bands played the Grenadiers' March. It was a noble sight. The French did a shabby thing: they cut the halyards to prevent our flags being hoisted on the flagstaff in the centre battery.' Sir Henry Bunbury, who was a contemporary, wrote that the success in Egypt revived confidence and an honourable pride in our military service. The British nation exulting in the proved valour and the triumph of their army, felt once more that they might rely upon their officers and soldiers as securely as they had long relied upon their seamen. The high character of the British army shone brightly forth after the clouds which had hung heavily over it. The miserable warfare in America, the capitulation of Saratoga and Yorktown, and the more recent disasters of our troops in Flanders and Holland had fixed a deep distrust in the public mind of our military men. It was believed that our commanders, nay, even our officers and soldiers, were degenerate and unequal to cope in battle with the conquerors of Italy and Germany. The trial which had now been made under great disadvantages first dispelled this prejudice. Our service regained its ancient standing in the estimation of the British people.'

If Wilson's praise of the steadiness and courage of British troops, of the behaviour and gallantry of their officers and the skill of their commanders seems overdone, he would have been thinking, consciously or unconsciously, of the shame and disasters which Bunbury mentions, and perhaps of what would happen if England were actually invaded by the veterans of Lodi and Castiglione, of Arcola and Rivoli; for it was these men that the British had beaten on the beaches of Alexandria. His attitudes and his language may seem theatrical, but they helped to bring about the transition from the likelihood of blundering, bloody defeat, to confidence in victory. His father, his brother-in-law and Mr Bosville had no doubts that the army was no place for a promising young man: Wilson and his like, beginning in Egypt, proved them wrong.

Once the fighting was over, Wilson used all his influence to get home quickly. He had every reason to do so. His friends had begun to call him 'Sir Robert' and there had evidently been an announcement of some sort in the Gazette. General Hutchinson had mentioned him in despatches and recommended him to the Duke of York, so he could count on a favourable reception at home, despite the troubles of the Hompesch. He also wanted to see Jemima: he had bought eight beautiful ostrich plumes in Cairo and hoped he would see them 'waving this winter on the hand of my dear wife.' With his usual luck or importunity, he found himself a berth on a naval vessel and sailed from Egypt on 11th September, praying that he might never set foot on its shores again. On the journey to Malta, which took four weeks, the second lieutenant of the vessel boasted that he would go up to the head of the top-mast and get down again before Wilson could get into the main-tops. He had picked the wrong man: 'I reached the main-tops before he had even got to the top-mast head,' Wilson wrote, adding, 'I had never gone aloft till then.' At Malta he heard that the preliminaries to a peace between Britain and France had been signed – it was the Peace of Amiens which was to last only until May 1803 – and Wilson was not the man to miss the opportunity that this offered of going home through France.

Before he was allowed to leave Toulon where he landed, he had to spend twenty days in quarantine. Among his fellow inmates of the quarantine station were Fourier, Monnet and Redouté, who had been members of the party of *savants* whom Bonaparte had taken with him to Egypt. He passed the time most agreeably and profitably with them, admiring Redouté's drawings and hearing from Fourier about Bonaparte's alleged massacre of Turkish prisoners at Jaffa and the poisoning of his own sick. Fourier also told him that he had discovered a temple in Upper Egypt 'with the signs of the zodiac so represented as to prove its construction eight thousand years. His delicacy, however, is so great with regard to any injury he might do by shaking the religious faith of the people in the Mosaic chronology *as received* that he is doubtful if he ought to publish the curious fact.' Wilson hoped to obtain through his new friends an introduction to Bonaparte in Paris, but when he got there, Bonaparte had left for Toulon.

Neither France nor French society were at their best in 1802 and Wilson's view of them was much like that of many of his countrymen since – he approved of the women and the food, thought the prices outrageous, and compared almost everything else unfavourably with the English equivalent. He was also shocked, no doubt agreeably. He did not like either the subject of *Phèdre* or its 'jingling rhymes.' 'The former,' he wrote, 'is certainly not fit to be presented before modest maidens; but the French are not particular in this respect.'

He cared greatly for the theatre and made a point of going to plays in the most unlikely places throughout his campaigns. In Paris he found that the great tragic actor Talma had a more expressive face than Kemble but ranted too much. During this trip Wilson claimed to have learnt much of French ideas and French manners which was not to their credit. With the smugness which has irritated our neighbours down the ages, he wrote in his Journal, 'I have some thanks to receive for my representation of English manners, women and husbands. Madame Gallois is a most charming person, and resembles Jemima so much that I could sit and think myself in her company; but I fear that such grace and loveliness cannot long bloom in pride of virtue and honour, in such an infected atmosphere.' At a ball in Paris he thought the women badly dressed and felt that the many diamonds they wore were in bad taste. He did not find a single decent village between Lyons and Paris. He describes that city, which had not then benefited from the services of Baron Haussmann, thus:

> I fear that my judgment of this city will not be deemed honest by many, yet I know it to be impartial. The spectacles, the gaieties, the vices of Paris intoxicate the senses perhaps, and obscure the discriminating powers of most English travellers. I have driven over the whole town, and seen certainly all its exterior beauty; I have now only to examine the rich interior of its palaces and museums. Any person who has been in Dublin can form the best idea of Paris: magnificence and meanness are only more frequently contrasted. The hotels are superb edifices; the Tuileries the noblest palace I have yet seen; the Louvre grand; all public buildings calculated to inspire admiration. But Paris has not a street so good as our Cheapside; all are narrow, dirty, unpaved; the houses old and mean in general, the shops without brilliance, and the tout ensemble bearing a strong resemblance to the worst parts of the City of London. Here are no open squares, no streets denoting wealth or comfort. Few equipages in the streets; but abundance of fiacres and cabriolets. The population seems scanty and both sexes are badly dressed. The women wear a costume which contrasts unfavourably with English neatness and decency in the clothing of the lower limbs. However I must allow that they are beautifully made and walk well.

The ruined state of the great hotels, which are almost all either converted into solitary offices of government or advertised to be sold, gives the town a very melancholy and sombre aspect. Paris is built aristocratically and seems to pine for Royalty. The traces of this bloody revolution are still too visible. When I passed the ruins of the Tuileries I felt a glow of admiration, softened by sorrow, for the fate of the brave Swiss.

On the political field, he found, or thought he found, much Royalist feeling, particularly in the south – France is too great a country for a republic, they told him. The people, he gathered, respected, even liked, Bonaparte, but had misgivings about the extent of his power: they were glad of the peace and well disposed towards things English: the Revolution was cursed everywhere. Wilson sensed the tension and the strain which lay close under the surface of life in France but he underestimated the length of time it could be endured, because he underestimated what the French will do for a leader who not only assures them that they are as superior to other people as they think they are, but who acts accordingly. Wilson's final word on the subject was:

Society is in the most abandoned state. There is no smile on the countenance of men. In short France is enduring all the miseries of the most despotic government and is verging fast to a fall. Organised as the country now is, it is impossible that it can hold together as an empire. Peace, however contradictory it may appear, has been the ruin of France: and within a few months the government wil be no more. The English government ought certainly to grant all the passports that may be asked for. The state of Paris – so different to expectation – the expense, the gloom and the consequent *ennui* will soon sicken our eager travellers.

A subjective judgment, wrong or, at most premature. But there was a lot in it that Bonaparte himself might have agreed with, for he was taking steps to carry out the re-organisation that was so obviously necessary and he was soon to renew the war: he was also careful, when he set up his glittering Empire, to do something about that *ennui*.

However, Wilson was a better patriot than a political analyst, and it was as an invincible believer in the superiority of his own tribe that he at last 'came in sight of our happy land: where all that remains of nobility in man or virtue in woman has found a refuge from all parts of the world.' He really felt like that, for when the small boat that took him off the packet touched the beach at Dover, he jumped out and kissed the pebbles.

CHAPTER FOUR

The Pen and more of the Sword

It was true about the *London Gazette*. His Majesty had been graciously pleased to grant the Royal Licence and Permission to Wilson and his brother officers of the Fifteenth to accept the rank of Knight of the Imperial Order of Maria Theresa. Henceforth he was Sir Robert and Jemima was Lady Wilson. But a terrible blow was about to fall on them both: Wilson may have seen the ostrich plumes waving on the head of his dear wife, but it is doubtful if any mirror revealed them to Jemima, for she was going blind. As hardly any private papers of Wilson's have come to light, we do not know exactly when this happened, but it was soon after his return from Egypt. She appears to have faced the disaster with as much resolution as her husband faced the enemy's guns, and Wilson says that she remained so animated that those who did not know did not realise that she could not see.

In the circumstances it was as well that there was now no active soldiering for Wilson. Along with Baron Hompesch and Bryan O'Toole (for the Hompesch were disbanded in 1802), he had spells of half-pay. The only military employment that he is known to have had between the end of the Egyptian campaign and the summer of 1805 was as Inspecting Field Officer for Devon and Somerset and this did not satisfy his restless spirit. Despite his apparently ceaseless exertions in Egypt he had found time to make notes and assemble materials for a history of the campaign. Within a few months of his return, his pen being as dashing as his sword, he had published in two volumes a *History of the British Expedition to Egypt, to which is subjoined a sketch of the present state of that Country and Its means of Defence, illustrated with Maps and a portrait of Sir Ralph Abercromby*. It created an immediate stir, went into several editions in a short time and was translated into French for circulation abroad. This was partly due to the book's undoubted merit, partly to Wilson's promotional activities, but above all to his bitter attack on Bonaparte's behaviour at Jaffa.

The book is dedicated to the Duke of York, and the dedication tactfully praises the Duke's work in improving the administration of the British Army. As a military historian Wilson performed creditably, describing not only the movements and battles, but also the country and its customs, the hardships of the soldiers in the intense heat, the sickness, the lice, the food. Nearly thirty pages in the appendix are devoted to The Diseases of Egypt, a subject which interested Wilson greatly, not least because it affected the welfare of the troops. In his detailed accounts of the various actions he is generous in his praise of gallant behaviour, French as well as British, for when he is writing of soldiers in action all his geese are swans. The near mutinous opposition by his own officers to Hutchinson's decision to march on Cairo is glossed over. But it was indeed a victorious campaign of which Britain might be proud, the first for a long time against the French. There is some lack of linking passages and exact directions which would explain how the troops got into their positions and why, and this suggests that the book was written in haste, as indeed it must have been. But the maps are good and the actions can be followed easily. His opening sentence expressly ruled out any probing into the political or strategic backround to the campaign, while suggesting delicately that there were things he could say if he were so minded. 'It is not my intention,' he begins, 'to discuss whether the direction of a British Force to Egypt, under the circumstances that Europe then presented, was the most judicious disposal of it.' But if he suppresses his political opinions, he makes clear his love of action and military display, his admiration of courage, his compassion not only for the troops, but also for the inhabitants of the country whose terrible conditions disgust him, while exciting his pity; his interest in new places and things; his fierce patriotism; even his eye for the ladies, however repulsive – this latter trait appearing in footnotes which are sometimes almost Gibbonian. Thus, after Rosetta had surrendered, he notes, 'several black ladies, with a pretty French woman, marched out. A comely face and a white straw hat, with a wreath of flowers, was an agreeable sight, where only the monsters had been before seen.' At this point an asterisk directs the reader to the following footnote.

An officer of the artillery asking how much a black woman cost, mentioned the word Espagnol (signifying Spanish dollars), which reminding the unfortunate female of that term so often made use of at her sale, she suspected a second barter, and giving a dreadful yell, ran and hid herself, but her pleasure was as great to find that her master did not mean to dispose of her. At the Alexandria camp, however, five sailors clubbed and bought a woman, brought by the Arabs to market, for seven dollars; she cried much during the auction, but when her lot was decided, quietly submitted to be led by a cord to the lake, where she was stripped naked, scrubbed well, then embarked in a boat and carried off to their ship.

Wilson also felt obliged to relegate his description of the Mamelukes' social system to a footnote, using a dash where Gibbon would no doubt have used Latin. 'It must be understood that the Mamelukes are all s————, Egyptians and Turks are also; but the former necessarily from their system must be, and when they become princes, they continue from inclination what in their early youth may be considered an involuntary act of submisssion.' His prim disapproval of belly-dancers – 'their movements instead of being graceful, are violent and disgusting distortions of the body' – also appears in a footnote, as does this observation on the capture of some French merchant ships. 'It is but too characteristic of the French, that on board of these ships amongst many other fantastical packages, was a cargo of fans most ingeniously indecent.'

Wilson did not rely on the book's merits and curiosities to achieve recognition, but sent copies to everyone he knew in high places – already a considerable number – and many whom he did not know but doubtless hoped to. The King of England, the Emperors of Russia and Austria, the Queen of Prussia and Nelson were among the recipients. Nelson replied from Merton on December 23rd, 1802:

Dear Sir,

I feel most exceedingly honoured and flattered by your present of your valuable book of the Egyptian campaign.

I really have always said, and I do think, that the landing of the British Army was the very finest act that even a British army could achieve. Aboukir will stand recorded in both our services; and I can assure you that I always hope that both our services will, with pleasure, enjoy the deserved success of either, and that our only emulation will be who can render most service by their exertions to our king and country.

The very handsome manner in which you are pleased to speak of my services demands my warmest thanks. Your gallant and ever to be lamented chief proved, by the manner in which he fell, what an old French general said when asked what made a good or a bad general. He replied, "Two words – allons – allez." Your chief and myself have taken the first and victory followed: and the medal which you so deservedly wear proves that your have imbibed the same sentiments.

With every good wish,

I am, sir,

your most obliged servant,

Nelson and Bronte.

In presenting the work to the Emperor of Austria, Wilson said that he was anxious to make known the brave conduct of his countrymen and to refute contrary imputations put about by an envious adversary; and he also wished to expose the barbarous atrocities that had been committed by the commander-in-chief of a French army; as an enemy of all tyranny and all usurpations, he wished to denounce actions which must give rise to the same feelings in all the sovereigns and the peoples of Europe.

The passage to which he referred was that in which he accused Bonaparte of massacring in cold blood a large number of Turkish prisoners taken in the assault on Jaffa, and of poisoning five hundred and eighty of his own men who were lying sick. The Turks, some 2,500 of them, were spared at the time of the assault, but a few days later, on the direct orders of Bonaparte, they were marched out to a chosen spot, formed into groups and systematically shot down by a French regiment. When all had fallen the French troops went among them and bayonetted any who appeared to be still alive. The basic facts have not been seriously denied even by Bonaparte himself; he merely claimed that the number was smaller than Wilson alleged and that in any case as the men had previously been taken at El Arish and set free on condition that they went to Baghdad, they had broken their parole and forfeited their lives. Wilson said they were compelled by the Turkish commandant to help defend Jaffa. However, it was not the killing of the prisoners that was so shocking – there was some legal justification and the the better customs of European warfare were not always applied to, or by, the Turks – but the calculating way in which it was done. Many French writers have described the scene, including Chateaubriand who claimed to have visited the spot and seen the heaps of bones. He also says that Wilson was the first to accuse Bonaparte of this crime.

The poisoning of the French sick seemed to contemporaries even worse than the massacre of the Turks. A hundred and fifty years later finishing off the wounded to prevent them falling into the hands of troops who have unpleasant ways with those they capture, may seem humane and sensible. Shooting down defenceless prisoners, however, would not now be condoned. In 1802 it was apparently the other way round. Moreover, in this incident the facts are disputed. Wilson asserts that Bonaparte sent for the chief medical officer of his army and ordered him to destroy five hundred and eighty men who lay in hospital with the plague: this would save them from falling into the hands of the Turks and would also prevent the spread of the disease to the rest of the army. The doctor, Desgenettes, was reported to have refused with the words 'Neither my prinicples nor the character of my profession will allow me to become a murderer; and, General, if such qualities as you insinuate are necessary to form a great man, I thank God that I do not possess them.' Later Wilson gave a different version, which he says he had from Desgenettes himself. This was 'I am a physician not a philosoopher. My duty is to preserve life, not to take it away upon abstract theories.'

Bonaparte, according to Wilson, was not put off by the refusal of Desgenettes and he found 'an apothecary' who dared not disobey and who mixed opium with the sick men's food so that they all died. The patients did not in fact all die, for Sidney Smith found some alive when he occupied the hospital some days later, and it was possible that none of the deaths were actually due to opium. Another possibility is that the opium was placed within the the men's reach so that they could take it if they wished. Whatever happened Wilson made the most of it: 'Is there a Frenchman,' he wrote, 'whose blood does not chill with horror at the recital of such a fact? Surely the manes of these murdered unoffending people must now be hovering around the seat of Government, and . . .' The dots are Wilson's and are presumably intended to convey that the manes were hovering around Bonaparte too. In a sense they did, for this story helped to maintain the morale of those who regarded Bonaparte as a tyrant and monster, and Bonaparte himself was by no means insensible to the harm it did him. He had an official complaint made to the British Government – for the two countries were briefly at peace and in diplomatic relations – and even on St Helena he was still muttering about the accusation. The official complaint, as such things often are, was a mistake from Bonaparte's point of view because it enabled Wilson, who had a lively sense of public relations, to repeat the attack in his reply. This was published in later editions of the *History* as an appendix entitled 'Sir Robert Wilson's answer to the observations contained in a note delivered by the French Ambassador to Lord Hawkesbury.' In it he justified not only his attack on Bonaparte but also his strictures on the conduct of the French troops towards the inhabitants of Egypt.

How true was the accusation? Certainly Wilson was wrong about the numbers involved: 580 was the total number of men sick in hospital, but the number who either were or were not poisoned was probably between twenty and thirty. The senior officers present with the French army believed that Bonaparte had given the order, as Bertrand told him on St Helena. Bourienne, Bonaparte's secretary but an untrustworthy source, declared firmly in his memoirs that it was true, adding these significant words, 'Opinions change with the times, and I am sure that if it were not for the immense power that Bonaparte achieved a few months after this event [he became First Consul and Ruler of France], it would now be no more than a historical fact and the only argument would be whether it was necessary or not.' Bonaparte himself always denied that he had given the order, but rather spoilt the affect by adding that it would not have been a crime to poison the men, but a sensible and humane act: if it had been himself or his son, he would have wished the same thing to be done. It has been asserted that Wilson later withdrew the charges or at least admitted that they were based on mere gossip. But no such recantation has been found and Randolph, wiriting in 1862, declared in italics that Wilson '*never did so.*'

Perhaps it does not matter much now, though, as Mr Vincent Cronin has pointed out, the publication in the pro-Government *Times* of a long and favourable review, complete with quotations, of Wilson's book provoked Bonaparte to publish in the *Moniteur* an anti-British and threatening report on Egypt written by a French officer, and this episode may have contributed to the breakdown of the always precarious peace. Certainly the charges did Bonaparte harm and Wilson good. Wilson became famous in Europe, and in England he acquired from Mr Creevey the nickname 'Jaffa.' The Queen of Prussia found comfort in her misfortunes by reading Wilson's descriptions of Bonaparte's crimes and Lady Holland took the book with her to Spain in 1803 to counteract insiduous French influence during her tour of that country. It also seems to have been of some comfort to George III. In the summer of 1802 Wilson was at Dorchester and went with Jemima to pay his respects to the King at Weymouth. The King asked him to go on board the Royal Yacht the next day to talk about Egypt, and turning to Lord Hawkesbury, the Foreign Secretary, he said 'These are atrocious crimes with which he has charged Bonaparte: I believe them all; do not you My Lord?' Hawkesbury declined to answer.

In May 1802 the war broke out again and this was the occasion of Wilson's appointment as Inspecting Field Officer. But he was not the only one who was eager for more active employment than that to which he was called: he shared this feeling with no less a person than the Prince of Wales, with whom he was now on very friendly terms. One evening at dinner at Carlton House there was talk about the possibility of the Prince serving in the army and after dinner the party went off to the Opera. On the way the Prince asked Wilson to draft a letter for him to send to the King seeking 'to serve in defence of His Majesty and the Realm.' With the help of his old commander, Lord Hutchinson, he complied and the letter was duly sent. Perhaps this was the origin of the belief that the Prince apparently held at the end of his life that he had served in the army and been present at Waterloo.

Wilson's non-belligerent service continued for two years and he employed what for him must have been a great deal of leisure in writing another book. Having dealt with Bonaparte in his previous publication, he now turned on his own superiors. The book was called *An Enquiry into the Present State of the Military Forces of the British Empire with a View to its Re-organisation,* and was addressed to Pitt. Wilson ingeniously defended his action in publishing his views in this form rather than submitting 'manuscript memorials' through the usual channels on the ground that memorials are intercepted by subordinates and seldom reach those for whom they are intended; but views that are published are read by the public and if found unworthy, will never come to Pitt's notice; but if the public attaches importance to them, 'they will be introduced under such patronage as will ensure the desired deliberation upon their practical expediencey.' This was simply appealing to the public over the heads of the Ministry, and his Whig friends were delighted. As the book urged the need drastically to reorganise the armed forces of the Crown, particularly the various kinds of reserve troops, and to improve the conditions of service, Wilson may have been right in saying that Pitt was not pleased. Still less can he have approved of a young officer criticising the policy of sending expeditions to the West Indies. According to Wilson, he complained to the Duke of York that Wilson had made an attack on his system, and the Duke, despite the fact that Wilson had taken the precaution of praising him for the reforms he had introduced, ordered him to India. Wilson regarded this as banishment and appealed to the King. His appeal was evidently successful as he did not go to India.

Much of what he said in the book was sound common sense and some has a modern ring. Elaborate uniforms, he maintained, were unnecessary for reserve troops; all that was needed was a grey coat with badges and a round hat with a cockade. Bravery was not enough, trained and experienced officers were essential. The mere donning of a uniform did not produce a trained soldier – though it did, of course, produce Cornet Wilson of the 15th Light Dragoons, a fact which he did not mention. The Volunteers, the Militia and the Army of the Reserve as then organised were not effective. Volunteer officers who had no experience of war should not be given high rank. The shortage of trained officers in the reserved forces should be made good by appointing regulars on full pay. This would reduce the need for officers to go on the 'absolute beggary' of half-pay. Reservists could stay at home and work, doing two months training a year. Every Sunday they should appear in uniform to draw their pay. He thought that the Guards had too many privileges and noted that the pay of officers had not increased since the time of Queen Anne. He had high praise for the men of the regular army and advocated a striking force of 40,000 men ready to intervene at decisive moments: such a force, he believed, could exert great influence on events. As it was, every time war broke out Britain was unprepared and had to create a new army.

All this was very reasonable, but Wilson's heart was with the army as well as his head. He was deeply shocked at the terrible and unnecessary sufferings that could befall a man who enlisted. He pointed out the appalling casualties caused by yellow fever in the West Indies, where regiment after regiment was sent to decimation for no sound military or economic reason; a hundred thousand of the best officers and men had died there in the previous year, he wrote. The colonies were, in his phrase, 'a charnel house,' and death from disease was 'inglorious.' Men were reluctant to enlist because they knew they might be sent to such places. Enlistment for life, which was then the rule, was another strong disincentive to recruitment.

The worst feature of all was the flogging. Wilson was one of the earliest and most vehement opponents of this barbaric punishment. Men were stripped to the waist and lashed to 'triangles', originally sergeants' halberds, and whipped for hours on end by the regimental drummers. The minimum sentence was twenty-five lashes, but this was hardly ever given. A hundred lashes was regarded as normal. Sentences of a thousand and fifteen hundred lashes were not unknown. The drummers were relieved every twenty-five lashes because their arms got tired. It took four hours to deliver a thousand lashes. The cat-o'-nine-tails had between six and nine tails of leather or whipcord, each tail being about two feet long. The punishment was inflicted in public, the whole regiment being formed into a square facing inwards, with the victim in the middle. A surgeon was present and could stop the flogging if he considered it too much for the victim to bear, but this rarely happened. If the man collapsed, he was brought round and the flogging went on. If it was stopped and the man went to hospital, he had to receive the rest of his punishment when his back was healed.

Some men died, some were permanently weakened and some were unfit for duty for weeks. This torture was inflicted for trivial offences as well as serious ones, and by 1812 it was virtually the only punishment in the British Army. Wellington and many other distinguished and civilised men defended it, partly on the ground that only the severest discipline could bring men through the ordeals of war, and partly on the ground that the men were so vile and degraded already that the lash was the only way of controlling them. It must be remembered that civil laws and punishments were also harsh at the time, and if the scum of the earth (as Wellington called them) were flogged unmercifully, so were the cream – Dr Keate, the headmaster of Eton, once flogged more than eighty boys in a day, though he used a birch and not a whip.

Wilson's opposition was forthright and uncompromising. 'Educated in the 15th Light Dragoons,' he wrote, 'I was early instructed to respect the soldier. That was a corps before which the triangles were never planted . . . corporal punishments never yet reformed a corps, but they have totally ruined many a man who would have proved under milder treatment a meritorious soldier. They break the spirit without amending the disposition. While the lash strips the back, despair writhes round the heart . . .' He never flogged any man under his command. Some years later, during the campaign in East Prussia, Wilson asked a young French prisoner

> whether the French soldier was on any occasion flogged. His countenance beamed indignation at the question, while he muttered, 'A blow! No. There is not a soldier who would submit for a moment such an outrage; and if one was dastard enough to bear it, his comrades would hang him like a dog.' How lamentable that such a sentiment should some from a Frenchman, and that a British soldier should be daily lashed to the last fibre of his bones . . . The fact is, that we are the greatest savages and the most ungrateful tyrants that ever ruled over their fellow men.

The publication of his *Enquiry* in 1804 was in a sense Wilson's entry into the political arena. There was then no rule against serving officers engaging in party politics and Wilson, seeing no immediate prospect of combatant service and having completed his written attack on Pitt's defence policy, looked for a seat in the House of Commons, where he no doubt hoped to be able to wage a more effective campaign for the reforms and changes that he believed necessary. He had in any case been influenced towards the Whigs when as a boy he had been so much in the company of Mr. Bosville and his radical friends. The Prince of Wales was still a Whig at this period, indeed he was the great hope of the party, and Wilson was already a familiar figure at Carlton House, as was his friend Hutchinson. He therefore asked the Prince if he would secure his return for Liskeard. He was too late, for though His Royal Highness 'would have been happy to have thrown a mantle' over him, his 'interest' had been promised to Tom Sheridan, the son of the playwright.

There was nothing for it but to go on seeking military employment and in typical fashion he did not try only the usual channels. For most people the performance of the Russian soldiery in Holland, to say nothing of Yarmouth, would not have been an inducement to seek closer involvement with them, but Wilson's contrary spirit was already well developed. He therefore wrote to the Russian Ambassador in London, Count Woronzow, and asked if he might enter the Russian service. The reply was a courteous but frank negative; the pay of a Russian officer, His Excellency wrote, was the worst in Europe, less even than a British officer's half-pay; and a knowledge of the Russian language was essential, since without it, it would not be possible to command so much as a company.

But his time as an Inspecting Field Officer was nearly over and he was allowed to purchase a Lieutenant-Colonelcy in the 19th Light Dragoons and then exchange into the 20th. This transaction enabled him to take command of the small cavalry detachment that formed part of an expedition that was about to leave the country under Sir David Baird. It is a measure of his determination to see action that Wilson did not know where the expedition was going and accepted the possibility that he might after all find himself in India. He hoped if that proved to be the case, Jemima might be able to join him. The greater part of the 20th Light Dragoons was in Sicily, but Wilson threw himself into the task of organising and training the rest with his usual enthusiasm and on 3rd August, 1805, he embarked at

Southampton with two hundred and thirty dragoons. In fact he was bound for the Cape of Good Hope, which, after having been taken from the Dutch in 1795, had been restored to them at the peace of Amiens. Now the Dutch were again in the French camp and it was dangerous for Britian to allow this key position on the route to India to remain in enemy hands. The convoy sailed via Madeira and San Salvador, or Bahia, in Brazil, and was plagued by the hazards and discomforts which ordinarily attended sea voyages at that time. Men went sick and were dosed with medicines which seem calculated to finish them off, though surprisingly most of them got better. Dysentry yielded to treatment with brandy laced with rust from the stocks of the anchors, and a sentry who fell down in a fit was revived by having his nose rubbed with an onion. Sick horses were cured by a mixture of oatmeal, gin and hot water. To get rid of bugs, lice and fleas, Wilson had his ship fumigated with gunpowder, brimstone and pitch. He did not, himself, entirely escape the general infection, suffering from dizziness and violent headaches, as well as from 'disturbing dreams respecting Jemima.' She was indeed much in his thoughts during this long voyage and as he enjoyed the candied mangoes that he had bought in Madeira, he wished that 'Jem and the brats" could share them with him.

There were the usual gales and calms, and two ships were lost when they ran on uncharted rocks. Through all this Wilson went to great pains to keep his men as fit as he could and to train them for the campaign that lay ahead. He wrote memoranda on tactics for the instruction of both officers and men, and made it clear that he would tolerate no looting, drunkenness of violence against the civilian population. There was musketry practice and on Sundays Wilson preached them a sermon. To encourage brisk rising in the mornings the men were awakened by trumpets and kettledrums. Apart from his genuine military zeal, Wilson realised that if his men failed the test of action, his own reputation and career would suffer. For all his royal friends, he lacked solid patrons at home, for he was both middle–class and a Whig, and it was an age when influence mattered more than merit.

He held firmly to his belief that discipline did not require brutality but depended on fair treatment, *esprit de corps*, and the example of the officers. He arranged that a sentence of a thousand lashes on four men for disobeying orders should be commuted to 'a booting from their comrades, who had been disgraced by the transaction.' A cook who stole the regimental madeira and porter was sentenced to receive a strong emetic and to have the word 'rogue' inscribed on his left sleeve. While he was being violently sick the regimental band played the Rogues' March. On going aboard one of the other transports, Wilson found a man serving there whom he had dismissed from his own regiment for theft but without further punishment: the man had 'acquired again a very good character.' On another occasion he refrained from punishing some drunken troopers because a young Cornet had been guilty of the same offence. There is confirmation of Wilson's attitude to punishment – and from the best possible source, the ranks – in Sergeant Landsheit's statement that in South Africa there were no punishments in the 20th because they were not needed. And yet Wilson was not above the ultimate violence, for he declared in his written orders for the forthcoming campaign that 'violence against their persons [the inhabitants of the country] or plunder of their property is immediate death without trial.'

The convoy put into Bahia on 10th November, 1805, to re-equip and to procure more horses. Wilson did not find it a pleasing spot. 'A more abominable, bad-stinking place is not to be named. Filth, horrible figures and ruins meet you in all the streets, which are in fact mere lanes. It is a medley of the worst Italian and Turkish styles of city. The blacks are all of enormous size – few are under six feet – the black women are hideous and display a naked left breast as flat as a deal board.' He set about his task of finding horses for his men with his usual energy, spurred on by the knowledge that if his men were not well mounted, his chance of glory would be small: he had not forgotten the Hompesch. 'I have toiled most severely,' he wrote, 'being always on my legs or on horesback for the purchase of horses; beside the trouble of getting money from the commissariat, and that of writing drafts for payment, arranging for forage etc. I have lost no opportunity of promoting the public service by want of activity or diligence and indeed my own honour is much implicated in the success of my present efforts!' He was forbidden by the Portuguese governor to buy horses outside Bahia itself, but he accepted the responsibility for disobeying this order, when Baird warned him that he would be disowned if he got into trouble. 'I could not,' he explained, 'tolerate the idea of being a mere spectator when fortune presented me with an occasion of being a distinguished actor. 'I could not bear the thought of having left my family and passed so many thousand miles with various anxieties, to reach the goal without being noticed as one of the emulous competitors for the prize of honour.' He found his Maria Theresa cross, which he always wore, a great help because the inhabitants took it to mean that he was no heretic but a Roman Catholic like themselves. He was also helped by being a Freemason – thereby having the best of both worlds. 'No sooner had I declared myself than houses, horses, servants, all things, were put at my disposal; for the institution is held in the highest esteem. 'Because the laws and bigotry persecute the professors with fire and sword, I dare not now mention the names of those who devoted themselves to my service; but some of the chief members of the government have in private made me their acknowledgements.'

Unlike so many Englishmen, then and since, Wilson went out of his way to respect foreign customs and win the friendship of foreign peoples. He did this from his genuine respect for humanity, and certainly not for his own glory – indeed it probably did him harm. He noted the ugliness and squalor of blacks or Arabs in offensive terms, but he protected them whenever he could and all his life he opposed not only oppression and excessive publishment, but colour discrimination as well. In a memorandum on the Cape of Good Hope, written immediately after the campaign, he wrote of 'those who arrogantly and impiously defend the Slave Trade with the blasphemy that the Almighty Creator stamped his indignation on the unoffending posterity of Cain (sic) by a black tincture of the skin, rendering his generations also worthless and abject in mind . . . ;' and he added, 'If they had reason, but bigots never have, they would in future attribute to physical, not to spiritual, causes, the variation of shade in human complexion.' Such views were probably not widely held among Colonels of Dragoons in 1806.

His views, did not of course, stem from egalitarianism or any theories about heredity and environment. He did not believe in equality and no one was less inclined to act upon abstract principles. The root of his beliefs was his horror of seeing human beings degraded. Harsh punishment, racial discrimination and slavery degraded people who, he believed, could be taught to lead useful and agreeable lives. In a book about the Russians published in 1810 he examined the question of serfdom and wrote that, notwithstanding his hatred of slavery, 'the greatest misfortune which could befall the Russian people would be a sudden and general emancipation. No measure could be productive of more misery . . . What would become of the sick, the infirm, the aged, when there was no provision for their maintenance? The revolutionist many startle at these embarrassments; but the statesman, the philanthropist and the good citizen will examine them and respect the consequences ere they adopt the theories.'

At Bahia, not all his companions shared his view of the respect due to foreigners or, for that matter, to honesty and good manners. He says that one party of officers tried to cheat their black boatman of the fare, and that one of his own officers took a crucifix under pretence of admiring it and gave it to Wilson's dog, Pacha. The boatman murdered the cheats and Wilson had no sympathy for them. He resolved never to trust his own officer again, but his account of the incident ends characteristically, 'but I will not urge his ruin,.' To make his own attitude quite clear he went everywhere unarmed, even after the officers' murder.

Early in December, 1805, the convoy sailed from Bahia and reached Table Bay on 3rd January, 1806. Wilson was full of confidence: he had an independent command, good troops, well instructed and well mounted, and he was to go ashore with the first wave. Glory seemed just a few miles away on the beaches and his only fear was that the Dutch might withdraw into the interior without a fight. But everything went wrong: in the end he had in fact left his family and travelled thousands of miles through great dangers, only to be what he most dreaded – 'a mere spectator.' He also had a quarrel with his superiors.

It was all because of the surf. The troops were rowed seven miles to within three hundred yards of the beach, where it became clear that the surf was too dangerous to allow a landing. Sir David Baird therefore decided to send Beresford with Wilson's dragoons and some infantry to Saldanha Bay, several days sail to the westward, to seize and hold a position inland, and to procure supplies and draught animals for the main force. Soon after they had sailed away the weather moderated and another attempt was made to land the main body. This succeeded, though with the loss of a boatload of Highlanders, and the next day a sharp action took place in which the Dutch were defeated. While this was happening Wilson, having landed successfully, was marching across very difficult country, thick scrub alternating with heavy sand, in what turned out to be the wrong direction. The dismounted dragoons suffered most as they struggled in the intense heat through the sand in their cavalry boots and heavy overalls. Once on the right road, Wilson's men laboriously occupied outlying farmsteads and rounded up horses and oxen. One march seemed to him to be worse than the retreat through North Holland in 1794 and on another he put a fainting infantryman on his own horse and walked six miles on foot, carrying the man's musket, his riding boots galling him severely. As typical of the man was his encounter with a couple of Boer farmers who tried to escape. 'I then drew my pistol. I could have shot the poor fellows and would have been justified in doing so, for they were armed against us and the country would by their escape, gain information of our approach; but other considerations weighed more with me and I replaced my pistols in their lodging without regret.' A much more illustrious horseman was one day to benefit by Wilson's reluctance to kill his enemies.

Wilson took his disappointment philosophically, noted that the vicissitudes of fortune must be expected in war, and made his way back towards the main body. Before reaching it he heard that Cape Town had surrendered and his last chance of glory in the campaign had gone; all that now remained was to round up the scattered garrisons and arrange for their despatch to Europe. The next three months must have been among the most miserable in his life. The heat and the lack of action at the Cape were getting on everyone's nerves: Cape Town itself was, in Wilson's view, one of the worst stations in the world, because of 'the offensive smells, the furnace heat of the atmosphere, the blast of the north-east wind . . . and the mercenary character and stupidity of the inhabitants.' There was much sickness among both officers and men, which Wilson put down to bad wine. All this could no doubt have been endured if the general had known how to handle men in such a situation. But Sir David Baird was, according to Fortescue, 'hard, rough, difficult and jealous of his own authority.' His answer to problems – he has had his successors in the British Army – was to impose ever more petty restrictions and vexations. 'Officers and men are discontented beyond expression,' Wilson wrote. 'The balance or *goose* step introduced for their practice excites a fever of disgust.' Officers were suddenly required to wear black leather stocks and Wilson protested personally to Baird, quoting the King's orders to the effect that velvet stocks were permissable. Baird replied that he was King there, whereupon Wilson bowed and promised to obey 'King David.' Not all the officers were so good tempered and there were many applications for leave and threatened resignations.

A more serious disagreement threatened when Wilson heard that the naval commander, Sir Home Popham, was proposing to employ part of the force in a descent on the River Plate, though he had no authority to do so. By chance, or because he was the sort of person who would possess such things, Wilson had a recent Spanish Army List with him which suggested that the enemy's garrison was stronger than Popham supposed. Wilson also knew a carpenter in the force who had lived in Buenos Aires and who drew him a sketch of the defences. Armed with this and his Spanish Army List, Wilson tried to dissuade his superiors from what he was convinced was a most ill-advised expedition. Baird was impressed with his arguments, but Popham was not and resented his interference. In the event Baird was over-persuaded and he allowed Popham and Beresford to make the attempt. Judgement is not usually regarded as Wilson's strong point, but he was not always wrong, and the expedition ended in the disaster that he had predicted.

An unfavourable inspection of his detachment caused another quarrel with authority. Only Wilson's defence, and not the accusation, survives amongst his papers, but the incident was serious enough to warrant an expression of censure on the 20th Ligh Dragoons appearing in General Orders and Wilson speaks of his having been 'removed in disgrace from the responsibility of my rank and station.' Apparently his horses were judged to be in bad condition. He defended himself vigorously, claiming that so many men were sick that proper grooming was impossible. All he will admit is that the men's hair was too long, that six German troopers had fastened their canteens in the wrong way and that some curbs were missing; and he appealed to 'H.R.H. the Commander-in-Cheif in England.' Apparently it was not thought necessary to bother the Duke of York with these matters, for a few days later Wilson was dining with his commander on the best of terms, and was still in command of his detachment. He was as easy to forgive as he was to censure.

He found relief from these irritations by taking his usual close interest in the country and it inhabitants. He admired the free and easy way of the Dutch colonists and, though he would not condone slavery, he praised them for at least treating their slaves humanely. He was bored by Dutch colonial society, but defended it from sweeping attacks, particularly from moralists. He believed that the Hottentots, those whom he called the 'Africans', and the Bushmen, would be capable of better things if they were well treated and kept off the drink: but 'to render the Hottentot women less hideous is beyond the power of legislation. Her features are all contrary to European ideas of beauty. Her limbs are well formed, but she appears bent in the spine from the immense rotundity of a certain quarter which, after child-bearing, becomes stupendous.' Wilson was not exaggerating: Francis Galton, the scientist and explorer, noticed the same phenomenon in 1851 and wished to record it scientifically. To have gone to work with a tape measure might have led to misunderstanding but, so prominent was the feature, he was able to stand well away and make the required observation with a sextant.

To add to the frustration of being shut away at the ends of the earth with no glory to win, the most momentous news was trickling in. In February, 1806, the garrison heard the news of Trafalgar, which had been fought in the previous October, and in April they learnt of Austerlitz and the peace between France and Austria. The following month brought the news of Pitt's death and the possibility of government changes in Britain. Wilson even envied the Dutch prisoners of war because they were at least due to be sent back to Europe. Baird had by now agreed to send him back with despatches but there was no ship. In May he wrote, 'To be absent from Europe when such great changes were in progress, and when the elevation of my friends to power offers opportunity for advantageous employment, is a hard destiny . . . Lord Hutchinson, the papers say, has an appointment . . . I am satisfied that he will have some good employment; and I calculate upon his friendly offices at all events to remove me from hence.' Accordingly he applied once more to Baird, putting forward family reasons for returning as well as the fact that his 'friends were come to office.' Baird was sympathetic and a ship, the *Adamant*, was available. On 7th June Wilson sailed for home via St Helena, and arrived off Start Point on 31st August. This time he did not record his joy at being home: he saw only the boats putting out to the returning East Indiamen in order to press the crews, who had already been away for two years. 'What a farce,' he wrote, 'to these poor fellows is the freedom of Britain.'

CHAPTER FIVE

Diversions and Disaster in East Prussia

To understand the 'good employment' that Lord Hutchinson did indeed obtain and the perhaps even better employment that he found for Wilson, it is necessary to look back on what had been happening in Europe while Wilson was away in Devon and Somerset, Brazil and South Africa. When in March 1803 the peace of Amiens broke down, Britain and France looked for military advantages and allies. Bonaparte, who in 1804 had crowned himself Napoleon, Emperor of the French, re-occupied Naples and Holland, and seized Hanover, of which George III of England was Elector, though the countries were not otherwise united. Napoleon also drew Spain even closer to France. On the British side, Pitt came out of retirement in 1804 and set about animating another coalition against France. Russia and Austria were willing to join in order to avenge past humiliations and forestall possible future encroachments by Napoleon in Italy and Germany – and neither of the hereditary Emperors looked with favour on a Corsican interloper appropriating so splendid a title – but Prussia hesitated, for though she feared the advance of the French, she feared the Austrians too.

At first Napoleon hoped to strike at the heart of the coalition by invading England – or at any rate he gave that impression, for there is some doubt about what his real intentions were. He assembled a huge army at Boulogne and directed his admirals to secure him an uninterrupted passage of the Straits of Dover by decoying the British fleet away. The Trafalgar campaign was the result, but even before it was decided, Napoleon began moving his great army towards Germany. Here Prussia's hesitation was fatal, for her potential allies as well as for herself: she had resolved to join them, but before she could do so, Napoleon had smashed the combined Russian and Austrian armies at Austerlitz in December, 1805. The Russians succeeded in retreating north-eastwards in some sort of order, but Germany lay at

Napoleon's feet, with only Prussia still undefeated – and still undecided. The King, Frederick William III, swung weakly from one point of view to the other, but eventually the decision was taken out of his hands: patriotic and war fever swept the country and Prussia marched to her destruction at the twin battles of Jena and Auerstadt in October 1806. The French occupied Berlin and much of the rest of the country. The King and Queen fled with the remnants of their beaten army towards the Russian frontier in the north-east corner of their dominions.

In England, after Pitt's death in January, 1806, Lord Grenville became Prime Minister, with Fox as his Foreign Secretary – these were the friends from whom Wilson hoped for advantageous employment. In March of the following year Grenville was succeeded by the Duke of Portland, with Canning at the Foreign Office (Fox had died soon after taking the post) and Castlereagh at the War Office.

In the aftermath of Jena the first essential for the new British Government was to find out what was happening. A British envoy, Lord Morpeth, had been sent to the Prussian court, but he had not had time to present his credentials before the disaster at Jena. After the battle, His Lordship ran for it and did not stop until he reached the sea at Hamburg. Even there he could not be persuaded to stay for longer than the time needed to find a ship to take him home. Young George Jackson was more in the Wilson mould: though only in his early twenties, he had been sent by Fox as a roving diplomatic agent to try to find out what was going on in Prussia outside Court and official circles. He not only stayed in the country but eventually established contact with the Court. However, the British government needed a more senior person on the spot, and in the circumstances there were advantages in appointing a soldier, particularly as the problem of how to bring military help to Prussia was bound to arise. The choice, though that might not have been the word that Ministers would have used, fell on Lord Hutchinson. That a man well known for indolence, slovenliness, ill-health, unsociableness and ungracious manners should have been sent on a delicate diplomatic mission to a much-battered Court, is perhaps surprising until it is recalled that Hutchinson was a crony of the Prince of Wales, indeed almost his military adviser. When there was another change of ministry in 1807,

George Jackson's brother wrote from the Foreign Office, 'If he (Lord Hutchinson) wishes to remain at the army as military commissioner, he will not be recalled. This is a ménagement for the Prince, for His Lordship is estimated by Ministers at his proper value.'

To assist him in this mission for which he was so generally considered unfit, Lord Hutchinson chose his old friend Wilson, his brother Kit Hutchinson, Colonel Eustace and Captain Harvey. They embarked in a frigate at Yarmouth on 3rd November, 1806. Wilson had been home for just over two months. Almost immediately they ran into gale-force winds and the passage must have been unusually dangerous even for those times. 'Surely there is a peculiar ill-fortune that persecutes me in navigation,' Wilson wrote. The gales continued and eventually the frigate was driven ashore on the Danish Island of Anholt. All the efforts to refloat her proved vain and the embassy prepared for death, Lord Hutchinson, his brother and Eustace quietly in their cabins, Wilson, characteristically, on deck. He had given up hope but was determined, somewhat illogically perhaps, not to die without a struggle, for the sake of his wife and family. As a last resort the Captain had the masts chopped down and this lightened the frigate enough for her to float off. Though still in great danger, they made port and Wilson sat up from midnight until three o'clock in the morning writing a description of the adventure 'to afford an interesting narrative for my wife's perusal,' and to record his gratitude to 'The Almighty Disposer of Events.'

In Denmark there were receptions at the British Legation and calls on the local dignitaries. These included the King who, like a surprising number of contemporary monarchs, was mad. Wilson says that he signed state papers, 'Christian Rex & Co.,' and that his penchant for drawing indecent pictures on the card table was such that an old lady had to sit beside him to wipe them off with her elbow. As seemed to happen everywhere that Wilson went, the people spoke enthusiastically of everything English. He went several times to the theatre and remarked on the beauty of the ladies. He and Kit Hutchinson toured the churches in Copenhagen and were surprised to find them equipped with tiers of private boxes like a theatre, each box having a green curtain to ensure privacy. 'If this were the case in England,' Wilson remarked, 'some of our crowded churches would soon have vacant places.' He was gratified to find that his book on the Egyptian campaign was known in Copenhagen, and he wished that the French edition were available there as 'two hundred copies would be sold, and this would extend my popularity as well as augment the hatred of the Danes against Napoleon.'

On 10th December the party embarked on a brig for Danzig and arrived there a week later. Wilson found the city so gloomy that he declined even to describe it. He went to the theatre twice, bought eight double-bottle cases of cherry brandy and two sets of amber jewellery for Jemima, and left for Königsberg. The King and Queen of Prussia were there with their Court and what was left of their army. Here too were young Lord Gower, who had 'a notion to see a battle,' and George Jackson.

Nothing whatever resulted from Lord Hutchinson's mission, except that the British authorities were kept informed, albeit tardily, of what was going on. In the circumstances no more could have been expected: hostilities were in progress, armies were in contact and Napoleon was in the field in person: diplomatic negotiation and offers of subsidies could no more affect the outcome than could the contingents of Asiatic archers who set out from the depths of the Russian Empire and marched towards the guns. Wilson realised that only military or naval help would be of any use, and when no British topsails appeared over the horizon, he was deeply ashamed. But what he could do by making the most of every crumb of good news, by cheerfulness, friendliness and encouragement, he did with boundless enthusiasm – and he did it in the gloomy wastes of East Prussia, a land ravaged by three armies and covered in mud and snow. Lord Hutchinson went to the opposite extreme. He was convinced that Napoleon, whom he much admired, would not be defeated by the Russians and Prussians, and he did not regard every check that the French received as a glorious allied victory, as Wilson was inclined to do. He had a lofty contempt for civilians whom he regarded as incapable of understanding military matters. He tried to ensure that only his version of events reached the British government by forbidding Wilson to communicate with Jackson on official matters. He prophesied disaster and did not conceal his satisfaction when it came. In short, Hutchinson made himself as disagreeable as possible and Wilson did the opposite. Since Hutchinson was generally regarded as "odd" and Wilson was himself well out of the ordinary, it is perhaps not surprising that their friendship should apparently have been strengthened by the endless arguments that they had during that grim and bloody winter: the contrary spirit was strong in them both.

One of Hutchinson's and Wilson's first duties in Königsberg was to make contact with the King and Queen of Prussia and their principal officers. Among the latter Wilson was delighted to find several admirers of his Egyptian book. Though he was strongly biased in favour of monarchs, he was not impressed by King Frederick William, finding him 'awkward in address and general manners,' and detecting a 'wildness of look that I could have imagined denoted an insane state of mind.' Quite different was his impression of the Countess Voss, Grande Maitresse to the Queen: 'a fine frisky old girl,' he wrote, 'who tempered gaiety with decorum, knew human nature well and had more courage than the men of Germany.' She was seventy-two. George Jackson, an amused spectator who had known the Countess in happier times, wrote in his diary,

> Lord Gower and Sir Robert have never failed to pay their respects to her. Little did I think when making her a formal visit at Berlin, that I should ever be admitted to her morning toilette; but so it is, and it is droll enough to see her under the hand of her friseur, while she is laughing and flirting, especially with the above mentioned gallants; for strange to say, Lord G., who is a handsome minor, and Sir Robert, are both deeply smitten with the ample charms of the Grande Maitresse. One day they send her a present of wine, another of tea, and so on . . .

With the Queen of Prussia it was a case of beauty in distress and Wilson was overwhelmed. The lady had indeed suffered much, for not only had she been bundled out of her capital and most of her country, but she had been the victim of vicious personal attacks in the French press. 'There is certainly something in the misfortunes of the great,' Wilson wrote in his Journal for Jemima, 'which touches the feelings of all men more sensibly than the sufferings of individuals in low estate; and the spectacle of a Queen in distress is universally acknowledged to be a more tragical sight than the more disastrous and general calamities of the commonalty.' He wrote this before he had even met the Queen, and after he and Hutchinson had been received by her, he added,

> The Queen was reclining upon the sofa and I approached expecting to see an individual languid in looks; but on the contrary I gazed upon one of the most animated countenances I ever beheld, and at the same time the most lovely, and a figure that was truly noble. Her affability, her interesting words and her presence, with the recollection of her fortunes which it called forth, could not but affect the feelings of the most indifferent stranger, and as my sensibilities are not torpid, I was moved by all the enthusiastic spirit of a true knight.

He found Hutchinson 'to have been no less moved than myself. I have, since this interview, felt more vindictive hatred, if possible, than ever against her unmanly enemies.' The Queen put the crown on his delight when she asked him to lend her his book. He found a copy in the town and had it bound specially for her. Here is Jackson's comment,

> A few days ago Lord Hutchinson and Wilson dined with the King and were afterwards admitted to Her Majesty; a very great compliment, for though she is no longer confined to her bed, she can scarcely walk across the room. Wilson, whom the more I see of him the more I like him, was as much pleased with the compliment she paid him in asking for a copy of his book, as he was enraptured by her beauty. If I were in the confidence of the Countess Voss I should certainly advise her not to allow her chevalier to have a second audience, if she values her conquest.

This interview took place in Memel, to which the Prussian Court had withdrawn when Königsberg was threatened by the French. They and Hutchinson's party had travelled along the narrow sand–spit which separates the Baltic from the Kurische Haff, an immense lake nearly a hundred miles long. It was January and the weather was appalling:

trees were blown across the road, there were hardly any places on the way where shelter could be had, there were very few horses and those that could be obtained were so small that Wilson called them cats. The overcrowding in the wretched inns was such that the English preferred to sleep in barns. At each stopping place there was competition for such miserable food as there was. The carriages and wagons stuck in the sand and overturned, they lost their way, and the wind blew so hard that the houses shook. Wilson, Jackson, Kit Hutchinson, Gower and Harvey, as well as various Prussian dignitaries with whom they shared carts and meals and inns, seemed to have enjoyed every minute of it. 'Count Lindenthal,' Wilson wrote, 'entertained us with many anecdotes, so that we did not get much repose.' 'The weather continued so frightfully bad that any attempt to continue our journey would have been madness . . . Lord Gower, I and Harvey, after a merry dinner retired to a barn and slept soundly in the hay.' 'We all laughed so much that sleep was impossible.' There can be no doubt that Wilson himself found hardship immensely stimulating; what is more difficult to accept is that in various parts of the world his companions in misfortune, whether princes or private soldiers, were equally delighted to slosh through freeziing mud to a cold dinner and a leaky barn. Wilson always claims that they were, and if he is right, his infectious enthusiasm and sanguine temperament could evidently turn even a nightmare into a lark.

It needed more than cheerfulness to transform the military situation. It is true that at the battle of Pultusk the French, though not defeated, were checked, and that in minor actions the Russian soldier was proving a tougher opponent than the French were accustomed to meet. Some of the Prussian units had rallied and were gaining confidence. But the Russian commanders were quarrelling amongst themselves and the problems of supply and food were beyond the capabilities of either side: the troops were perpetually hungry, their clothes were in rags and they slept in the snow. The country had been so ravaged that nothing more could be wrung from those of the inhabitants who still remained. The problem of finding shelter was aggravated by the Russians' habit of feeding their horses on thatch, no other forage being available.

Much as he enjoyed the life at Memel, his audiences with the

Queen and what he called his 'noble arguments' with Hutchinson, Wilson was impatient for action. Hutchinson's mission was to the King of Prussia, but clearly the main action would be between the French and Russian armies. At last on 25th January, Wilson was able to leave Memel with Kit Hutchinson and attach himself to the Russians. Soon after setting out he came upon the French Consul in St Petersburg and his wife and family stuck in the snow. 'Intense as is my *national* enmity to the French,' he wrote, 'I could not *humanly* do an inhuman act, and therefore we gave them the assistance of our horses.' A few days later he wrote, 'I hate the French nation from my soul for their aggressive wars and their violation of all the rights of a common humanity; but as a man I cannot treat individuals of that nation ill, although I often profess to show them no goodwill.' The Consul's name was de Lesseps and his family included his infant son Ferdinand, the builder of the Suez Canal.

As soon as Wilson and Kit Hutchinson reached Russian headquarters they were involved in the confused but bloody skirmishing that preceded the battle of Eylau. For four days Wilson did not take his clothes off or lie on a bed, and in order to get his shirt washed he had to buy another from a peasant for seven shillings. The two British officers were also in danger from their own side as their uniforms were unfamiliar to the Russians: on one occasion Wilson narrowly escaped 'a dexterous poke from a Cossack lance.' He wrote detailed accounts of his activities both to Lord Hutchinson in Memel and in his Journal for Jemima. This latter he sent home whenever a safe hand was available and he directed Jemima to show it to Canning. He also wrote to George Jackson. Hutchinson's attempt to stop him sending out information other than through himself was thus in vain, but it was not unreasonable, for Wilson's optimism certainly needed tempering. Not only did he hate the French, but he soon began to love the Russians: 'I confess that I do feel a great and inalienable attachment to the Russian nation,' he wrote some years later. He became in fact emotionally involved with those to whom he was accredited, a serious fault in a diplomat. He saw all the defects of the Russian military machine and he never underestimated the French. But he so passionately wanted the Russians to beat the French that, perhaps unconciously, he played up the desertions, sickness and other problems of the latter, while concentrating on the courage, endurance and devotion of the Russians. In this way he produced a picture that he did not entirely believe in himself, for while he was writing so optimistically to Hutchinson, he was advising the Russian Commander-in-Chief, Bennigsen, not to risk a battle. Fortunately his temperament was well known, and sensible men, among whom was young Jackson, valued his reports and knew how to interpret them.

The main Russian and French armies met on the snow covered plain of Eylau on 8th February, 1807, and slaughtered one another from dawn until night, for much of the time in a blinding snow-storm. At the end of the day Bennigsen had to withdraw, having neither food nor ammunition for his troops. This enabled Napoleon to claim the victory, though he himself was obliged to fall back a few days later, with his army badly mauled and his reputation for invincibility impaired, Wilson, of course, claimed that the affair had been a great victory for his beloved Russians; Hutchinson told Jackson that it was nothing of the kind.

Wilson and Kit Hutchinson were with Bennigsen throughout the action; Wilson's cheek was grazed and his horse was wounded; he was forty hours without any food 'except a *crumb* of the sourest black bread given me by a Cossack;' and even he was 'almost exhausted by excessive fatigue.' But this did not prevent him from writing a long account of the battle to Lord Hutchinson followed on successive days by supplementary despatches. He wrote a shorter account in his diary for Jemima and sent her a piece of the captured standard of the French Forty-Fourth Regiment. Two days after the battle he was asking his friend Worontzow, the son of the Russian Ambassador in London, who was going to St Petersburg with the captured standards, 'to bring a beautiful Russian cap for Jemima.' He was also wishing that he had twelve thousand men under his command with which he 'would undertake to put the whole French army in retreat,' for he was convinced – rightly as it turned out – that the French had been so badly mauled at Eylau that they were incapable of another attack for a considerable time. He even won a five-guinea bet on the point with General Tolstoy. But as usual he went too far: he begged Lord Hutchinson to assure the British government on his, Wilson's, authority that 'Eylau was decisive of the fate of Europe.' A week after the battle, his romantic temperament still exhilarated by the experience, he wrote in his Journal, 'I confess to get in the rear of Bonaparte is one of my objects; for somehow or other I think that his capture is not impossible and perhaps I might be the instrument to avenge the world.' He has left no record of how he felt when he learnt, if he ever did, that Hutchinson did not forward his account of the battle to London for a fortnight.

After the battle both Russia and Prussia begged Hutchinson for British money and for British troops to be sent to the Baltic. The latter was, of course, impossible in mid-winter, but in March Hutchinson did urge that a force be sent. Among Wilson's papers is a sensibly argued memorandum dated February urging that a subsidy should be given to Prussia lest she should accept peace offers and become a vassal of France. Castlereagh sent Hutchinson's proposal to Lord Cathcart, an officer who had experience of the area and whose path was destined to cross Wilson's at an even more perilous time. Cathcart pointed out that as Britain could spare only twelve thousand men (the exact number, curiously, that Wilson wished he could have) they could make no real difference in East Prussia where the Russians and Prussians already had 100,000. If landed anywhere else, and Cathcart mentioned a number of possible places, such as Danzig, they would not only be too few to achieve anything, but would risk being ignominiously bundled out again. 'The truth was,' wrote Fortescue, 'that England was impotent for the moment owing to the mismanagement and misapplication of her military resources.' Attempts were made to co-operate with Sweden, which was hostile to France and then ruled part of Pomerania on the southern shore of the Baltic. Unfortunately, the King, one learns without surprise, was mad and nothing could be concerted with him. In any case Napoleon had apparently obtained a copy of Cathcart's report and had posted troops at all the possible points of disembarkation that he had mentioned. Nevertheless a detachment of the King's German Legion did occupy the island of Rügen, off the Pomeranian coast.

In East Prussia the French retreated from Eylau, and Wilson revisited the battlefield and the surrounding villages. He saw files of corpses lying where they had fallen under the grape-shot or cavalry sabres, houses filled with the dead and the dying of both armies, ruined hamlets, plundered houses, snow, mud; over all was the stench of death. Many additional Cossack regiments had joined the Russian army, and as the main body cautiously followed the retiring French, the Cossacks harried them without mercy and brought in a stream of prisoners. One of these, Montgaillard, admitted under interrogation that he was an aristocrat and was promptly threatened with death for having served Napoleon. Wilson commented,

> Why commence an argument with a prisoner, and when he manfully defends his country from aspersions, abuse power by unjust punishment? If I had been the prisoner I should have felt honoured rather than disgraced by the cords that bound me. I hate the savage atrocities of the French, and it is almost a pain when one of them compels my admiration. Nevertheless, if I could, I would do Montgaillard a sly service, and perhaps it may be in my power.

As a light cavalryman himself, he admired the Cossacks almost to idolatry, while fully aware of their darker side. He attributed their marauding to the need to find forage for the many horses they had with them, and to bad habits acquired in the Turkish wars. He recognised that 'they could be more fatal to friends than foes,' but thought that if their 'licentious practices' were stopped and their discipline tightened up, their dash and ingenuity would be impaired. He made a great friend of the Cossack Hetman, Platov, and indeed of all the Russian senior officers from Bennigsen downwards. But he was under no illusions about their competence and was aware of their incessant quarrelling. He fretted that he was not himself in command of such fine troops as the Russians; and it comes as a surprise, though it is probably true, to read in his Journal that there was no officer in the Russian army who had seen so much service against the French as he had, no one who knew their stratagems better or was less likely to be deceived by them. 'I am not presumptious 'he went on, 'when I wish that the command of the advance guard was under my control.' The provoking negligence, the apprehensions and ignorance of the enemy's character are so egregious that a military man who aspires to excel those who have the immediate conduct of the light troop service may still be humble. Perhaps Europe is fortunate in the fact that the Russians have not intelligence equal to their courage.' George Jackson's comment on the Russian High Command was pithier: 'Consultation follows consultation, but nothing is done.'

As winter changed into spring and the roads became easier, ministers and other civilian dignitaries began to arrive at Russian headquarters. Wilson distrusted these arrivals because he thought that they would bring with them a tendency towards peace. Bennigsen seemed to be thinking less and less of taking the offensive, and the usual quarrels continued. The absence of help from England even though the Baltic was now free of ice was a further discouragement to the Russians. Hopes of Austrian intervention seemed unlikely to be realised, and Napoleon made several offers to Frederick William. The arrival of the Emperor of Russia seemed to Wilson a sign that negotiations might be about to begin. Nor was he much impressed with Alexander at first. 'I confess that with all my reverence for distinguished personages I thought the scene resembled much a representation I once beheld at Bartholomew Fair.' The first conversation that Alexander and Frederick William had at headquarters was about dress – the dress, as Wilson scornfully put it, of officers 'who had been serving the rudest campaign in the history of the world.' Lord Hutchinson was not present, which was probably just as well. However, Wilson soon succumbed to Alexander's charm, which worked with people far less susceptible to great personages than Wilson was. They were the same age, 30, and soon were great friends: there were dinners when Wilson laughed himself 'almost into a fit,' and where the party 'were unable to recover their gravity.' With ministers and staff officers there were mock tournaments and water-fights. George Jackson wrote home that,

> Colonel Hutchinson [i.e. Kit] and Sir Robert Wilson have made themselves much liked here. Both of them behaved so gallantly on the 8th [at Eylau] that they are to have the Order of St George of the Third Class; and the Emperor has asked for Wilson – who rattles away with him at a great rate, as if laughing and joking with a fellow comrade – to remain with him as military resident, in the event of Lord Hutchinson leaving. All this suits Wilson

exactly, and makes him very happy here. I am heartily glad that it is so, for though it cannot be denied that he is perhaps one of the most harum-scarum fellows that perhaps ever existed, yet there is an immense deal of good in him, and much sound judgment at bottom. Better tempered it is hardly possible to be, and I must say he has full need of good temper, for the more he gains ground with the Russians, so much the more do Lord Hutchinson's attacks on him increase in severity. We know that nothing is seriously meant by them and, as Wilson parries so well His Lordship's thrusts, to bystanders the spectacle is amusing enough. On the other hand Lord Hutchinson was always 'in the Slough of Despond . . .' loud in deprecating our own resources and magnifying those of Bonaparte . . . exalts Boney . . . is incoherent.

However, good diplomatic relations are no substitute for real help, and Wilson's popularity could not make up for the absence of British men and money. Jackson reported that 'at the Army . . . loud complaints were flung continuously into the teeth of our countrymen.' The taunt that most hurt Wilson was that while Russian and Prussian troops were dying in battle against the common enemy, British troops were acquiring colonies. He was as much opposed to this policy as his friends were, and longed for 'forty-thousand British soldiers, with bayonets poised and step as firm as that of the Russians.' Unlike Napoleon, he had not seen Lord Cathcart's report. He also thought that 'Shrapnell's shot, that murderous invention,' would be most useful in East Prussia, and he asked that the word should be passed to Shrapnell. He was impressed by the number of desertions from Napoleon's multi-national army: Poles and Piedmontese were coming across in a steady stream, and men from the smaller German states were anxious to join the Prussians. He was convinced, and remained so for the rest of his life, that almost any people when properly led would make good soldiers and he continuously asked that the deserters should be formed into a corps under British officers. He was later to prove his point in Portugal. At this time he even went so far as to take a captured Lorrainer as his orderly, despite the fact that he was an enemy national and simply because he looked trustworthy. The trust was not misplaced and Captain Charles, as the man became, remained with Wilson for many years as orderly and aide-de-camp. Wilson was a strong believer in the theory that if you expected people to behave well and assumed that they would, they normally did.

Although the skirmishing was becoming hotter as the weather improved, Wilson and his friends, both British and Russian, were sometimes bored. In 1807 in East Prussia, great ingenuity was shown in warding off ennui. Wilson took particular pleasure, he claimed, in writing his Journal for Jemima. 'Although within two hours of marching,' one entry begins, 'and invited to repose by fatigue and example, I prefer that employment which gives my mind most content as affording future pleasure to the object for whom I write my Journal.' 'I have just been at luncheon,' he reported at the beginning of June, 'Grits with butter, lights of beef, herrings mashed, caviare, salt sturgeon of the Don, gin and sour quashi formed our repast. How the mouth of my lady fair will water at this description of a luxurious déjeuner, if she had as much taste for epicurean dainties as I have.' A few days later he was describing an entertainment devised by one of the Cossack generals.

> We were received by a band of music; and on entering the room we saw sixteen extremely well-dressed girls, many of them very pretty. It appeared to me as an enchanted castle. I could not comprehend that within two miles of the enemy, at a solitary house in the Cossack quarter such a society could be collected. The fiddles struck up; and Polish dances, waltzes, Scotch and Cossack dances were called for in rapid succession, and the Hetman himself led off to the admiration of the company. At one o'clock in the morning supper was served; at two dancing again commenced; but Morpheus had such a leaden influence over me that I went to sleep and continued in a delightful slumber until eight o'clock this morning, when I was interrupted by the arrival of the courier to the Hetman. At that hour the music had ceased, the ladies had disappeared, and my eyes were thrown upon a wretched dwelling with naked walls: so that the cobbler in the entertainment could not have been more magically deceived nor more cruelly disappointed.

For fear of any sarcastic smile at the idea of my Polish belles I will give you a description of the dress of one who was *demoiselle* of the house where we had the dance. Her hair was bound up and round à l'anglaise. She had a chemisette with a high and stiff frill – a kind of demi-Mary Queen of Scots costume; a blue silk dancing short gown, the skirt open behind from the waist downwards but kept from flying forward by pink ribbon bows; a very white petticoat, with an imitation of a lace flounce in cotton; clean stockings and good shoes, with an ankle and foot sufficiently handsome to remind me of my own property. Having avowed this I expect that all surmise of scandal is anticipated; but the fact is also that I was too weary to notice the fair maidens beyond this outward observation of those points which move female sympathies at home – I mean face, form and costume – and I retired too early for more accurate investigation.

The young colonel could describe the flounce of a petticoat with the same accuracy and enthusiasm as the defence works of a fortress, however tired he was.

Though he felt no need to apologise for dancing, he was ashamed to confess that he and his companions were so bored that they descended to reading novels. He deprecated the works of Mrs Opie because in seeking to promote virtue she could not avoid mentioning its opposite, which 'must frequently cover the cheeks of a pure reader with a blush. These cautions act always as attractions; and therefore as no story is thought interesting where there is a monotony of virtue, all such novels are bad reading for young people. I am now about to read *The Discarded Son*.' A few days later, apropos of nothing in particular, he recorded that he was reading a new French novel called *Mons. Botte* 'which amused me but which I cannot recommend to others.' If he does not appear at his best in these passages, no doubt Jemima was comforted by the thought that neither Polish belles nor naughty French novels, nor even Mrs Opie, could corrupt her faithful husband. We have, of course, no word but his that this was so.

The climax of the campaign was approaching and Wilson and his friends cannot have been bored in the fighting which eventually led the two great armies to Friedland on 14th June. The Russian soldiers fought with all their accustomed courage and tenacity; the Russian high command with their accustomed stupidity. This time there was no doubt about the French victory, nor indeed about the magnitude of the Russian losses, which might have been even greater if Wilson had not helped to unblock a bridge over which the beaten troops were retreating. He was of course overwhelmed by the defeat.

> I am sick – quite sick with grief and vexation; and when I think that to Bennigsen's folly must be added my own country's humiliaton, my heart utterly fails me. I fear she will pay dearly for the relinquishment of her duty and neglect of her continental alliances. As for Austria, I hope that Vienna will be sacked. Bonaparte has passed the Pragel beyond Tapiau, which is evacuated, as is Königsberg . . . The Baschirs are arrived to succour us with their bows and arrows! Of such defenders Europe does not stand in need, nor is the occasion fitting. The new divisions are, however, on the march, and Bennigsen says he will renew the offensive in future days – but this is childish.
>
> I have not yet said anything of myself, but I escaped all perils with my usual fortune. The fatigue, however, has been excessive. On 14th I was twenty-one hours on horseback. I have only undressed once since 1st June and have never slept with my boots off. I am meagred to a skeleton, my nose is broiled to flaming heat, and I am suffering the greatest inconvenience from the loss of my baggage, which I fear the enemy has taken, with my servant, at Königsberg.

If even Wilson was momentarily demoralised, the effect of Friedland on those of less robust temperament can be imagined. Bennigsen's resolve to maintain the struggle did not last, and though some of the senior Russian officers, particularly Wilson's friends, regained their spirit, Alexander did not: he never tired of seeing his soldiers on parade, but he could not easily contemplate them lying dead in heaps on the field of a disastrous battle. Prussia was finished and Austria could not now resume the struggle; Britain had brought no help and seemed interested only in colonies and the sea. The Tsar was disposed to make peace, and rumours of an armistice began to circulate. Wilson heard them and needed neither prompting nor instructions: he wrote off to Alexander, to Hardenberg, who, almost alone among the Prussians remained resolute, and to those Russians whom he thought anxious to continue in the field. 'This correspondence,' he wrote in his Journal, 'may appear very presumptuous; but in fact it is not so in the existing state of affairs and from my relations with these personages. At all events I am satisfied that I have acted rightly.' His action had no effect: Tilsit followed Friedland because the Russian leadership had lost the will to fight.

CHAPTER SIX

Tilsit and the Drawing Room War

The meetings at Tilsit between Napoleon and Alexander, with the wretched King of Prussia in humble waiting, marked the zenith of Napoleon's power. Austria was cowed, and so was Spain: Prussia had almost ceased to exist except as a geographical region, and the rest of Germany and much of Italy were under French tutelage: the Kings of Holland and Westphalia were Napoleon's brothers, the King of Naples his brother-in-law: the Ottoman Empire, which included the Balkan countries, was in no condition to make trouble, and now Russia was beaten. Only Britain remained in the field, and Napoleon had no reason to fear British troops, who had been so ineptly led in Europe and whose numbers would always be small so long as they were frittered away in expeditions to Buenos Aires, the West Indies or Java. Even though British supremacy at sea meant that invasion of the British Isles was impossible, Napoleon believed that Britain could be subdued by cutting off her trade with the rest of Europe. In 1806 after Jena, he had issued the Berlin Decrees, forbidding his allies and vassals to admit British goods; if he could now close Russia's ports to the British by agreement with Alexander and, with Russia's help, dragoon the Danes, Swedes and Portuguese into doing the same, the reverse blockade would be so nearly complete as to bring the nation of traders to bankruptcy and ruin.

Considering the magnitude of Alexander's defeat at Friedland and his previous losses in that appalling campaign, the mere closing of his ports to the British did not seem much to ask in return for peace and the friendship of the most powerful man on earth. No territory need be required of him, indeed Napolean could let it be known that so far as he was concerned, his friend the Tsar could help himself to any parts of Finland or the Ottoman dominions that he particularly fancied; in fact such seizures could only be of advantage to the French, because

Sweden would be weakened by a Russian occupation of Finland, and Turkey would be weakened if any of her European provinces were lost. Furthermore, Austria would be alarmed by any Russian advance into the Balkans and less likely to make common cause with Russia against France.

This was the hand that Napoleon and his Foreign Minister, Talleyrand, held at Tilsit. Against them, apart from Lieutenant-Colonel Wilson's unauthorised letters arguing against an armistice, there could be counted only the commercial interest that Russia had in maintaining trade with Britain; and a strong anti-French (because anti-revolutionary) and pro-British faction at the Russian Court centered round the Empress-Mother. In the circumstances the French could hardly lose; nor did they, but Wilson, sanguine as ever, continued his opposition to the end. The part he played was typically dashing, but inevitably unsuccessful.

The meeting at Tilsit took place in a two-roomed 'maisonette, très joliement meublée,' as one of the Russians put it, constructed by the French army on boats moored in the middle of the River Niemen, which formed the frontier between Russia and what had been Prussia and was now the empire of Napoleon. Napoleon contrived to reach the raft first and so was able to play the host when Alexander stepped on board a few moments later. The Tsar's first words were ominous for Britain. 'Sire,' he is reported to have said to Napoleon, 'I hate the English as much as you do.' Napoleon is supposed to have replied, 'In that case the peace is made.' Whether the story is true or not, it foretold the outcome accurately.

While the preliminaries were in train, Wilson and the rest of the British party remained at Memel with the Queen of Prussia. He kept away from both the Russian and the Prussian military headquarters for fear of embarrassing his friends. There was evidently not much to do at Memel and the Queen suggested a party on board a British frigate lying in the roads. It turned out to be the one on which Wilson had so nearly lost his life on the way out and it brought back unhappy memories. In any case, it needed more than boating parties and the society of the Queen and her ladies, greatly though he enjoyed it, to restore Wilson's spirits, particularly as the news and rumours from Tilsit were so dreadful: the two emperors had actually *embraced*: the poor King of Prussia had been kept waiting in the rain for four hours before being allowed into the presence of those who were dismembering his kingdom; the wronged Queen was to be sent to plead with the conqueror; and the crowning infamy – the Tsar and the King had dined with the usurper, 'broken bread with him,' as Wilson put it in his Journal. Indeed Alexander had even spent a night on the French side of the river, under the protection of Napoleon and the French Guards. 'What in the counsels of the Almighty can be the purpose of this human degredation?' Wilson asked in his Journal. 'What foul offence can have merited such retribution?' His usual exaggerated language of course; but many in Britain would have felt the same if things had gone differently at Dunkirk, in 1940, and King George VI had embraced Hitler, spent a night under the protection of the S.S. and exchanged the ribbon of the Garter for a swastika brassard.

When Wilson found that his friends in the Russian army were still anxious to see him, he waived his scruples and set out for Tilsit, accompanied by a Mr Mildmay who had arrived on the scene. It is surprising how casually people visited battlefields, congresses and courts in the past. Pierre's presence at the battle of Borodino, as described in *War and Peace*, would no doubt have seemed quite normal at the time. A Captain Alison, an Irishman, was also at Tilsit during the conference and was arrested by the French, but he satified even Talleyrand that he was there simply as a tourist. Wilson found his Russian friends as much against the peace and as disgusted with the imperial fraternization as he was himself. He may well have been right in his impression, but there is, of course, a great difference between hating the idea of defeat and being willing and able to carry on the war. What many influential Russians felt and what the Tsar had the will to carry through were also different, and in the coming months Wilson was led astray by his failure to appreciate this.

In the Russian camp Wilson was invited by Worontzow to meet him at the bridge, for Worontzow's battalion was stationed in Tilsit itself, on the French side. The temptation was too strong. He and Mildmay rowed across the river in disguise and presented themselves at Worontzow's mess. A few days later they dressed as Cossacks and paid a second visit to enemy territory. It was a most imprudent thing to do: Wilson was well known to, and hated by, the French, and his tall, commanding figure did not sink easily into a disguise. Britain and France were still at war, and if he had been taken by the French in disguise, it could have gone hard with him. Certainly Worontzow *père* thought so and wrote him a reproving letter when he heard about it. 'How can you put yourself in such great danger', he wrote, 'you who have published a book in which you give irrefutable proof that the infamous Corsican massacred enemy prisoners and poisoned the sick of his own army? Who, knowing the atrocity of this monster, could doubt that he would have seized you and produced some French rogue from his household who would have sworn that you had tried to suborn him to murder his master? After which he would have had you sent to France in chains where you would have been put to death in dreadful agony.' It was not only Wilson who used strong words about the French.

Wilson enjoyed himself behind the enemy lines. The danger, of course, stimulated him, and he had the satisfaction of being able to make disparaging remarks about his enemies after close personal inspection. Murat was dressed like a May Day chimney-sweep, he wrote, 'and his staff were in fancy dress.' The Marshals of France wore 'gingerbread clothes' and did not look in the least like warriors. Napoleon himself 'was grossly corpulent and his countenance presented no commanding talent . . . his face was pale and unheathily full.' Alexander, of course, was "Majesty itself" despite his fall from grace. The contrast between the two emperors was reflected, for Wilson, in their guards: 'I hardly saw one gentleman among all the French and their troops. Their imperial guards were not worthy to be seen after inspection of the Russians.' The trouble was that the French had won.

As he rode back to Memel, Wilson was greeted by the King of Prussia, who was badly in need of a cheerful friend. Napoleon had refused to accept the able and patriotic Hardenberg as the Prussian negotiator, and the aged Marshal Kalckreuth counted for nothing. Frederick William was not admitted to the business meetings where the fate of his country was discussed, but he was obliged to attend the social functions. It is not surprising that he did not add to the gaiety of these occasions. His humiliation naturally aroused Wilson's sympathy. 'All his offences should be forgiven; he has expiated them all by this draught of woe.' His sympathy for the beautiful Queen was even greater and better deserved. When the Prussians tried to replace Kalckreuth by Goltz, Talleyrand refused to receive him, and to get round the difficulty it was decided to ask Queen Louise to plead with the man who had plundered her country and publicly impugned her virtue. Her sense of duty to her country overcame her repugnance, for the conditions that were being prepared for Prussia were disastrous: half her territory was to be taken away, a huge indemnity was to be demanded, and key fortresses like Magdeburg would have to be given up. Perhaps the Queen could soften the conqueror's heart. She put on a floating white dress embroidered with silver and a pearl tiara, and set off to dine with the Emperor. He paid her compliments, discussed her dress, and parried her every attempt to talk business; when she asked for Magdeburg, he offered her a rose. Finally he promised to think over what she had said and asked her to dine with him again the following day. When she had gone he ordered Talleyrand to have the Prussian treaty signed at once, and he wrote to Josephine that the Queen of Prussia was charming, that she had flirted with him, but that there was no need for Josephine to be jealous. The Queen returned to her lodgings believing that there was still some hope. But when she set off for dinner the next day, this time in a splendid dress of red and gold, with a muslin turban on her head, it was seen that she had been weeping. She had just learnt that Goltz had at last been received by Napoleon and informed that his words to the Queen had been mere politeness, that the House of Prussia was lucky to have a crown at all, and that they owed even that to the pleading of the Tsar: Goltz must therefore sign the treaty that was put before him and do so without discussion. Goltz told Wilson that he had refused to do so, whereupon Napoleon had seized him by the ear and pulled his head down to the document, saying, 'You will sign.' He had signed. So poor Louise had to go through it all again. 'Why is the Queen of Prussia wearing a turban?' Napoleon asked brightly. 'It can't be to please the Emperor of Russia, for he is at war with the Turks.' 'It is to please Rustem,' the Queen replied, indicating Napoleon's Mameluke who stood behind his chair.

It must have been a grisly meal.

Besides carving up Europe and making peace, the two emperors addressed themselves to the problem of the only other major power still in the field, Britain. With Russia and Prussia obliged to comply with his wishes, Napoleon could now shut their ports against British ships and commerce, along with those of France and Spain, most of Italy and Dalmatia, the Low Countries and North Germany, for all these were already in his hands or under his influence. Portugal and Denmark, though they possessed useful fleets, could hardly stand against the victor of Austerlitz, Jena and Friedland, where one after the other, Austria, Prussia and Russia had been knocked out. Sweden was still regarded as a considerable power, but her King was mad and her people is no mood to fight Napoleon. It seemed that the reverse blockade of the British Isles could at last be made complete. To this end Alexander and Napoleon agreed on 7th July in secret articles that Russia should offer to mediate between Britain and France, and that if Britain refused to make peace, Russia would declare war and the two emperors would make common cause. In that event, Portugal, Denmark and Sweden would be summoned to declare war on Britain and shut their ports to her: any of these countries which failed to comply would be treated as an enemy.

These secret articles were ratified on 9th July and Canning apparently learnt of them some days later. Historians have been discussing ever since how the news got out, and at one time Wilson was believed to have been the 'spy on the raft'. It was natural enough: he was present at Tilsit, in the midst of events and in disguise; he was on terms of close friendship with those elements in the Russian camp who most disliked the treaty; and he also came across several of the tourists who had made their way to the area and who could have taken the news out. But the evidence of Wilson's diary is against the theory, for it is unlikely that, if he had known what had been agreed on 7th July, he would have written on 15th July. 'The English ships are all clearing as fast as possible from Memel under an apprehension that Bonaparte may send an order to detain them; but I imagine that the fear is groundless.' He mentions a number of other things that he hears have been agreed by the parties and they are often only half right. In any case once he was safely home his feat could have been revealed if he had performed it.

A more likely candidate is the French Comte D'Antraignes, a professional spy who had worked for the Bourbons, the British and the Russians, and who may even have worked for Napoleon at one time. At the time of Tilsit he was working at the Russian Embassy in London and apparently taking money from the British Government as well. Shortly afterwards he was dismissed by the Russians and given an increase in pay by the British. In 1812 he was murdered in Barnes and Canning went to considerable pains to ensure that incriminating papers were not found among his effects. The theory is that D'Antraignes obtained the secret articles either from a disgruntled Russian or through one of his network of correspondents in Europe, and sold them to the British; and that after his death Canning was anxious to ensure that the name of the informant should not be revealed.

This seems the best explanation if it is accepted that actual information was passed. Probably it must be, for it was so often said at the time that it had been, and so many people in high places believed it. But it does not seem that there need have been a spy at all. Neither Canning nor Leveson-Gower, the British Ambassador, doubted that secret articles existed, and rumours and reports about them flowed in continually: it cannot have been difficult for a trained mind to piece them together, relate them to the likely course of events, and arrive at the right answer. On 4th July, three days before the treaty was signed, George Jackson wrote in his diary, 'I fancy they will . . . propose peace to us, which, if not accepted, we may see another attempt at a Northern Neutrality, which I hope and trust another Nelson may arise to dissolve.' On 15th July he wrote that he had been 'positively assured' that Napoleon had ordered Denmark to shut the Sound to British shipping. If Jackson had sent information of this kind home, it would have been enough to cause British ministers to look hard at the position of Denmark. Certainly it was his duty to have sent a report if a courier could be found. But if he did, it is strange that the fact has not been revealed, for there is no need to conceal for ever that a member of the Diplomatic Service has secured some useful information. As will be seen, over two months later Canning's Private Secretary did not know for certain whether any secret articles had been agreed or not.

However that may be, immediately after Tilsit, ministers in London were worried about Denmark, and George Jackson's brother,

Francis, then serving in the Foreign Office, was woken up at one o'clock in the morning on 18th July 'in consequence of something I had written . . . some days previously on the subject of our discussions with Denmark,' and ordered to set out for London, eighty miles away, at once. When he got there he was told to be ready to leave for Copenhagen in a few days. He told his mother something of this in a letter dated 19th July and was in a panic for a few days when he heard that his letter had been wrongly delivered. He talked of 'near ruin if this business got abroad' and of the seriousness 'not to me only, but even to Canning himself in a public and official point of view.' A most important action was obviously under consideration in London within ten days of the secret articles being agreed by the two emperors. Ministers may have known of them through D'Antraignes, or Jackson or someone else at Tilsit, but the courier would have had to make exceptionally good time. Or else ministers and their staffs could have asked themselves after Friedland what was the most likely turn that the war would take if Russia and Prussia were constrained to make peace with France; and they could have arrived at the right answer. It was not as though the same road had not been travelled by a British government before: as Jackson had noted, the Danish fleet had been destroyed by Nelson in 1801 to prevent it being used against Britain. With the Continent united against her, Britain could not stand by and allow a powerful fleet to fall into the hands of her enemies. Frenchmen who knew what had happened at Copenhagen in 1801 and 1807 cannot have been surprised at what happened at Mers-el-Kebir in 1940. Ministers in 1807 may not have needed a spy to tell them what to do about the Danish fleet.

Whether they had definite information from Tilsit, or whether their deductions were subsequently confirmed by definite information, or whether they acted solely on inferences and put it about that they had information – and the truth will probably never be known – ministers moved with great despatch, aided by the fact that an expedition was being prepared anyway to evacuate the troops that had been landed at Rügen. It was just as well, for on 31st July, Napoleon told the Danish minister that if England refused to make peace, Denmark would have to choose between war with England and war with France. For once Napoleon was too late: the British

expedition sailed for the Baltic and Francis Jackson set out for Denmark
to persuade the Danes to hand over their fleet peacefully. The Danish
Prince Royal indignantly refused, saying that nothing whatever was
to be feared from the French. This was on 8th August, six days after
Napoleon had appointed Marshal Bernadotte to command the French
troops being prepared to back his demands. On 16th August British
troops landed at Copenhagen, with Sir Arthur Wellesley in command
of a division, and by 2nd September the Danish fleet, 18 sail of the
line and 15 frigates, had been secured. Napoleon was filled with
righteous indignation at the perfidy of the British, and so was the
Opposition in London: they called it the most immoral, iniquitous
measure ever conceived. Lord Holland commented in his Memoirs,
'The Danish fleet, neither formidable nor useful to us, was wrested
on very flimsy pretexts from an industrious nation. Some secret articles
in the treaty between Russia and France were alleged to justify the
outrage.'

These events formed the background to Wilson's next activities.
Leaving Memel on 20th July for St Petersburg, he called at Mittau in
Courland on Louis XVIII, the rightful King of France, who was living
there in exile and poverty. Wilson thought that this was bad public
relations on the part of Louis's brother sovereigns who ought to have
seen to it that due honour was paid to a crowned head. For lack of
money the dinner was bad and the house was so dilapidated that the
Queen needed an umbrella when she walked round the billiard room.
In Riga Wilson went to the theatre but found the house badly lit and
the acting and singing wretched. Lord Hutchinson fell ill there and
gave Wilson permission to go on alone. He obtained a britska, a low,
unsprung carriage with just room for one person, and set out, following
his 'golden rule of travelling . . . never stop till you have reached your
goal.' He claimed to have covered three hundred and thirty miles to
St Petersburg in sixty-five hours, arriving on 9th August.

He was not the only new arrival. Napoleon had grasped the need
to keep up the pressure on Alexander, particularly as so many of the
Russian nobility were against the peace. The Tsar would need constant
support and perhaps constant reminding of the engagements he had
undertaken. Napoleon did not wish to choose an Ambassador until
he knew more exactly what qualities such a man would need and

what the real situation in St Petersburg was. Meanwhile someone must hold the fort. Napoleon's choice for this was General Savary, one of his aides-de-camp, who had worked with him closely for ten years and knew his mind. He had been implicated in the kidnapping and murder of the Duc d'Enghien and was later to give something like a repeat performance in Spain. Later still he became Napoleon's Chief of Police. For the next few weeks this tough character was to be Wilson's antagonist in what a French historian has called 'la guerre des salons.'

The British Ambassador, Lord Granville Leveson-Gower, suffered from two handicaps: he disliked diplomatic life in St Petersburg, where he had only just completed one tour of duty and, according to George Jackson, the Tsar did not like him. However, Jackson may have been partly wrong, for he believed that the Tsar's dislike resulted from the two men being rivals for the favours of the same lady. In fact, though Leveson-Gower did spend a great deal of his time in St Petersburg pursuing Princess Galitzin, his rival was Prince Dolgorouki and not the Tsar. Nevertheless, in the eyes of the French the British Embassy was one of the main centres of opposition to the Tsar and the French alliance. The other was the Court of the Empress-Mother who was against her son's policy at this juncture. All that was smart, gay and patriotic in St Petersburg's society was seen at these two centres and at the houses of the great nobles of the 'English' faction. The French envoy was not received in such houses, but Alexander received him the day he arrived, 23rd July, and commanded him to dine on the following day. The Tsar's enthusiasm for Napoleon and the French alliance seemed no less than it had been at Tilsit.

This was the situation into which Wilson dashed. It was impossible for someone of his temperament to believe that all was lost, that the new policy was irrevocable, when all that was best in Russia – in his eyes, at least – hated it. Although diplomats normally dislike the unsolicited assistance of amateurs – often with good reason – Granville Leveson-Gower may have been glad of the help of one who adored the society of the great, their receptions and dinners and balls, who apparently needed no sleep, and who was on terms of great friendship with the Tsar. Wilson immediately began a round of visits to his old friends, Strogonov, Czartoryski, Novosiltzov and the rest, and was gratified to find that none of them would receive Savary; but he was shrewd enough to notice how often the Frenchman visited the Tsar. However, his own turn soon came and Alexander's charm found a particularly easy victim. Wilson was flattered to be seated on the Tsar's right, to be chatted to by the Empress (which was more than Savary could claim) and to enjoy a 'lively and unceremonious' talk with Alexander. However, neither in his talk with Alexander nor in his social visits does he seem to have engaged in serious political discussion; he apparently confined himself at this stage trying to ensure the continued social ostracism of Savary and his staff. 'From Lord Gower's,' he wrote, one evening in August 'I went to Strogonov's and there I rattled on all subjects indiscriminately; but much about the French and the pollution of their acquaintance.' Leveson-Gower, though irritated by Savary's chauvinism, derived amusement from his unpolished and uninhibited manners. 'He imitates the brusque *ton* of his master,' the Ambassador wrote, 'mixing in his conversation innumerable 'morbleu', 'parbleu', etc., etc., then softended down by a 'mon cher milord' . . . He talks of massacres with the most perfect sang-froid . . . He abused us for the abolition of the slave trade'. The Ambassador was also slightly surprised when Savary remarked that in order to restore Santo Domingo to France it would be necessary to massacre the whole population.

Savary pretended not to mind, or perhaps really did not care about, his exclusion from the best society, and showed extraordinary thickness of skin and devotion to duty in presenting himself time after time at the same houses and being refused admission. But Alexander could not allow his hero's envoy to be treated with such contempt. He had to proceed with care, for the Russian nobility had a way with Tsars who tried to force them to accept policies of which they did not approve; Alexander's own father had been one of their victims. But his intervention soon began to take effect: after over a month of quarantine the doors of a few great houses were opened to the Frenchman. One such house, that of the Narishkins, became the centre of a combined operation. 'La belle Narishkine' was Alexander's mistress and it was said of her that, though she did not like France much or politics at all, she did like Alexander and would do anything that she believed to be in his interests. Savary decided to make use of her. She was well known to be interested in fashion and clothes, and Savary, appreciating that the way to her heart was through her wardrobe, proposed to Napoleon that she should be dressed in the best that Paris could produce and at French expense. Napoleon was delighted with the idea. 'The dresses shall be sent,' he wrote, 'and I will pay. When you hand them over, say that I opened your despatch by mistake and insisted on choosing them personally. You know I am very knowledgeable about dresses.'

At the end of August, Leveson-Gower decided that Wilson should return home with despatches. He was all the more ready to go as he had received news that Jemima was ill. No doubt too, even he was somewhat depressed at the number of doors that were now opening to Savary. On 2nd September he was summoned to a farewell audience with the Tsar who talked for an hour 'on important political subjects: a conversation very interesting to England.' From there he went to General Budberg, the Foreign Minister, where the 'conversation was of a most important character.' He hastened to report these two conversations to his Ambassador who gave him 'very important letters' and asked him to hurry.

Never was such advice less needed. This time in a springless teluga, Wilson rushed off. Through Russia, Finland and Sweden, by sea and land, he reached Gothenburg in nine days. From there he took ship for Harwich, arriving at midnight on 18th September sixteen days after leaving St Petersburg. He reported at once to Canning and other ministers, and then went to Bognor where he found Jemima much better.

The reception of his and Leveson-Gower's despatches is described in a series of letters from Ross, who was Canning's Private Secretary, to Lord Malmesbury. Ross wrote on 21st September.

> the despatches he brought are of much more conciliatory nature than any we have received since the peace of Tilsit. Lord F. (sic) L. Gower found Budberg in his last conference more unreserved and less overbearing than in any previous one. General Budberg assures Lord F. L. Gower that there are no secret articles hostile to Great Britain, nor a word respecting the shutting of Russian ports against our commerce. After his last official conference Lord

F. L. Gower had a long private conversation with the General, in which he said he did not consider the peace as a lasting one, that the French were not cured of their revolutionary restlessness: he viewed the peace as affording a breathing time and wished to profit by it to renew a confidential intercourse with Austria and Great Britain. The Emperor's language to Sir R. Wilson was much of the same tenor. Mr Canning seems to think from all this (I should observe that no secret articles have been communicated) that there may be no secret articles, but he seems convinced that a general understanding was agreed upon between the two Emperors which was hostile to us. We attribute a great deal of this mild spirit to our expedition [to Copenhagen] . . . it has created a great 'deal of apprehension at St Petersburg. At Cronstadt they practice firing red-hot shot every day.

Before Wilson's return the Russians had made their formal offer of mediation, and Canning had replied that he would like to know the basis on which the French were prepared to negotiate, and that the secret articles of the treaty should be communicated to him. This request produced nothing, as Ross noted, but it is strange that, if Canning knew for a fact that there were secret articles and was aware of their contents, his Private Secretary should report him as thinking that there might not be any. Private Secretaries normally know about such matters.

In no doubt that the Tsar's soft words to Wilson were the result of the expedition to Copenhagen, Ross believed that Wilson would be sent back with instructions to try to extract some advantage from this change of attitude. On 29th September, Ross wrote

Wilson did not go yesterday, he will to-day. If he had related merely *his own opinions*, I should certainly have hesitated to give implicit confidence to them, but what he has stated is the Emperor's conversation with him, confirmed subsequently to him by General Budberg, with the collateral proof afforded by Lord F. L. Gower of the change in Budberg's tone and manner. "Under these circumstances it is good policy, I think, to send Sir R. Wilson back; he is a military man, has served with the

Russians, has been spoken to confidentially by the Emperor, and may do better than a better man. Nothing important, however, should be left to his sole discretion."

So back went Wilson again, this time with formal instructions from Canning and his arguments strengthened by the presence in the Baltic of a victorious British fleet and army. There was a chance, it seemed to Ministers and to him, of preventing Russia from committing herself entirely to Napoleon. Even if there were not, no harm would be done by trying. He set off on 2nd October and was dining once more with Leveson-Gower on 17th, having called on the way on Louis XVIII, then at Gothenburg, and on Alopeus, the Russian Minister in Stockholm. He seems to have been unwise enough to say something to Alopeus to the effect that the Tsar would not be displeased if British troops remained in occupation of Danish territory. Alopeus reported this to the Tsar, who was naturally annoyed. It was a bad start to the mission, and worse was to come. For one thing, the French began to take him seriously. Four days after his return, Savary referred to him in a report to Napoleon as 'a postillion of intrigue and corruption.' The French historian, Albert Vandal, writing at the end of the last century, has a picture of Wilson at work in St Petersburg which, though doubtless coloured by the view which was held for many years by the French that the world was full of British agents working against the interests of France, no doubt also reflects the opinion of Savary and his master. 'He was a young British officer named Wilson,' wrote Vandal, ·

one of those agents who formed what might be called the mobile diplomacy of the coalition; with no fixed base, no permanent status, they were ceaselessly on the move, going from capital to capital, rekindling the zeal of our opponents; as the case might require, they could be acknowledged or disowned, treated as simple messengers or promoted to authorised negotiators; their activity maintained invisible links between the powers, while the knots which bound together the coalition were cut by Napoleon's sword.

Never was there a link less invisible than the dashing cavalryman in his red coat, over six feet tall, who was the life and soul of every dinner and ball

Vandal's portrait of Wilson goes on, 'Of good family, intelligent, well educated, Sir Robert Wilson had fought honourably, always against us, and earned his colonelcy on the field of battle.' In fact he was middle class, had purchased his colonelcy, and fought against the French because no other enemies had been available in his time. 'Studying the portraits of him that have come down to us,' Vandal continues,

> his handsome, almost feminine features, his fine profile, his look, penetrating but at the same time charming; or reading the reports on him by our own representatives, as well as the Journal he has kept during his stay in St Petersburg (a veritable society column where politics are mixed with accounts of social function and piquant appreciations of the ladies) – such a study reveals a man for whom the intrigues of court and cabinet were his natural element. He now plunged happily into them, for they offered one more way of hurting his hated enemy. Bonaparte personified all that he detested, France, the Revolution, the triumph of popular forces over the rights of birth and eduction; for the conqueror he maintained an implacable hatred compounded of bitter patriotism and caste prejudices, the hate of an Englishman and an aristocrat.

Some of this Wilson himself would have accepted: he certainly hated Napoleon and was deeply, though not bitterly, whatever that may mean, patriotic. He had mixed feelings about the Revolution, but he did not regard it as something that should be exported by force. He was actually less well born than Napoleon, and would have appreciated being called an aristocrat, but would have settled for the title of English gentleman. He did have caste prejudices as his remarks about Napoleon's Guard show, but they did not lead him to hate his inferiors; they led him rather to wish to do something to help them. He never hated France or individual Frenchmen, and apart form a curious but not unusual reverence for royalty, he was very far from being a reactionary. His subsequent career was to demonstrate how inaccurate Vandal's portrait was.

In one respect Vandal and Wilson were both wrong, for Wilson was nothing like so skilled in intrigue as both of them apparently thought. Indeed his days as a drawing-room warrior in St Petersburg were ending, though there were some brilliant occasions still to come. On one of these, at a grand ball, the Tsar's sister asked him to dance the Polonaise with her and this, he said, 'completed my English triumph, as it was decisive proof of her disposition in the present times, and under existing circumstances a daring confirmation. I have no doubt that Savary will notice it with displeasure.' He went often to the theatre where he made a point of going round the boxes 'to show that the English are well received here and have powerful friends.' The French version of this is that he was 'to be seen making the rounds of the boxes, going from one to the other like a general inspecting his troops and arousing their fighting spirit.'

The first serious check came when his letter to the Tsar seeking an audience was returned unopened, on the grounds that it appeared to be concerned with public business and should therefore have been sent through the Foreign Minister, Rumyantsev, who had just succeeded Budberg, and was pro-French. Indeed Wilson was not able to speak to the Tsar at all, but had to be content with an interview with the Minister. Though he appears to have put his case well and with moderation, the British had really nothing to offer – or at any rate nothing that would seem to Alexander to be comparable with what Napoleon had offered at Tilsit. The Tsar may not have appreciated how important British trade was to Russia, until after he had agreed to stop it.

A week after the interview, Russia declared war on Britain. The French believed that the breach was hastened by the imprudence of Wilson and his friends in making available copies of an English pamphlet which denounced the proceedings at Tilsit. Wilson thought that Alexander had acted on receiving a peremptory despatch from Napoleon reminding him of the obligations that he had undertaken; but although such a despatch was sent, it arrived after the rupture. In fact no such explanations are necessary for, as Canning's private Secretary had understood, the friendliness of the Russians' tone was due to the presence of the British force in Denmark. So long as there was a chance that it might sail eastwards and turn its guns on Cronstadt, it was only common prudence for the Russians to practice a little deception on Leveson-Gower and Wilson. But by the beginning of November, the situation had changed: the British troops had evacuated Danish territory and the British fleet had left the Baltic. Soon the sea would be frozen over and the garrison of Cronstadt could put away their red-hot cannon-balls for the winter. There would then be no danger in honouring the promises made at Tilsit.

Wilson and the Ambassador had lost a game that was never winnable. Even the most skilful diplomacy is powerless against victories like Jena and Friedland; and Napoleon had also won the battle for Alexander's mind. No doubt the two Englishmen should have been less impressed by their drawing-room victories and more aware of the possibility that when the Tsar and Budberg assured them that nothing hostile to Britain was intended, they were simply lying. However, this was not Wilson's last skirmish in the salons of St Petersburg, for he was to return five years later with more effective ammunition.

Once again he was sent on ahead with despatches announcing the rupture, and he had more reason than usual for making a non-stop journey: a Russian courier had been sent off ahead of him, and Wilson was determined to overtake him. He did so at Stockholm where he arranged for a British messenger to delay the Russian for as long as possible, while Wilson himself pressed on. He was much held up by gales and contrary winds, but he reached Darlington on 30th November. He set out at once for London, which he reached at four o'clock in the morning. Despite the hour he called on Canning and gave him the news. Canning, according to Wilson, approved everything he had done, in particular his rapid journey, for it enabled the British to detain a Russian warship which happened to be in the British waters.

CHAPTER SEVEN

Lusitanian Partisan

Among the ten thousand papers of Wilson's now in the British Library, there are hardly any that relate to his private life. There is one charming love-letter in French, in which a certain Sidonie, writing from Erfurt, laments that she can no longer hold her Bouchu in her arms, but there is no evidence that it was ever intended for Wilson, let alone the British Library. It must have been one of those taken by Wilson and his men from the unfortunate victims of his next campaign. There is no information about how Wilson spent the last months of 1807 and the early part of 1808, but presumably he was with 'Jem and the brats.' However, so patriotic a soldier would not remain unemployed if he could help it, and on leaving Russia he had written, 'I would hang the first pusillanimous knave that whispered peace; for at the moment peace is the confession of weakness and terror. If peace could be honourable, with joy I would promote it; for as a man I am weary of this war, never ending, still beginning, and which renders my life a distraction: but I cannot dismiss patriotism for my heart; for not even Pitt loved his country's fame more than I do.'

His patriotism did not involve despising foreigners: he was, of course, convinced of the superiority of the British, but his belief that the men of any nation could be made into good fighting soldiers if they were properly trained and were led by men who respected them as human beings and set them a good example, extended, as we have seen, even to Hottentots. In 1808 there were probably no Hottentots in England for him to practice on, but there were plenty of Portuguese. Like the Danes, the Portuguese had a fleet which they could not defend, and consequently they figured in the secret articles of the Treaty of Tilsit. It was no easier in 1807 than it has ever been for a weak country to remain neutral when it has assets that warring powers want. Napoleon did not mean to be forestalled by the British a second time, and on 19th July, he told the Portuguese that they must close their ports to British commerce and sequestrate all British property. Ten days later he ordered Marshal Junot to concentrate troops at Bayonne on the Franco-Spanish border to ensure compliance. The Portuguese monarch, Queen Maria, was – it is tempting to add, 'of course' – mad, and the country was ruled by her son as Regent. He was weak and vacillating and believed to be under the influence of his valet, but it should be said in mitigation that he had much to be weak and vacillating about. If he had reason to fear Napoleon by land, he had no less reason to fear Britain by sea; for if he let the French into his country, he could expect the British to compensate themselves in Madeira, the Azores and Brazil. Since he obviously could not keep the French out, he made a deal with the British in which he agreed that, if his country were invaded by the French, he would emigrate to Brazil and take his fleet with him.

In October, 1807, Junot's troops crossed from France into Spain and France declared war on Portugal. The Regent promptly declared Portuguese ports closed to British ships and gave orders for British property to be confiscated and British subjects detained; but he did not seem to be in any hurry to leave for Brazil. Thinking, no doubt, that it was time the Regent and his valet vacillated in the direction of Britain, the British authorities sent Sir Sidney Smith with six sail of the line ostensibly to escort the Royal Family to Brazil, but also bearing instructions to see that the Portuguese fleet either sailed at once for Brazil or was surrendered to the British. After some days of hesitation, the Regent accepted the inevitable, and when Junot's men, exhausted, ragged and starving from the rigours of their march, staggered into Lisbon on 30th November, they were just too late to see the Portuguese warships, bearing the Regent and escorted by the British squadron, sailing away to Brazil.

The Spanish Royal Family were not actually mad, though in the case of the King it would have been difficult to be certain on this point, but they were contemptible, as Goya's portraits of them show, and Napoleon can have expected no difficulty in placing his brother, Joseph, on their throne. Already in military occupation of northern Spain in furtherance of his designs on Portugal, he decoyed the Spanish King and his heir into France – Wilson's old antagonist Savary was used for this dirty work – and forced them to renounce their rights. He then had Joseph proclaimed King and, with Junot in control of Portugal, it seemed that the whole Iberian peninsula was in his power and denied to the British. But regrettable though their own rulers might be, the Spanish people had no wish to exchange them for a foreign conqueror. On 2nd May, 1808, the people of Madrid rose against the French garrison. After some hours of savagery in the streets, Murat, the French commander, succeeded in restoring order. Some of the rioters were rounded up, taken outside the city and summarily shot. Goya's picture, in the Prado at Madrid, records this terrible day and foreshadows the cruelty, ruthlessness and horror of the next six years; for the revolt spread rapidly throughout Spain and the Peninsular War – the Spanish 'War of Independence' – had begun.

The Portuguese followed their neighbours' example and rose against the French. A small British force under Wellesley was sent to help them and inflicted two sharp defeats on Junot at Rolica and Vimeiro, but after Wellesley had been superseded by two more senior but less competent generals, the French troops were allowed to evacuate Portugal unmolested under the terms of the Convention of Cintra. There was an outcry in Britain and all three commanders went home to face an enquiry. The British government now had no choice but to appoint as the new commander-in-chief, Sir John Moore, who was widely regarded as the ablest general in the British service and who would no doubt have been appointed in the first place, but for the fact that some Ministers did not like him. By the end of October, 1808, he was leading his army north-eastwards out of Portugal to help the scattered and hard pressed Spaniards. The command of such British troops as were left in Portugal devolved upon Sir John Cradock.

We must now return to the Portuguese who were gathering in London. Most of them had either fled from their homes when the French marched in, or had deserted from the French forces. The deserters were received in London by the Portuguese Minister, the Chevalier de Sousa, another extraordinary figure in this age of extraordinary men and women. He was fifty years old and married to the Comtesse de Flahaut, the mother of Napoleon's aide-de-camp. Small, ugly, passionate and gay, he did everything with immense gusto and without shame, pursuing women and the interests of his country with equal energy and success. He brought a refreshing directness to diplomacy: if he wanted something he importuned and nagged until he got it, without any noticeable regard for the traditional diplomatic concept of 'good relations' which he evidently thought were of small account compared with the attractions of mutual interest and the fear of a common enemy. In the crisis of 1808, he badgered Canning, apparently without any fear that his importunity might be counter-productive, for he could be as sauguine, zealous and intemperate in language as Wilson. Both men saw a great opportunity in the crowds of homeless Portuguese in England: for de Souza they were the means of building his country's armed forces, with British help, and for Wilson they could be not only an outlet for his ambition and his deep desire to serve, but also a chance to put into practice his belief that to make a man a good soldier was to do him a great service. De Souza succeeded in persuading the British Government to give the help that was essential and on 4th August, 1808, the Secretary of State for War, Lord Castlereagh, appointed Wilson to raise a Portuguese corps of some 3,000 men horse foot and artillery. Most, but not all, of the officers were to be British and the cost of the force was to be borne by the British government until it landed in Portugal, and thereafter by the Portuguese. Wilson was given the rank of Brigadier-General in the Portuguese service.

Two weeks later Wilson arrived in the Peninsula in enthusiastic command of a body of men in bright green uniforms grandiloquently styled the Loyal Lusitanian Legion. The situation was dangerous, later even desperate, and ideally suited to his talents. He was bound to two masters, one British and one Portuguese, and had no intention of taking orders from either. He was particularly clear about how he stood vis-à-vis the British command: 'To unite with the British Army would be no advantage to my ambitious projects,' he wrote in his Journal, 'the Order and System of such a force would be fatal to my adventures. I must have freedom of action; and my head shall never lower from the weight of responsibility.' In Oporto he soon found a potential third master, the local Bishop, who was also head of the Junta which controlled the town, and who regarded the Legion as his own private army. In his time Wilson had had more than his share of difficult colleagues of various nationalities and religions, and at first a

Portuguese Bishop seemed no worse than an Ottoman Grand Vizier or an eccentric Irish peer. Wilson installed himself in a fine house – 'quite the Pallace of a Dictator' – and set about the task of recruiting his Legion up to its full strength and obtaining supplies and clothing for it. The difficulties were great, for he was no longer entitled to draw equipment from the British, and the Portuguese administration had completely broken down. He soon found himself with many more recruits than he could clothe and some of the officers sent out from England proved 'rebellious' and had to be removed. The Legion had to be drilled and trained, and Wilson felt – and he was certainly right – that he had to supervise everything himself.

Nevertheless, he enjoyed himself immensely. Whatever pond he was in, he liked to be a big fish, or, at any rate, to swim with the big fishes, and in Oporto he was regarded as a saviour, fêted and cheered in the streets, the recipient of turgid addresses, sprinkled with holy water and a great success with the ladies. He got on well too with the Bishop whom he described as 'an amiable old woman' who overwhelmed him with kindness, and served him 'Plumb Pudding' at dinner. Later he had reason to doubt the Bishop's good intentions. As always, he did not confine his attention to the big fish. Once as he rode through the streets he saw 'a naked wretch' rolling about in the gutter, foaming at the mouth. Many people passed by and others looked on from their windows, but no one made the slightest effort to help. 'Never . . . in all the scenes that I have passed through did I see such horrible apathy to Humanity.' He jumped off his horse and 'by striking his head continually, hastened the circulation so that the jaws unlocked and the convulsion greatly eased.' Eventually he ordered two soldiers to take the man to hospital. As in Egypt and Brazil he was disturbed by the squalor in which ordinary people lived, and shocked by the contrast with the opulence of the houses of the wealthy and the elegance and jewellery that were nightly on display at the Opera, which of course he attended in the best box.

Both his labours and his pleasures were interrupted in October by several days of serious rioting. Fourteen hundred French troops were being embarked at Oporto under the terms of the Convention of Cintra, when the rumour spread that they had plundered churches and convents and were taking their loot away with them. The dangerous combination of patriotism, religious fanaticism and a desire to get their own hands on any treasure that there might me, inflamed the mob. The Portuguese troops in the town, themselves disgruntled by a pay cut, were not only useless but inclined to join the rioters. Wilson ordered out the Legion and was supported by a few British and, subsequently, Spanish troops. With these and by his personal courage in facing the mob and by the steadiness of his men, he averted a massacre. His conduct was officially commended to Castlereagh, and many years later it was remembered to his credit by the French and may have helped him through a disagreeable predicament.

As the Autumn of 1808 faded into winter, Wilson felt that his troops needed action. In October he wrote that such a corps was best in the face of the enemy, and that was, of course, his own favourite situation. Though the conditions which prevailed in the Peninsula were anything but favourable to the Allied cause, Wilson thought that it was by no means desperate, and indeed his appreciation of the part that his own corps could play was far-sighted and sound. 'A handful of men' he wrote, 'may be of great service, and the enemy may not easily ascertain their numbers.' He was increasingly harassed by conditions in Oporto, where complete anarchy often seemed imminent, so much so that on several occasions he tried to have the Bishop removed, and he even asked for British troops to come and keep order. Both requests were turned down by General Cradock in Lisbon, the second because so few British troops were available. Cradock had generously sent troops north-east to reinforce Moore, and Lisbon was almost defenceless. In November Moore had been obliged to accept that his thrust to Madrid and Northern Spain could not succeed and that if he went on he would lose the only field army that Britain had. He turned back to the westward and after a terrible retreat through the mountains of Galicia, his army – or most of it – was safely embarked at Corunna in mid-January, 1809, leaving its gallant commander dead on the field.

In December, Wilson at last got away from Oporto, profiting by the fact that no one could really prevent him, and Cradock gave him the opportunity that he wanted by 'recommending' that he should move to Vila Real, east of Oporto. Before they left Cradock inspected the Legion and reported favourably to Castlereagh, adding, 'Sir Robert

Wilson certainly is entitled to much approbation for his exertions.' Even so, only part of the force was well enough equipped to move, the rest being left behind under Baron Eben to await the clothing that Wilson still could not get from either the Portuguese or the British. The winter weather which so battered Moore's men as they struggled westwards towards Corunna, was no kinder to Wilson's Portuguese advancing to Almeida on the Spanish frontier, which was indeed east of Oporto but well beyond Vila Real. Young Captain Lillie, one of the Legion's British officers, wrote of the rain that came down in torrents for days on end, of swollen rivers across which the cavalry had to swim their horses and the gunners manhandle their guns, often up to their shoulders in water. Wilson was in the water with his men, refusing to ride while they faced such conditions on foot. Hardship exhilarated him, particularly when he faced it in company with soldiers – he had reacted similarly in East Prussia. Now he wrote in his Journal that in spite of the rain and cold, his men 'marched with one perpetual Song and Cheer. It was a pleasure to be even in this distress with them. The Bacchanalians were never more joyous in their orgies than the soldiers were with this first debut of military service.' The language is exaggerated, as usual, and not every private soldier enjoys himself as much as his officers like to think. But Wilson's ability to inspire men by his own spirit and by his respect and care for them, was amply proved in the next few weeks. In fifteen days they covered two hundred miles and reached Almeida on the last day of the year, 1808. Wilson was quite clear what he wanted to do – probably the only British commander in the Peninsula, apart from the retreating Moore, who was. His plan was to act so aggressively in the area to his immediate front that no French attack could be mounted on northern Portugal from that direction. To accomplish this he had under command just 700 men.

On New Year's Day, 1809, he wrote, 'We have only to play on and play high,' and though this may look like just another example of his over-optimism, he had in fact perceived that the situation was ideal for guerilla or partisan operations. Napoleon's plan of campaign at this stage, that is after Marshal Soult had chased Moore's army on to their ships, was for Soult to come down from the North, taking Oporto on the way, with Victor supporting him by advancing towards

Lisbon along the valley of the Guadiana. Between the corps of Soult and Victor, General Lapisse was to occupy the area between Zamora and Salamanca, covering the left flank of Soult's advance through Galicia. When Soult had reached Oporto, Lapisse's division was to become part of Victor's corps, to take Ciudad Rodrigo and advance into Portugal towards Abrantes. This plan was set out in an order from Napoleon to King Joseph in Madrid dated from Valladolid on 17th January, 1809. So far as Lapisse's movements were concerned, the order is not a model of precision, and its successful execution depended on reliable and quick communications between the French corps. The responsibility for ensuring such communications would have rested primarily on Lapisse in the centre. It was in any case a difficult task, as the population was hostile, and the mountain ranges and rivers ran roughly east-west, thereby imposing successive barriers against north-south communication. Wilson spent the rest of the winter making the task impossible.

He began at once at Almeida. Warned by Cradock that the British garrison of two battalions was being withdrawn, and also that the British might have to evacuate Portugal altogether, Wilson installed Colonel Mayne, his second-in-command, as Governor, with a few troops of the Legion, and assumed command of the local Portuguese levies. Then he set off for Ciudad Rodrigo, across the Spanish frontier, in complete disregard of Cradock's wish that he should not go beyond the limits of Portugal. He explained cheerfully that he really could not be expected to act on an opinion given without any knowledge of the local situation. Like Almeida, Ciudad Rodrigo had recently been evacuated by British troops and the inhabitants were expecting the French. Wilson's reception was therefore all that he could have wished; it was like the early days of Oporto, but without the Bishop. Better still, some two thousand Spanish levies were placed under his command by the local authorities. Within a few days, by his enthusiasm, determination and willingness to lead where others were dithering, he increased his force to some three thousand, though many of them were raw levies. With this not very formidable force he completely dominated the 9,000 troops under Lapisse. The French knew that Moore was in full retreat and that the Spanish armies in the area had disintegrated, and they assumed that the British would be evacuating

Portugal. Suddenly they found themselves faced by troops in green uniforms like those of British riflemen, and under British officers. They had no idea how many there were as the peasantry put it about that the countryside was swarming with them and Wilson's energy emphasized the deception. His detachments raided up to Ledesma, north-west of Salamanca, threatening such of Lapisse's communications with Soult as still existed, beat up any French post within reach, seizing their supplies and their money. The spirits of the Spanish rose with each small success, and Wilson made the fullest use of their goodwill and hatred of the French. He practised all the techniques of partisan warfare, even to the extent of distributing handbills in the appropriate language in order, to induce the foreign troops in the French service to desert, which many of them did. No doubt he remembered the troubles of the Hompesch Hussars in Egypt. The French prisoners he took, many of whom were surprised in their quarters, provided not only love-letters from Sidonie and her like, but almost the only intelligence that was to be had of what was going on. 'For God's sake,' wrote Frere, the British envoy in Seville, where the supreme Junta was established, 'tell us everything you know and take it for granted that otherwise we shall know nothing.'

He took great pains with the morale of his own men. On one occasion he wrote to a Portuguese woman to praise the conduct of her husband and son who were serving with him. She replied that if other leaders would write such letters of appreciation, there would be no difficulty in getting more officers and defending the country. Such actions were very much a part of his character. At this time a passage in his Journal tells how incensed he was when a British officer died of wounds and no brother officer had bothered to write to the widow or send her a lock of hair or other memorial: 'There is a manly sympathy for affliction,' he wrote, 'which I hope will never abandon me.' As a partisan leader he knew that he had to be ruthless too, when the safety of his band was at stake: when a sergeant deserted and took thirty men with him, Wilson had no hesitation in having the man shot when he was recaptured.

So completely were the French confined that Wilson was eventually able to establish a permanent post in the Pass of Bãnos, thus cutting Lapisse's communications with Victor in the south. With the fortresses of Ciudad Rodrigo and Almeida in front of him, garrisoned and protected, as he believed, by a powerful force, and without direct communication with Victor, Lapisse must have felt that Napoleon's plan for him to take Ciudad Rodrigo and advance on Abrantes was no longer feasible. He had no idea where Soult was, since the Galician insurgents had by now severed such communications had survived the attentions of Wilson's men, and he decided that his best move was to fight his way south and join Victor. To do this he needed to seize the Roman bridge over the Tagus at Alcántara. He achieved this with great skill by concentrating a considerable force before Ciudad Rodrigo as if he was about to do what he should have done weeks before. Wilson failed to recognise this as a feint and brought in his scattered posts to parry the thrust. Whereupon Lapisse struck suddenly southwards in the night. Wilson, who was joined by Mayne and the garrison of Bânos, pursued closely, but was unable to prevent Lapisse from occupying Alcántara. There he was safe for the time being, and was again in communication with Victor. Tactically successful though Lapisse's southward march was, Napier may have been right in saying that 'this false movement greatly injured the French cause' for when Soult in Oporto extended his left wing to feel for the troops of the central prong which should have supported his further advance, they were far away massacring and mutilating the inhabitants of Alcántara before moving off to join Victor at Mérida in mid-April. Lapisse never marched on Abrantes, Soult did not get beyond Oporto, and Victor hardly moved at all.

It was well for the Allied cause that someone in those first months of 1809, was willing to try and frustrate Napoleon's plans. Indeed there was very little else in the Emperor's way. Moore was dead and his army was sailing home; the Portuguese army, in Cradock's words, scarcely deserved the name of a military force; and the British troops under Cradock's command could hardly have defended Lisbon, let alone Portugal, not least because their Commander was timid and pessimistic, and fully accepted Moore's view that Portugal could not be defended against a superior force coming from Spain. So Cradock was obliged to make preparations to evacuate the country. He could not issue direct orders to Wilson to retreat because Wilson was nominally in the Portuguese service, but he did 'suggest' that Wilson's

British officers should rejoin their countrymen round Lisbon. 'The situation of yourself and the English gentlemen attached to the Legion,' wrote Cradock's secretary, 'appears to be very embarrassing and it would be difficult for His Excellency to hazard with any chance of being right, a suggestion upon the line of Conduct they should pursue. The determination is of a nature so exclusively personal that it would seem to rest solely with the Breasts of the individual concerned.' Wilson did not find the situation in the least embarrassing and replied that as he had not heard of any intention on the part of the British government to abandon Spain, he had no intention of doing so either: he was acquainted with the situation of the enemy in front of him and would maintain his ground with the Spaniards until he had orders to withdraw. He was conscious of the serious damage to the Spaniards' morale that a retreat would cause and he proposed to stay where he was until the last moment. He asked that his decision should be attributed not to obstinacy, but to 'a sober reflecting perseverance.' 'When retreat is necessary', he went on, 'and when honour sanctions the measure, I must conform, but I certainly prefer to defend the last ruin and therefore am inclined in such a misfortune to make for Andalusia.' He evidently had no thought at all of quitting the Peninsula. His officers, to whom he left the decision whether to stay with him, agreed with his views and decided, as one of them put it, that it would be 'disgraceful . . . and inconsistent with the honour of a British soldier to desert their comrades.'

This exchange took place towards the end of January, 1809, and Cradock repeated his 'suggestions' on several subsequent occasions, but he bore no resentment over Wilson's rejection of his advice. Indeed he praised his 'indefatigable exertions' and spoke warmly of him in his despatches. 'You really have done wonders with your little corps . . . I have, so far as my feeble powers allow, done you ample justice by letters home.' Others were equally impressed: Lord Holland had been in Oporto just after Wilson left, and years later he wrote

that sanguine officer, Sir Robert Wilson, with a miserable band of ragamuffins called 'the Loyal Lusitanian Legion,' contrived, by threatening proclamations, letters purposely thrown in the way of the enemy, and other devices, to preserve Ciudad Rodrigo from attack and to keep on the alert a French force considerable enough to have taken that fortress and made a fatal inroad on Portugal itself. He remained where he was in spite of the orders of Sir John Cradock and the remonstrances of almost every English officer with whom he communicated. The value of this service can only be estimated by those who were in the country at the time. Such was the consternation at Lisbon that his retreat would have been the signal for embarking every British soldier in that capital or its neighbourhood.

His Lady agreed with him: 'Whatever blemishes he may have had in rodomontading,' Lady Holland wrote of Wilson, 'I know from experience, having been in the country at the time, that when every other English officer took to his heels, he alone remained, and by setting a good face upon matters, kept in check at Salamanca, a French corps of 6,000 [in fact 9,000] men, when he was in Ciudad Rodrigo with only a few half-dismounted cannon and some of his miserable Legion.' Frere was delighted that Wilson had refused to retreat and urged him – as if it were necessary – to be 'an active Cossack.' De Sousa wrote from London in terms as extravagant as those which Wilson himself was accustomed to use, for Sir Robert had vindicated them both, and Portuguese military virtue as well. A Portuguese historian described the Legion's actions at this time as 'one of the most glorious campaigns of the Portuguese troops in the Peninsula War and one whose greatness most historians have not understood.' Considering how well the Portuguese were to fight later on under Wellington, this was high praise. Some British historians, notably, Sir John Fortescue and Sir Charles Oman, have appreciated Wilson's vital role.

Wilson's Whig friends claimed that he saved Portugal during those early months of 1809 when the only effective British field army had been chased out of the Peninsula and neither the British government nor the remaining British commanders knew what to do. This view has, of course, been challenged, but it is permissable to wonder what would have happened if Wilson had obeyed Cradock and fallen back? Fortescue has a harsh passage on Pitt's policy of sending expeditions to Europe and snatching them out again, a policy which, he says was inherited by Pitt's successors.

Again and again he sent Generals to different quarters of Europe with vague orders to do something, no great matter what, but at any rate something, which would show that England was an active ally . . . by this purposeless distribution of troops the armed force of England was frittered away in paltry and useless detachments . . . It demoralised the men; it discouraged the officers; it took the heart out of the generals. More than any other cause it brought about that readiness to re-embark and to abandon enterprises which made the British Army the laughing stock alike of its own nation and Europe.

If Wilson had gone back and Lapisse had entered Portugal and Cradock had abandoned Lisbon, would the British government have accepted local defeat as it had so often in the past, and indeed as it was shortly to do again in Walcheren? The war was not popular in Britain, the Cabinet was divided on what should be done, and there was Moore's pessimistic opinion about the possibility of defending Portugal. In a passage defending those concerned in both Lisbon and London against the charge of having dithered, Fortescue wrote,

Only a few months had passed since the Spanish armies had been scattered to the winds, and Moore's troops had re-embarked after a terrible retreat. It was not obvious at first sight that there was still a chance of success in the Peninsula; and since Castlereagh, with Wellesley's help, realised within six weeks of receiving the news of Corunna that there was such a chance, and converted his colleagues to his view within two weeks more, we have hardly the right to criticise either his insight or his courage.

Certainly, but we may wonder whether another expedition would actually have sailed, if by the time the Cabinet had come to their decision and collected their troops, Cradock had left Portugal, taking every British soldier with him. Cradock wrote at the end of February that '*he was sure* that another army would not be sent.' If the expedition had not sailed, the most glorious series of campaigns in British history would not have been fought, and Napoleon's path to glory would have been smoother. This may be no more than a possibility, but perhaps it serves to justify for Sir Robert Wilson a small niche in the history of his country, as well as the one he occupies in Westminster Abbey.

The commander-in-chief of the new force was Sir Arthur Wellesley, but he was preceded by General Beresford under whom the Portuguese government agreed to place what passed for their army. At last Wilson had a master, for Beresford became his direct superior. He lost no time in setting up a Portuguese army headquarters and on 24 March ordered Wilson to hand over the command of the Legion and report to him. Wilson was shattered. A month before he had made contact with the Spanish General Cuesta, one of the least co-operative of a thoroughly unco-operative body, and had made a favourable impression on him – the only British general known to have achieved this. As a result he had been promised 5,000 Spanish troops, who would have brought the force under his command to 8,000 men. His dreams of a great independent command seemed about to come true and the glory he so ardently sought might now be attainable. Then he was summoned like a junior officer to attend the headquarters of a man whom he knew to be a capable but rather orthodox and ordinary soldier.

He does not seem to have obeyed the summons immediately, waiting until the pursuit of Lapisse to Alcántara was over. He then set out for Portugal in a philosophical frame of mind, resolved, as he had been after his disappointments in South Africa, to accept the blows of fate as a disciplined soldier should. At least he was to be actively employed. Sir Arthur Wellesley's plan was to concentrate first against Soult at Oporto, deploying part of Beresford's Portuguese force to advance northwards on the right wing of the British in order to prevent Soult from breaking out eastwards, and if possible to get round behind him. Wilson was to take a force of Portuguese from Almeida, amounting, apparently, to two battalions, and join Beresford's advance. Wellesley, in one of his most brilliant actions, forced Soult out of Oporto and drove him north into Galicia, where he escaped being cut off only with great difficulty. Wilson seems to have done more marching than fighting, but there is amongst his papers a copy of an order from Beresford, which appears to relate to these operations and which reads, 'To Brigadier General Sir Robert

Wilson – He gives his most perfect approbation as well as to the Corps under his command, whose exact observance of Discipline and Regularity on the March, honours as much the Commander as the troops. So that both the Commander and the troops assured the Marshal [Beresford] the means of attacking the enemy who they had hopes to find in this town and which attack would no doubt have conferred glory on the troops and their country.' To this is appended a footnote which reads, 'The Marshal afterwards said – I meant to make Sir Robert Wilson Commander of my Advance Guard, but the Advanced Guard composed my army.'

But Wilson was not the man to be satisfied with commands that he did not get or glory that he might have won. Shorn of his independent command and back in the region whence he had set out with such hopes and plans six months before, his philosophical frame of mind collapsed. On 23rd May he wrote to Beresford saying, 'I can only connect myself with the Portuguese service by the Legion which His Majesty directed me to raise, discipline and command, and if the command should be adverse to Your Excellency's plans, so that it cannot be combined with more general service, I must request [you to accept] my resignation as Chief of the Legion and Brigadier-General in the Portuguese service.' Beresford replied that it was incompatible with all military system for a general officer to limit his service to one corps or place, and hoped that Wilson would reconsider the matter. At about the same time Wilson learnt that plans were being made which included a satisfactory role for him and his Legion, so on 2nd June he wrote a gracious letter acknowledging Beresford's kindness and agreeing to continue to serve.

The part that was allotted to Wilson was one that he might have chosen himself. Wellesley, having driven Soult into the north-west of Spain, felt himself strong enough to challenge Victor for the prize of Madrid. Victor had been obliged to leave his positions round Mérida and Alcántara owing to lack of supplies, and he had made his way north-east towards Madrid. Wellesley planned to strike boldly in the same direction, join Cuesta's Spanish army west of Talavera and fall on Victor with the combined force. Wilson, with the Legion and a regiment of Portuguese caçadores under command, was to form the northern flank guard of Wellesley's army. 'The appointment,' he wrote, 'heals all my woes and reconciles me to service in the Peninsula.' He threw himself with great gusto into the work of preparing the Legion for its exacting task. His presence was very necessary, for Mayne had absented himself without explanation and the force seemed to have gone to pieces. The men were dirty, ragged and unpaid, and they had indeed been officially reported as unfit for service. Within a few days Wilson had had '800 pr. of trowsers made, 300 pr gaiters, all the jackets mended, the Hairs Cut, the bodies purified and then decked with 600 new shirts and the Feet consoled with as many pr of Shoes.' He exercised the men night and morning. Even the second battalion joined them at last, having been detained in Oporto first by lack of clothing, then by the Bishop and finally by their involvement in Soult's rout of the Portuguese defensive screen which had tried to prevent his capture of the city in the spring. The overall commander of the Portuguese in that disastrous action had been Baron Eben, Wilson's original second-in-command, but he did not now rejoin his old chief. Perhaps he had heard that the first battalion were referring to his men as 'Eben's runaways.' With the prospect of action all was forgotten and Wilson was able to write, 'I noticed my *old* Legion worthy of itself. The jackets covered with leather suited well the soldier-like countenance and Veteran hue of the men. Their white trowsers and Gaiters gave them an air of Lightness and Gaiety which was more congenial to the smiling Fortunes of the time and the commencing Spring Season.'

He marched on 4th July, promising to do more mischief to the French with the Legion alone that the whole British army was then doing. In the first two days he covered sixty-eight miles. On the 10th he had a gratifying interview with Wellesley who told him that Cuesta had spoken highly of him and was sending two Spanish battalions to join the Legion. His objective, Wellesley said, was Escalona, thirty-eight miles from Madrid. Wilson was delighted with his new Spanish battalions, the Mérida and Sevilla, except that they were reluctant to ford rivers – a serious handicap in such a campaign. He got over the difficulty by issuing a proclamation suggesting that the ladies of Mérida and Seville might be surprised to learn that mere water could deter those whom the bullets of the enemy could not – a typical Wilson alternative to the lash. He reached Escalona on 23rd July, but here again the temptation to push on and to disobey orders proved irresistable. On 26th he entered Navalcarnero to the great alarm of the French: they were already facing the joint force of Wellesley and Cuesta at Talavera and a potential threat from a Spanish force under Vanegas coming up from the south: now they found Wilson behind their right rear with a corps which they estimated at 15,000. Though troops which should have gone to Talavera were sent to contain him, he resolved to press on. To the now continuous cheers of the crowds by the way, he marched down from Navalcarnero on the almost defenceless capital – almost defenceless because King Joseph had marched out to join Victor at Talavera – and reached Mostoles, only fifteen miles from its gates. His dream had nearly come true. But before he could summon the city to surrender, as he intended to do, he was ordered by Wellesley to bring his corps back to Escalona and to go in person to meet Wellesley and Cuesta at Talavera. The great battle had taken place and resulted in a victory for the allied armies; and Wellesley, so far from reproaching Wilson for exceeding his instructions, received him cordially and reported to Castlereagh that he had made himself very useful. The difficulty was that Wellesley's communications were threatened. In striking eastwards from Portugal towards Madrid he was aware that Soult in the north was a potential threat, but he believed that Soult's army had been so badly mauled at Oporto and in the subsequent retreat that he would be incapable of moving fast enough and with sufficient force to constitute a serious danger to the British communications. He now learnt that Soult was threatening Baños and he was reluctant to press on to Madrid or allow Wilson to do so, until he knew the exact nature of Soult's threat. However, he sent Wilson back to Escalona and added that he might go nearer to the capital if circumstances permitted. No sooner had Wilson left than serious news began to come in: first that Soult had actually got through the pass at Baños and was nearing Plasencia, and then that he had been joined by Ney, whom Wellesley believed to be far away in Galicia, and had 40,000 men under command. A retreat through Plasencia, by which Wellesley had come, was no longer practicable, though the more southerly road through Badajoz was unlikely to be seriously threatened provided that Wellesley moved fast.

So Wilson went off gaily to maintain his position above Madrid, while the rest of the allied army prepared to retreat. He captured a courier on 3rd August, from whom he learnt that Soult was at Baños, but he had no idea that Ney was with him. It was some days before he found out the true state of affairs, and then his position was critical. The French had sent a division under General Villatte to attack him from the east, and Soult and Ney lay across his line of retreat. But Wilson was a true partisan leader: finding that Talavera had already been evacuated by the allies, he struck westwards in the hope of overtaking Wellesley on the march. But Villatte caught him up and he turned towards the mountains, with the aim of escaping along the northern bank of the Tietar. Here he lerned from Spanish peasants that Soult had detached General Foy from Plasencia to look for him, and that the Governor of Avila had marched down to block his escape northwards. Although almost completely hemmed in, he kept his nerve and struck north-west unto the Sierra de Gredos, snow-capped, rugged and generally thought to be impassable to armies. He had to abandon his guns and fight his way through several French posts in the mountain villages, but on 11th August he emerged at the pass of Baños. Here his talents as a partisan were overborne by his thirst for glory: from the top of the pass he saw a French column approaching from the south. It was Marshal Ney with 10-12,000 men returning from Soult's army at Plasencia and heading north for Salamanca. There was no valid reason why Wilson should try to stop them; they were marching away from the British further south, they greatly outnumbered his own force and he was without artillery. But it would be too much to expect a man of Wilson's temperament to stand aside; and after all, one of the objects of war is to damage and destroy the enemy. So Wilson gave battle. At first he fell back steadily but the Mérida and Sevilla battalions were no match for the French, who worked their way round Wilson's flanks. The big battalions with their guns were bound to win in the end and eventually Wilson's troops gave way and ran for it over the hills. They did not rally until the next day, but Ney admitted to the loss of thirty-five killed and a hundred and fifty wounded, and it was generally believed by the British that the French were in the habit of putting their losses at about one third of the true figure. Wilson lost under 400 killed, wounded or missing. After rallying his men Wilson resumed his westward march and rejoined the allied armies on 24th August. He duly reported to Wellesley on his affair with Ney, and Wellesley sent his report to Castlereagh under cover of one of his own. Wellesley's despatch ends with the following paragraphs:

> I enclose Sir Robert Wilson's account of the action. He as well as the other British officers of his corps, have been very active, intelligent and useful in command of the Portuguese and Spanish corps with which they were detached from the army.
>
> Before the battle of 28th July [Talavera] he had pushed his party almost to the gates of Madrid, with which city he was in communication; and he would have been in Madrid, if I had not thought it proper to call him in, in expectation of that general action which took place on 28th July. He afterwards alarmed the enemy on the right of his army; and throughout the service showed himself an active and intelligent partisan, well acquainted with the country in which he was acting, and possessing the confidence of the troops which he commanded.
>
> Being persuaded that his retreat was not open by Arzobispo, he acted right in taking the road he did, with which he was well acquainted; and though unsuccessful in the action which he fought (which may well be accounted for by the numbers and description of the enemy's troops) the action, in my opinion, does him great credit.

Wilson in his despatch reported that he had been 'obliged to retire on the mountains' and laments that he could no longer arrest the progress of the enemy, but he did not say – and it appears to have been the case – that his men, after a creditable resistance, simply took to their heels and disappeared into the mountains, accompanied, of course, by their commander. According to Lord Londonderry, this had been previously arranged, and as the men rallied again the next day and marched westward in good order, this seems probable. It was no doubt a good guerilla tactic, for a parade-ground withdrawal in the circumstances would almost certainly have resulted in much heavier losses, particularly from the enemy's cavalry and guns. Many years later the Tory *Quarterly Review*, seeking to blacken Wilson's character for political reasons, accused him of having falsely claimed the action at Baños as a victory, and a public slanging match ensued. Wilson replied to the attack with a pamphlet and the *Quarterly* replied to that with an article belittling Wilson's defence of Northern Portugal in 1808-9. Wellington was not deceived for his despatch contains the words, 'though unsuccessful in the action he fought . . .'. What did irritate Wellington was Wilson's attempt to disguise the manner of his retreat, for he wrote that he did not understand how troops could have behaved so well and yet dispersed so completely. Wilson replied that the defence was a series of isolated posts and that 'the dispersion was a separation by detachments over the mountains.' It would have been better if he had admitted that his troops had had to run, but he did not deny that he himself 'owed his safety to the fleetness of his horse,' for he explained to Wellington that he had stayed on the road as the only place where he could remain on horseback (and so survey the action), and when the French cavalry broke through on the road, he had no choice but to flee. He had tried to show the action in the most favourable light, but as he reported that he had been 'obliged to retire' and 'could no longer arrest the progress of the enemy', it is nonsense to accuse him of claiming a victory.

CHAPTER EIGHT

The Scene Shifter

The affair at Puerto de Baños was Wilson's last service in the Peninsula, or rather, in the Peninsula War, for we shall see him once more on a Spanish battlefield. For twelve months he had worked and fought without rest. He had raised, trained and equipped his Legion in the face of enormous difficulties, politcal, administrative and personal. His officers were not of high quality, and the inspiration, the infectious enthusiasm, came from Wilson. When he was away the Legion deteriorated. After the training came the months of guerilla warfare in the mud and the rain of the Sierras, followed by the shock and disappointment at finding himself marching and counter-marching at Beresford's command, just another subordinate officer with no freedom of action. From the near despair of this period he was back in the clouds again when he was restored to the Legion with an important part to play and the 'vivas' of the Spanish townsfolk in his ears. But his exertions in the Talavera campaign were very great and they ended not only in a sharp defeat, but with Beresford's resumption of control over him. Already in April 1809, before his attempt to resign, he was wondering whether there might not once again be war in the North and a chance for him to serve with his beloved Russians. Though the Talavera campaign temporarily restored his spirits, by the time he reached the Portuguese frontier depression had set in again. There could well have been an element of mental exhaustion, of battle-fatigue, in his condition, mingled with professional frustration, for under Beresford's supervision there was no prospect of his spending the coming winter as he had spent the last, beating up French convoys and insulating their outposts. Above Beresford was Wellington (Wellesley had become Viscount Wellington after Talavera) and Wilson must have sensed that there would be no scope for his particular talents – or his insubordination – under such a commander. As Sir

Charles Oman put it, 'There was hardly an officer in the Peninsula Army to whom he [Wellington] would grant a free hand even in carrying out comparatively small tasks. His most trusted subordinates were liable to find themselves overwhelmed with rebukes delivered in the most tempestuous fashion if they took upon themselves to issue a command on their own responsibility, even when the great chief was many leagues away.' Wilson had already had a taste of the treatment; when in the Talavera campaign he was behind the French right rear and threatening Madrid, with the Commander-in-Chief's knowledge and approval, he received a letter from him beginning, 'It is difficult for me to instruct you, when every letter I receive from you informs me that you are further from me, and are carrying into execution some plan of your own.' However, later in the year Wellington wrote, 'I should like to have Sir Robert Wilson on this side of the Tagus in our front. We must have somebody within the Spanish frontier; and we ought to have with this army some troops belonging to the country. Sir Robert is much liked here, and I should prefer him to anybody else.'

Even if he had seen this letter, it would probably not have made any difference to the despondent mood which is revealed in one of his few surviving private letters. Addressed to Jemima and dated 2nd September 1809, it is not all legible, but his low spirits and frustration are unmistakable. He would like, he says, a change from service in the Peninsula and hoped to go to Russia. But he has no idea how things are going at home 'or if H. M. Ministers now deign to contemplate me with good disposition.' He has heard nothing from them and is

not ashamed of owning that any praise would have been acceptable. The withholding such expressions, after all that has happened, is no great encouragement for greater service, epecially when coupled with actual neglect of every application . . . But I have received no instance of support from the Government and I have had to battle more impediments than the enemy presented . . . The greatest kindness they could show me would be to give me the appointment before-mentioned [that is, in Russia] should opportunity offer.

He believes that the Russians would ask for his services, that his 'interest requires another theatre of service' and that he is losing 'valuable connection in Portugal.' The letter also asks Jemima for news of how the action at Puerto de Baños was received – 'if justice is done, all must agree that we did our duty' – and ends 'God Bless you my d...g Jem.'

The letter gives a conventional picture of an able middle-class man trying to make his way in an aristocratic society and turning away from those who did not appreciate him, to foreigners who would: others in the same position went to India or the colonies. However, although Wilson did not always behave impeccably when in this mood, at least he seems to have been free of that personal prickliness which often afflicts its victims. In the same letter he wrote, 'Although Beresford's military views and mine are not in the same accord, he presently shows me the most distinguished notice and friendship.' In fact, Wilson's charm seems usually to have been proof agains this despondency, and it was difficult to be upset with him for long. Beresford was not only personally friendly but, to his credit, in his despatches home he recognised the importance of Wilson's services. So did the French. General Foy, who had hunted him in the mountains, wrote some years later (in a letter that Wilson may have solicited) that he 'had very definite ideas about the effect of Sir Robert Wilson's operations on the campaign of 1809, not only in preventing Lapisse's division from entering Portugal, and thus paralysing Marshal Soult's army, but also later when he alarmed Madrid and produced a greater effect with two or three thousand men than Sir Arthur Wellesley and Cuesta did with sixty thousand.'

After a final interview with Wellington and more melancholy entries in his Journal, in one of which he said that, though he loved the Spanish theatre, if there was no part for him except that of a candle-snuffer, he would rather be a scene-shifter, Wilson decided to leave. Ostensibly he went home to sort out some of the administrative problems of the Legion, for there were irregularities in the accounts and it transpired that its administration had been chaotic, though Wilson himself was never seriously thought to have misappropriated funds. It is unlikely, however, that he really intended to return –

indeed for a while he was technically absent without leave. His scene had shifted.

Unfortunately no other theatres were open to him for the next two and a half years. Inaction did not suit his temperament, and in his frustration his attitude and conduct fell short of that generosity which he admired and normally showed. It is not so much that he pestered those in authority and enlisted outside help for his causes: that was the usual way of getting things done, and if Wilson was perhaps more active and persistent than other people, he was not only a more active person than most, but he was a Whig and therefore without direct influence on the government; for Canning, who did look favourably on him, had left the Foreign Office after his duel with Castlereagh. What is less acceptable is that Wilson took to disparaging Wellington and the Peninsula army. It must have been galling for him, who had played a gallant and successful part in the days of defeat, to watch the Spanish theatre under Wellington's direction get on well enough without him, and to see others – lesser men, he no doubt considered them – gaining the glory that he so much coveted. The fact that he had separated himself from the scene by his own act, cannot have made it any easier for him to bear the applause that his erstwhile comrades were winning. He spent much of his time with his Whig friends at Brooks's and they did not support the continuation of the war. Personal and political feeling thus inclined him in the same direction and distorted his judgement. He seems to have taken upon himself the task of keeping the Whig leader, Lord Grey, who lived a great deal at Howick in Northumberland, in touch with both the military and political situations, and this was the beginning of a correspondence between the two men which was to last for many years. During 1810 and 1811, a stream of letters went northwards suggesting that Wellington's successes were less than they turned out to be and his set-backs worse. They make Wilson look foolish to judges who have the benefit of hindsight. At the time, however, there was some justification for his pessimism as it did take Wellington nearly four long years after Talavera to make his final victorious advance, an advance which must have been made easier by Napoleon's loss the year before of half a million men in Russia. Sergeant Bourgogne was not the only French soldier who marched from Spain to Moscow in 1812. What Wilson failed to see was the spark of military genius in Wellington which enabled him to defeat the attempts to trap and destroy him and to exploit every sign of enemy weakness. Four years later Wilson was guilty of the same failing and on that occasion he was recorded in Mr Creevey's pages.

In March 1810, his campaign for recognition from his own government reached the House of Commons, where Hutchinson proposed that his distinguished services in the Peninsula should be recognised by a vote of thanks. Unfortunately the actions in question did not come within the definitions laid down and the motion was withdrawn but not before Perceval, Canning and Castlereagh had all paid tribute to Wilson's services. He was also appointed A.D.C. to the King at this time, but he failed on a technicality to get the medal which was conferred on all general officers who had served in the Peninsula; it was denied to him on the ground that his rank of Brigadier-General was Portuguese and that his British rank was Lieutenant-Colonel. In vain did he point out that he had commanded several thousand troops in the field, and in vain did he make a nuisance of himself by petitioning the Prime Minister, the Duke of York and the Prince Regent. He supported his petitions with testimonials from British, Portuguese and Spanish authorities, at least some of which seem to have been solicited for the purpose. It is easy to imagine the indignation of a man who set so much store by marks of distinction and who had done so much to deserve them; but he made so much fuss that even Sousa, who had done his best to help, begged him to restrain himself.

Fortunately Wilson's writing at this time was not confined to seeking decorations and disaparaging Wellington. As he had done before and was to do again, on returning from fighting a campaign, he sat down to write about one. This time his subject was the Russian army in East Prussia and the book was published as *Brief Remarks on the Character and Composition of the Russian Army; and a Sketch of the Campaign in East Prussia in 1806 and 1807*. Apart from some justified objections to its florid style, the book was well received, even by the Tory *Quarterly Review*, for although it was the work of a Whig, it reflected Wilson's belief that Napoleon could and must be beaten. This was the Tory, but not the Whig, view. The book also reflected

Wilson's admiration for the Russians and no doubt he chose that time to bring it out in order to further his chances of eventually serving again in eastern Europe: to make sure that the right people read it he dedicated it to the Duke of York and sent a copy to the Tsar.

War between Russia and France was not imminent in 1810, but Russia was not the only country in eastern Europe in which Wilson knew all the leading men or claimed to: there was also Turkey. He felt sure that Turkey would sooner or later be embroiled with France and would then need the services of an officer well acquainted with French tactics and a known friend of Turkey. Failing that perhaps he could be of service in patching up the never-ending quarrel between Turkey and Russia, for was he not persona grata to both parties? All this he explained at length to Lord Wellesley, Wellington's brother, who was now at the Foreign Office and was well-disposed towards Wilson. In the end his importunity bore fruit. In September 1811, he was promised an appointment under Mr Liston who was going to Turkey as ambassador. Even so there were still delays and Wilson was so frustrated that he considered going to South America to seek his fortune there. No papers tell us about his private life at this time, but it is clear that so long as the war continued, he was unable to settle down with Jemima and the children.

It was not until April 1812 that Liston and his military adviser set out, Wilson having been promoted to Brigadier-General – in the British service this time. He was to be under Liston's orders and he was instructed not to correspond with anyone else. On the voyage out he read Byron and a History of the Turks. He approved of Byron's work and noted in his Journal that, though he could 'not perhaps be a favourite with any public, he will survive the more popular compositions of Walter Scott, Mr Wharton or Lord George Grenville.' The first port of call was Cadiz where Wilson, as always in such circumstances, inspected the fortifications and the women, called on the leading personages and attended the theatre. The fortifications did not impress him at all, but the women did. He also reviewed a regiment and dined in a Spanish Mess for 1/4d. which included a pint of Catalan wine. He arranged for two shawls to be taken back to England, one for Jemima and one for Lady Grey. The mission next called at Gibraltar, from where Wilson explored the neighbouring area of Spain. Before leaving he 'wrote to the Duke of Gloucester, Lord Grey and Lord Hutchinson many sheets of paper containing such matter as I thought would be interesting to them; and suggested some subjects for very early attention if they saw power to regulate them in sufficient time.' This habit of writing to the opposition leaders (for the Duke of Gloucester, nephew of George III and cousin of the Prince Regent, was also a prominent Whig) was resented by the Tories and was probably a major cause of their refusal to accord Wilson the recognition that he deserved. Moreover, it was entirely contrary to his instructions. However, in considering Wilson's penchant for insubordination it should be recalled that Wellington in 1812 wrote that 'nobody in the British Army ever reads a regulation or an order as if it were to be a guide to his conduct, or in any other manner than as an amusing novel!'

In May the mission reached Sicily which, with the southern part of the Italian mainland, had formed the Kingdom of the Two Sicilies. In 1812 the mainland part was under French occupation with Napoleon's brother-in-law, Murat, as King; Sicily itself was occupied by British troops. The rightful King of the Two Sicilies, Ferdinand, was, if not mad, at best incompetent; and Queen Caroline, a bad and intriguing woman, a sister of the late Marie-Antoinette, exercised the royal power. As she exercised it in the oppressive manner traditional in those parts, the British were in a position of great discomfort, with which they were to become increasingly familiar until they finally gave up their empire and passed the identical problem on to the United States. The problem was – and is – that in order to preserve law and order, and a secure place for ships or troops or commerce, an imperial or dominating Power soon finds itself propping up corrupt and tyrannical regimes. To deal with such a situation in Sicily, the British Government had sent out a member of the Portland family, Lord William Bentinck, in the dual capacity of Minister and Commander-in-Chief. The Bentincks were Whigs, and Lord William was a strong supporter of the party's ideals.

This was the situation upon which Brigadier-General Wilson came with his usual curiosity and impetuosity. He rushed round Palermo on foot and on horseback, seeing everybody and everything. He was delighted to find that the 20th Light Dragoons, the regiment that he had commanded at the Cape, were stationed in the town and he spent much time with them. He found only one woman with any pretentions to beauty and she, by virtue of her *déshabille*, he considered was cheating. He questioned everyone about the political situation, and his Journal records not only his views on the opera and Princess Paterno, but some shrewd and prophetic observations on the snowball effect of acquiring territory overseas and on what he called the 'march of usurpation in English policy.' Bentinck thought that the problem of Sicily could be solved by imposing democratic government by force of British arms and by removing the King and Queen if they stood in the way. Wilson saw how easily intervention with lofty motives led ineluctably to permanent commitment and occupation. Though he too was a Whig and imbued with liberal principles and compassion for the oppressed, he also understood the strength of national feeling and knew that most people would rather be badly ruled by their own tribe than well ruled by another. In fact his understanding of the feelings of foreigners seems to have been a good deal deeper than that of most Englishmen of his time. He warned Bentinck that if the British were entitled to do as they liked in Sicily in the name of democracy, they could hardly blame Napoleon for similar interventions, past or future.

Wilson, of course, secured an interview with the Queen. She was no doubt glad to have someone to whom she could pour out her troubles, particularly a handsome young general wearing the Cross of Maria Theresa, her mother. Soon she was showing him Bentinck's threatening letters and assuring him that she would die rather than see a revolutionary committee established in Sicily under the guise of a parliament: of course there were abuses, and she would be glad to see them put right, but though England might give advice in such matters, it was an extraordinary abuse of power to give orders to a sovereign state. Wilson claimed that he was far too accustomed to the company of sovereigns to be influenced by their flattery, and on this occasion – if his account be true – he counselled moderation. He made a report to Bentinck and urged on him that it was wrong and dangerous for Britain to seek to impose her will, even in the cause of freedom. But he also sent a detailed account of the whole proceeding to Lord Grey, which greatly and rightly annoyed Bentinck.

This episode helps to elucidate Wilson's complex and apparently inconsistent political beliefs. He believed that the dignity of man led on to the dignity of nations; that if you violated the latter, you violated the former as well. He felt too that just as the English had a right to govern themselves, so had the Sicilians and the Spanish. He might not have agreed that the Hottentots were ready for independent statehood, but he insisted on their right to humane treatment. At the same time he had a great reverence for monarchs, in spite of the fact that numbers of them in his day were either mad or despotic or both. These beliefs in nationalism and monarchy and human dignity coalesced into the ideal of a national monarchy in which the monarch treated his subjects as human beings. Wilson was opposed to any movement which might upset the proper working of a benevolent monarchy, such things, for instance, as Roman Catholicism in England (though he came to modify this view) republicanism and foreign intervention. These, he thought, caused such conflict and misery that they were worse than the evils that they were intended to remove. Colonialism stood in the way of a people's right to nationhood, and the revolt against monarchy that wars of colonial liberation inevitably involved, did not seem to worry Wilson, presumably because human and national dignity seemed more important than monarchy in the colonial context. In the years after 1815, when monarchy became synonymous with despotism over most of Europe, and nationalism became identified with revolt, Wilson's simultaneous belief in freedom, nationalism and monarchy looked decidedly odd – particularly to the monarchs.

On 20th May, 1812, his establishment strengthened by a corporal and four troopers of the 20th Light Dragoons, Wilson set sail for Constantinople. On the way his ship called at Malta and a number of Greek Islands. On one of them he remarked that 'further acquaintance with these people has proved to me that the moralities are not regulated by the length of petticoat.' As the Journal was intended for Jemima, he probably did not mean what he seems to imply. On another island, aided by two dragoons, two sailors, a lieutenant of Marines and a priest, he 'removed' a large Greek altar and had it put on board ship. He denies that this was pillage on the ground that he 'had the sanction of the chief person of the island and also of the priest.' He added in a footnote, 'I gave it to Mr William Hamilton, who set it up in Chelsea.'

He also visited Troy after a most arduous journey, and wrote a long and exceedingly dull memorandum about it. He reached Constantinople at the end of June, a few days after Napoleon had crossed the Niemen and invaded Russia with over half a million men. His usual inspection of the city's attractions was somewhat frustrated by the women's yashmaks, but he claimed that the pretty ones contrived to wear them in such a way as not to conceal their most attractive features. He took care to wear his Turkish decoration, but shocked his English companions by going out in the mid-day sun and by dismissing his Janissary escort: he thought it showed a lack of trust in the people to go about with a guard.

He had, of course, no intention of remaining quietly in Constantinople as military attaché at the British Embassy: his aim was to take part in the great struggle between Russia and France, and first to do what he could in the Balkans to ensure that Russia was not distracted by hostilities with Turkey from the main business of resisting the French invasion. This was not his own original idea and the greater part of the work had been done by Stratford Canning, then a young man, who was in charge of the Embassy before Liston arrived. Stratford Canning saw how vital it was that the Russian-Turkish war being fought in the region of Roumania should be brought to an end before Russia had to fight the French. Though without instructions, he used all his influence in favour of peace and a treaty was signed at Bucharest at the end of May. This should have been the end of the matter but fortunately for Wilson, the treaty satisfied neither side and it seemed likely that one party or the other would refuse to ratify it in the hope of getting better terms. The French would press the Turks to try. How Wilson persuaded the British and Russian ambassadors that he could be of use in this situation is obscure, but he evidently did and was about to set out when there was a last minute hitch: all public business was suspended because the Sultan's son had died and Wilson's passport could not be signed. He regarded this as particularly unreasonable since four of the Sultan's wives were pregnant at the time and the late prince was clearly not irreplaceable. When the passports did arrive he dashed off in his usual headlong fashion for Shumla on the Danube, where the Grand Vizier was encamped with the Turkish army. After a journey of 200 miles in 70 hours, he set about persuading the Grand Vizier not to make trouble. He claimed to have received assurances that the Turks had no such intention, though they felt that concessions by the Russians would improve relations. Wilson then crossed the Danube and found himself, to his great joy, once again among Russian soldiers. He urged their commander, Admiral Chichagov, to march his troops north towards the Russian main front instead of west through Turkey's Balkan provinces. Once again he claimed to have been successful, though the Admiral was, in fact, ordered north by the Tsar.

Wilson then dashed off to St Petersburg to tackle the Tsar in person. He realised that it was somewhat irregular for an officer without any official standing in Russia to make diplomatic representations to the Tsar over the head of the duly accredited Ambassador, but he naturally assumed that the importance of the matter and his own past friendship with the Tsar justified any flouting of diplomatic protocol, for which he did not have any high regard. Modern diplomatic practice, in which special emissaries are more and more used for delicate negotiations, has moved towards Wilson's ideas. The Tsar made no bones about receiving him, though that too was probably irregular. It was the light cavalry approach to diplomacy and no harm was done, except perhaps to the relations between Wilson and the Ambassador, and they could hardly have remained easy for long. The task itself Wilson says was 'to induce the Emperor to secure the amity of Turkey by restoring the acquisitions in Asia obtained by that treaty; a propositon to which the Russian Generals had added their concurrence as they attached no military importance to the new boundary line . . .' The quotation marks are in Wilson's own account and suggest that the words may have been Liston's. It was a forlorn hope, but both Castlereagh and the Ambassador, whom Wilson had kept informed, thought it worth trying. Wilson presented his case skilfully, appealing to Alexander's generosity, but nothing happened. However, the Turks did remain quiet, and Chichagov's army was able to march north and take its part in the repulse of the invaders. There were other factors at work besides Wilson's private diplomacy, but Liston at least thought that he had done well. 'I cannot but feel very high satisfaction,' he wrote, 'in the able manner in which you

The patriotic dinner to the Spanish and Portuguese Ambassadors held at the London Tavern on March 7th 1823.

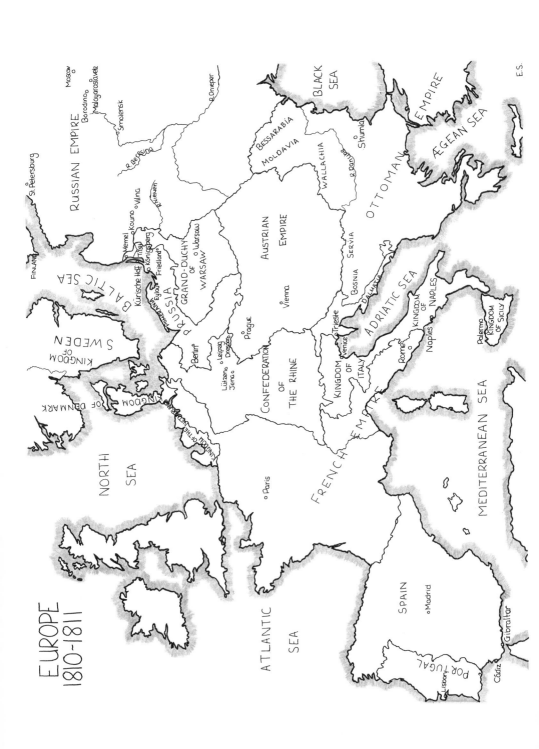

EUROPE 1810-1811

RUSSIAN EMPIRE

Moscow
Borodino
Maloyaroslavetz
Smolensk
R. Dnieper
R. Beresina
St. Petersburg
FINLAND

BESSARABIA
MOLDAVIA
WALLACHIA
R. Danube
Shumla

BLACK SEA

OTTOMAN EMPIRE

AEGEAN SEA

E.S.

BALTIC SEA

Memel
Tilsit
Kurische Haff
Königsberg
Friedland
Eylau
Kauno
Vilna
R. Niemen

PRUSSIA

GRAND-DUCHY OF WARSAW
Warsaw

AUSTRIAN EMPIRE

Vienna

Prague

Berlin
Leipzig
Dresden
Lützen
Jena

SERVIA

BOSNIA

DALMATIA

ADRIATIC SEA

Trieste
Venice

KINGDOM OF ITALY

KINGDOM OF NAPLES

Rome
Naples

Palermo
KINGDOM OF SICILY

CONFEDERATION OF THE RHINE

SWEDEN
KINGDOM OF DENMARK
KINGDOM OF

NORTH SEA

KINGDOM OF THE NETHERLANDS

FRENCH EMPIRE

Paris

MEDITERRANEAN SEA

ATLANTIC SEA

SPAIN
Madrid

PORTUGAL
Lisbon
Cádiz
Gibraltar

Corunna

Vigo

o Braga

o Vila Real

Oporto o

R. Douro

Almeida o

PORTUGAL.

R. Tagus o Abrantes

Lisbon

o Badajoz

R. Duero

Salamanca
o

o Ciudad Rodrigo

o Baños

Sierra de Gredos

Plasencia o

R. Tietar

Escalona o

Alcantara

Arzobispo

Tulavera o

o Toledo

R. Alberche

o Navalcarnero

o Madrid.

SPAIN.

Cádiz

Gibraltar

Morocco

ATLANTIC

OCEAN

MEDITERRANEAN

SEA.

E.S.

Wilson, Hutchinson and Bruce in the exercise yard of their prison. A contemporary print reproduced by courtesy of the British Museum.

have executed the commission I had ventured to entrust to your charge.' He expressed a similar view to Castlereagh.

The Ambassador at St Petersburg, Lord Cathcart, was, not surprisingly, rather less happy at Wilson's appearance on the scene. An elderly general, much concerned with his own dignity and with the minutiae of diplomatic communication, Cathcart was regarded as incompetent by the professional diplomats and disliked by successive members of his staff, who complained that he did not take them into his confidence or make use either of their abilities or of the information that they obtained. His treatment of Wilson was in accordance with his usual practice. It is impossible, however, not to have some sympathy with him over the predicament in which Wilson placed him. He was the Ambassador, the accredited representative of his sovereign; suddenly there arrives from the south – actually from the last charge of the Russians at the battle of Smolensk, as we shall see – a dashing British officer who turns out to be an intimate friend of the Tsar and the darling of the pro-British faction in the Russian capital: and this officer has proposals and representations to make the Tsar which are of the highest importance and some of which emanate from members of the Russian High Command. Obviously the task could be carried out only by Wilson, however much he was, in fact, usurping the Ambassador's place. It is to Cathcart's credit that he accepted the situation with no more ill-grace than was human. That he subsequently tried to put Wilson under proper restraint was both human and sensible. It was agreed with the Foreign Office that Wilson should be formally attached to Cathcart's staff and should serve as British Commissioner with the Russian army, but Cathcart told him in writing that he should have no 'public character' but only a military one, and Castlereagh instructed him to confine himself to matters of military detail. This naturally made not the slightest difference to Wilson, who concerned himself with everything that came under his eye and intervened equally readily in politics, battles and Russian internal affairs. What is more, though he knew that his despatches were opened by the Russians (because Cathcart repeatedly told him so) he nevertheless made the most indiscreet observations in them and caused poor Cathcart agonies of embarrassment. Any ambassador who had Wilson on his staff was to be pitied.

Wilson's road from Moldavia to St Petersburg had taken him across Napoleon's line of advance on Moscow, and on 14th August 1812, he made contact with the Russian armies in the neighbourhood of Smolensk. He at once went to dinner with his former chief, General Bennigsen, and had the pleasure of finding his old friends, Worontzow, Galitzin, Bagration and the Cossack, Platov. The Commander-in-Chief, Barclay de Tolly, a Balt of Scottish origin, immediately invited Wilson to join his staff. He soon distinguished himself by directing a Russian battery which silenced some French guns which were cannonading a key Russian position, and he was then sent into the city of Smolensk to find out from the Russian commanders there whether they could hold out. Both officers, Wilson says, were confident that they could, but Barclay, as Wilson sensed, had already decided to retreat. Wilson's friends in the High Command also perceived what they considered to be signs of defeatism in Barclay, and they begged Wilson to use his influence to persuade him to stand firm. He did his best, but Barclay's mind was already made up and the Russian troops began to evacuate the town. There is no need here to examine whether Barclay's moves were really inspired by defeatism or by a proper wish to avoid the encirclement of Russia's main army. The French did make great efforts to cut off its retreat and at one point they nearly overwhelmed a Russian detachment posted to keep open the road along which Barclay himself with the rearguard was to withdraw. Wilson was there and thus described the episode in his despatch to Cathcart: 'General Barclay . . . opportunely arrived at this moment, and seeing the extent of the danger to his column, galloped forward, sword in hand, at the head of his staff (including myself with two Russian officers attached to me as aides-de-camp), orderlies and rallying fugitives, and crying out, "Victory or Death! We must preserve this post or perish" by his energy and example re-animating all, recovered possession of the height, and thus, under God's favour, the army was preserved.'

The evacuation of Smolensk was a bitter blow for the Russians, and Wilson's friends were in a state of near mutiny at what they felt was an impending betrayal by the civilian ministers and foreign officers on Barclay's staff. They knew, of course, that Wilson was on his way to St Petersburg to discuss the Turkish situation with the Tsar, and they begged him to use the occasion to put their demands – there is no other word – before him. Wilson agreed, and not for the last time, played a part in Russian affairs, which today seems almost incredible, particularly when it is recalled that he was a foreigner, a mere brigadier, and not much more than a free-lance. What he had taken upon himself was to act as spokesman for a group of officers who were prepared to defy their own sovereign and dictate his choice of ministers. That, as Alexander, saw at once, was tantamount to military rebellion. Alexander's own father had been destroyed in such a plot and it is small wonder that Wilson's friends were chary of undertaking the task themselves, for if the Tsar chose to regard their demands as treasonable, the consequences for them could have been disastrous. Indeed the consequence for Russia could also have been disastrous, for the most formidable army in the world was inside the gates. If Wilson's handling of this affair averted such disasters and stiffened Alexander's resolve, as it may have done, though there can be no proof, his service to the allied cause was indeed remarkable. He recorded his discussions with the Tsar, both those on the officers' discontent and those on the situation in Turkey, and embodied the record in his *Narrative of Events during the Invasion of Russia by Napoleon Bonaparte* which he put together in 1825 for posthumous publication. There is no reason to doubt the general accuracy of his story and it deserves to be told in his own words.

> When Sir Robert Wilson reached the Russian army he found the Generals in open dissension with the Commander-in-Chief, General Barclay, for having already suffered the enemy to overrun so many provinces, and for not making any serious disposition to defend the line of the Dnieper . . . Before his departure for St Petersburg, however, it had been resolved to send to the Emperor not only the request of the army, but a declaration in the name of the army, 'that if any order came from St Petersburg to suspend hostilities, and treat the invaders as friends (which was apprehended to be the true motive of the retrograde movements, in deference to the policy of Count Romanzow*), such an order

---

*The pro-French Chancellor Rumyantzev who, when Foreign Minister, had helped to thwart Wilson after Tilsit.

would be regarded as one which did not express His Imperial Majesty's real sentiments and wishes, but had been extracted from His Majesty under false representations or external control; and that the army would continue to maintain his pledge and pursue the contest until the invader was driven beyond the frontier.' Since the execution of such a commission might expose a Russian officer to future punishment, and the conveyance of such a communication by a subject to the Sovereign was calculated to give pain and offence, when no offence was proposed, it was communicated by a body of generals to Sir Robert Wilson, 'that under the circumstances of his known attachment to the Emperor, and His Imperial Majesty's well-known feeling towards him, no person was considered so properly qualified as himself to put the Emperor in possession of the sentiments of the army; that his motives for accepting the mission could not be suspected; and that the channel was one which would best avoid trespass on personal respect, and prevent irritation from personal feelings being humiliated.'

Sir Robert Wilson, after that deliberation which such a grave proposition required, agreed to be the bearer of the message, as far as the question of war and peace was concerned; but agreed solely that he might mitigate the unavoidable distress which the Emperor must experience during the execution of such a commission.

The dismissal of Count Romanzow was not made a *sine qua non*; but Sir Robert Wilson was directed to state 'that his removal from the ministry could alone inspire full confidence in the Imperial councils'.

Evidently Wilson did not undertake to ask for the removal of Barclay, but his mission was certainly intended to bring about the dismissal of the Chancellor. In fact the Tsar had already decided to appoint Kutusov Commander-in-chief of both western armies over Barclay's head. Kutusov was 67, a veteran of the Turkish wars, where he had distinguished himself, and of Austerlitz, where he had not. He was dilatory, unwilling to commit himself, fond of good food, good wine and a good sleep in the afternoon. But he was a true Russian, not a

German or a Balt, and he owed his new appointment to popular demand rather than to any great confidence in him on Alexander's part. On his way to St Petersburg Wilson fell in with Kutusov who was travelling south the take up his command. They talked for an hour beside the road most cordially, and Wilson reports that Kutusov urged him to rejoin the Russian army as soon as possible as he had 'great need of such a comrade as yourself in the cabinet and in the field.' Later on he probably regretted those words.

In St Petersburg The Tsar entertained Wilson to dinner and his *Narrative* tells what happened.

When dinner was over the Emperor withdrew with Sir Robert Wilson to his cabinet, where the conference commenced by Sir Robert Wilson glancing over the subject of his mission from Mr. Liston, the state of Turkey, and the details of the battle of Smolensk. The Emperor, having satisfied himself on all these points, directed the conversation to the dissensions existing among the Generals, observing that 'he had heard that Hetman Platow had even said to General Barclay, on the evacuation of Smolensk, 'You see I wear but a cloak: I will never put on again a Russian uniform, since it has become a disgrace.' These expressions having been used in Sir Robert Wilson's presence, he could not pretend ignorance of them. The Emperor then asked 'whether Sir Robert Wilson thought that Marshal Kutusov (who had been appointed Commander-in-chief) would be able to restore subordination?'

Sir Robert Wilson observed 'that Marshal Kutusov, whom he had met going to the army, was fully aware of the temper in which he would find the army; that he had thought it his duty to communicate to the Marshal the facts with which he was acquainted, and that the Marshal had conjured him to conceal nothing from His Imperial Majesty; that he, Sir Robert Wilson, had undertaken a charge which his affection and gratitude towards His Majesty had made a duty under all circumstances; that in incurring the chance of displeasure, he was devoting himself to the Emperor's service, and for the protection of his dignity;' and then, entering at once into the matter (carefully avoiding the designation of individuals who might be regarded as leaders) he concluded 'By earnestly imploring His Majesty to bear in mind the perilous state of the Empire, which might justify patriotic alarm, and which alarm, from the gravity of its cause, extenuated a trespass on authority instigated by the purest motives, and intended for the permanent preservation of that authority itself; that the chiefs were animated by the most affectionate attachment to the Emperor and his family; and if they were but assured that His Majesty would no longer give his confidence to advisers whose policy they mistrusted, they would testify their allegiance by exertions and sacrifices which would add splendour to the crown, and security to the throne under every adversity.'

During this exposition the Emperor's colour occasionally visited and left his cheek. When Sir Robert Wilson had terminated his appeal, there was a minute or two of pause, and His Majesty drew towards the window, as if desirous of recovering an unembarrassed air before he replied. After a few struggles, however, he came up to Sir Robert Wilson, took him by the hand, and kissed him on the forehead and cheek, according to the Russian custom. 'You are the only person,' then said His Majesty, 'from whom I would or could have heard such a communication. In the former war you proved your attachment towards me by your services, and you entitled yourself to my most intimate confidence; but you must be aware that you have placed me in a very distressing position. – Moi! Souverain de la Russie! – to hear such things from anyone! But the army is mistaken in Romanzow: he really has not advised my submission to the Emperor Napoleon; and I have a great respect for him, since he is almost the only one who never asked me in his life for anything on hiw own account, whereas everyone else in my service has always been seeking honours, wealth, or some private object for himself and connections. I am unwilling to sacrifice him without cause; but come again to-morrow – I must collect my thoughts before I despatch you with an answer. I know the generals and officers about them well; they mean, I am satisfied, to do their duty, and I have no fears for their having any unavowed designs against my authority. But I am to be pitied, for I have few about me who have any sound education or fixed principles: my grandmother's [Catherine the Great's] court vitiated the whole education of the empire, confining it to the acquisition of the French language, French frivolities and vices, particularly gaming. I have little therefore on which I can rely firmly; only impulses; I must not give way to them, if possible; but I will think on all you have said.' His Majesty then embraced Sir Robert Wilson again, and appointed the next day for his further attendance.

Sir Robert Wilson obeyed His Majesty's commands, who renewed the subject almost immediately by saying 'Well *Monsieur l'Ambassadeur des rebelles* – I have reflected seriously during the whole night upon the conversation of yesterday, and I have not done you injustice. You shall carry back to the army pledges of my determination to continue the war against Napoleon whilst a Frenchman is in arms this side of the frontier. I will not desert my engagements, come what may. I will abide the worst. I am ready to move my family into the interior and undergo every sacrifice; but I must not give way on the point of choosing my own ministers: that concession might induce other demands, still more inconvenient and indecorous for me to grant. Count Romanzow shall not be the means of any disunion or difference – everything will be done that can remove uneasiness on that head; but done so that I shall not appear to give way to menace, or have to reproach myself for injustice. This is a case where much depends on the *manner of doing it*. Give me a little time – all will be satisfactorily arranged.'

Turning to the idea that Russia should give up territory acquired under the Treaty of Bucarest, Wilson says that he then, told the Emperor, 'that the Turks attached the greatest value to the recovery of the ancient limits, and that the Grand Vizier had offered him purses to the amount of 50,000l., exclusive of great rewards from the Sultan, if he succeeded in his negotiation.' – 'And what reply did you make?' asked the Emperor, – 'A laugh, and a hope that the Grand Vizier did not found his proposition upon any purchased experience of English envoys' – 'on which,' said Sir Robert Wilson, 'the Grand Vizier gave an Allah il allah, and joining in the tone of my mirth, he told me that the moment he saw a smile on my countenance he was convinced he could not drive a bargain; for all the diplomatic jobbers he had ever had to do with pretended great wrath until he had soothed it by offering at least double that sum.' The Emperor in great good humour remarked that 'he knew, to his cost, how the Turks spoiled the market by their extravagant prices;' 'for', he added, 'we generally employ the same contractors and agents.'

During the stay of Sir Robert Wilson at St Petersburg, His Imperial Majesty continued to heap distinctions on him, as if anxious to make more manifest through him his sentiments and feelings towards the parties whom he had represented; and when the Emperor sanctioned his return, His Majesty, with the greatest solemnity, 'declared upon his honour, and directed him to repeat in the most formal manner the declaration, that His Majesty would not enter into or permit any negotiation with Napoleon as long as an armed Frenchman remained in the territories of Russia.' His Imperial Majesty said, 'he would sooner let his beard grow to his waist, and eat potatoes in Siberia.' At the same time he *specially authorised Sir Robert Wilson* (who was to reside with the Russian army as British Commissioner) *to interpose, and intervene with all the power and influence he could exert, to protect the interests of the Imperial Crown in conformity with that pledge, whenever he saw any disposition or design to contravene or prejudice them.*' (Wilson's italics).

On the subject of Turkey, the Emperor acceded to the principle of the cession solicited, provided that the Turks maintained peace inviolably, but said, 'he would conclude that negotiation with Lord Cathcart.' Sir Robert Wilson despatched that information to Mr. Liston, and Lord Cathcart undertook to bring the transaction under the Emperor's notice at a suitable moment, but thought it not delicate to press him further at the instant: nevertheless, in consequence of waiting for a more decorous opportunity, the object was never accomplished, for after the retreat of the French, the Emperor waived all attention to the application . . .

After his discussion with the Tsar, Wilson spent some time in St Petersburg writing despatches and doing the social rounds. Though too prone to act on his own, he cannot be accused of not telling his superiors what he had done. He was particularly careful to keep Liston, in Constantinople, informed of the true state of affairs in Russia, for the Ambassador found the information of the greatest use in counteracting the versions that the French were always quick to put out. In an age when news travelled at the speed of a horse, the advantage of being first with a story favourable to one's self was great and prolonged. The French understood this and so did Wilson. Liston apparently forwarded his news to the British in the Mediterranean, such as Bentinck in Sicily, and they too profited.

In the drawing rooms of St Petersburg it was 1807 over again, la belle Narishkine and all, but this time the tide was with the British. Wilson found la Narishkine 'greatly attached to the English,' so perhaps the destinies of Europe were not, after all, swayed by a few Paris dresses, even if chosen by Napoleon himself. But in spite of the delights of such a life, Wilson was anxious to return to the army, and on 15th September he was able to get away, parting on the best of terms with everyone, including Lord Cathcart. He was accompanied by young Lord Tyrconnel, a friend of Castlereagh's who, it has been suggested, might have been sent to keep an eye on him. If that was the intention, it miscarried, for the Earl succumbed first to Wilson's charm and, before the end of the year, to the Russian winter. Wilson should also have been accompanied by Baron Brinken of the Russian Hussar Guards, whom the Tsar had assigned to him as a mark of favour, but the Baron's tailor was unable to finish his uniform in time.

CHAPTER NINE

The Pursuit from Moscow

While Wilson was concerning himself with high politics and high society in St Petersburg, Napoleon's huge army was rolling towards Moscow. It had suffered severe losses already, not only in the battle of Smolensk and the other delaying actions fought by the retreating Russians, but also from sickness and lack of supplies. The peasants scorched the earth in the Grand Army's path, and the Cossacks cut down foragers who strayed from the main body. At the village of Borodino, outside Moscow, Kutusov turned and gave battle. At the end of the day he withdrew what was left of his forces in good order and unmolested by the French, who had been fought to a standstill. They had lost some 33,000 men to the Russians' 44,000 – probably the bloodiest eleven hours the world had ever seen, or was to see again for over a hundred years. Moscow was evacuated by its inhabitants, and Kutusov's men marched through the empty city and out again, turning southwards into a region which could supply them with arms, recruits, horses and food, and where their presence would deny all those things to Napoleon. On 15th September, Napoleon waited outside the walls of the city for the Russians to surrender it. By the usual standards he had won the war: he had killed and wounded huge numbers of Russian soldiers at the battles of Smolensk and Borodino; he had penetrated hundreds of miles into the heart of Russian territory and occupied the ancient capital. But no peace offers came.

On 22nd September Wilson rejoined the army, having ridden round the east side of Moscow. Much had been done to make up the losses suffered at Borodino, but the dissension among the generals was as bad as ever. This time it was a deep and widespread dissatisfaction with Kutusov on both personal and military grounds. He was clearly ailing – in fact, he had only a few months to live. Whether for these reasons or from some basic factor in his temperament or political outlook, he seemed in no hurry to destroy his enemy or even meet him in the field. Napoleon, still in Moscow awaiting offers of peace, was becoming more and more uneasy about his position, but refusing to believe that in the end Alexander would not come to an arrangement with him. When no reply came from St Petersburg to the message that he had sent to the Tsar on 20th September, he ordered General Lauriston to seek an interview with Kutusov. Since it had been laid down by the Tsar that there was to be no negotiation while a single Frenchman remained in Russia, Kutusov should have refused to receive Lauriston at all. In fact, he agreed not only to meet him but to do so some way beyond the Russian outposts. The Russian generals were outraged, and none more so than Wilson. The Tsar had solemnly authorised him to intervene if he saw any disposition to disregard the ban on negotiation, and now a dozen generals formally asked him to 'act as Commissioner for the Emperor under his delegated authority' and 'as an English commissioner charged with the British and Allied interests' – hardly an accurate description of his position; and they added that he should convey 'the resolve of the chiefs, which would be sustained by the army, not to allow Kutusov to return and resume the command if once he quitted it for this midnight interview in the enemy's camp.' These words are taken from Wilson's own account, which goes on to describe how he immediately saw Kutusov and reported the news of the proposed meeting as a rumour, thus giving him an opportunity to avoid a confrontation. But Kutusov confirmed that it was true, adding that he was commander-in-chief and knew best what should be done: he had agreed to a night meeting, he said, in order to escape notice and avoid misrepresentation. He did not deny that the move was a peace feeler, but said that in his opinion it might lead to an arrangement which would be satisfactory and honourable to Russia. He ended by remarking sarcastically that he hoped that Wilson would allow his affection for the Emperor and Russia to prevail over his well-known hostile feelings towards the Emperor of France. Wilson reminded Kutusov of the Tsar's pledge that there should be no negotiation, and lectured him on the strength of the Russian army's position: he passed on the generals' threat to remove him from his command and added for good measure that he himself would report the matter to St Petersburg, Vienna and Constantinople.

Kutusov was unimpressed. Wilson then sought reinforcements in the persons of Prince Volkonsky, aide-de-camp general to the Tsar, who had just arrived, and the Dukes of Würtemberg and Oldenburg, respectively the Tsar's uncle and brother-in-law. All three supported Wilson, but Würtemberg suggested a compromise whereby Lauriston should be received at Kutusov's headquarters, with Wilson and others close at hand. Kutusov accepted grudgingly. When Lauriston arrived, Kutusov presented him to the Russian generals in attendance and to Wilson. The latter reported that Lauriston afterwards said that 'he immediately comprehended from what quarter the obstacle had come to the execution of the original agreement.' Many of Wilson's accounts of his exploits end with similar little blasts on his own trumpet, but attributed to somebody else; they can seldom be checked. Kutusov's staff withdrew during the interview which lasted for an hour: Lauriston did propose a truce, but Kutusov told him that he had no authority for such a thing.

There were a number of interviews at the outposts during this period, for Lauriston's move seems to have led to something like a tacit armistice. Murat was particularly keen on fraternization and once even obtained an interview with Bennigsen. When the Tsar heard of these meetings he sternly reminded Kutusov of the Imperial orders on the subject, and ordered him to reprimand Bennigsen – which Kutusov no doubt enjoyed – and to prevent such things happening in future. Wilson, from his usual mixture of motives, turned these encounters at the outposts to his own and British advantage. He would never actually converse with French officers, not even with Murat who made several advances, but he showed himself ostentatiously, escorted by one of his Light Dragoons, and made sure that the whole Grand Army knew that there was a British general with the Russians and that he was the famous Sir Robert Wilson, the scourge of the French. This intelligence certainly reached Sergeant Bourgogne of the Imperial Guard who mentions Wilson by name in his memoirs. Many years later, in 1825, Wilson told Creevey when they were out riding in England, 'it was just about the length of that village that I rode after Murat, with my pistol cocked, quite within reach of him, but I could not find it in my heart to fire at him, and no reflection has gratified me more than my not doing so.' When the two men met in Italy two years later, Wilson went on to tell Creevey, with another little flourish on his trumpet, 'Murat. . .said he had always wished to see him and thank him for his noble conduct, for. . .he fully expected his death from him.' It is likely that this incident took place outside Moscow at this time.

Meanwhile in Moscow the discipline of the Grand Army was breaking down, and even outside the city Murat's cavalry, already badly mounted, was becoming demoralised. At Vinkovo they were caught off their guard by a Russian attack and badly beaten, losing over 4,000 killed, wounded and captured. This was on 18th October, and it seems to have finally decided Napoleon that he must leave. On 19th October the retreat from Moscow began. When he heard the news Kutusov fell on his knees before his icon and gave thanks to God. Russia was delivered and in the view of its commander-in-chief, all that the Russian army needed to do was to follow the retreating enemy, keeping some way behind and to the south of their line of march to prevent them from drawing supplies from the unscorched south.

To the other generals, and to Wilson, this was feebleness if not cowardice. Already Kutusov had needed much persuasion before he could be induced to agree to the attack at Vinkovo, and during the battle his slowness in committing his left wing had allowed Murat to escape a much worse defeat. Before that there had been the interview with Lauriston. Six days after Vinkovo there was Malo-Yaroslavets. Napoleon's advance guard had swung south after leaving Moscow, and Kutusov sent two corps to intercept them. The two forces converged on the town of Malo-Yaroslavets and a bloody battle ensued, with Wilson playing a distinguished part. At the beginning of the encounter he appreciated that in order to mount an effective attack the French would have to pass through a narrow approach and cross a bridge which could be commanded by Russian guns: summoning a battery he placed it and directed its fire so accurately that the French were held up for a vital hour and the Russians given time to organise the defence. However, with French reinforcements pouring into the line, the defenders were forced out of the now burning town. Only one corps reinforced them because Kutusov refused to send more, though he could easily have done so. His critics say that he was unwilling to face Napoleon in battle; his defenders ask why, with the Russian winter approaching and the Grand Army already on its way out, he should risk another Borodino.

All the way back to the Niemen and beyond it was the same story. Kutusov could not be persuaded to close in for the kill, though most of his generals and above all the English Commissioner, believed that he could and should have done so. They were certain that Napoleon's armies could be so completely destroyed in battle, or by capture, that they could never recover. His power to dominate France would be broken, and with it his power to dominate Europe: tyranny and war would be removed together. But if he were allowed to escape, even with the heavy losses that the Russian winter and the Cossacks would inflict, his powers of recuperation were such that he would contrive to maintain his dominion and raise new armies to continue the war.

Kutusov's view was that there was no point in interfering with the doom that was about to fall on the enemy troops: when Russia was free of the invader that would be the end of the matter. Arguments about Napoleon's boundless ambition and freeing Europe from his tyranny meant nothing to Kutusov: he cared nothing for Europe and everything for Russia. The Soviet historian Eugene Tarle takes Kutusov's side in the controversy, and has some fine denunciations of Wilson's motives. He asserts that Wilson 'regarded Russian soldiers as mere material on which to found the new post-Napoleonic greatness of the British Empire . . . According to Wilson, Malo-Yaroslavets should have been the scene of a new attempt to 'save' the London merchants, the Liverpool shipowners, the Manchester textile manufacturers, from the effects of the continental blockade.' Shorn of its rhetoric and its marxist overtones this seems to mean no more than that Napoleon was trying to strangle Britain's trade and Britain was trying to stop him, with Brigadier-General Wilson doing his best for his country. The sneer at Wilson does nothing to explain why so many Russian officers were equally opposed to Kutusov's tactics, nor does it take note of the fact that Napoleon did recover from the Russian disaster, did raise new armies and did carry on the struggle through several brilliant campaigns. Moreover by the time the few thousand survivors of the invading army had limped out of Russia, the Russians themselves had suffered terrible losses and were to suffer many more in the ensuing campaigns. The real question is whether, if Kutusov had been bold and swift at Malo-Yaroslavets, at Krasnyi and at the Beresina, fewer Russians – and fewer French, British, fewer men, women and children from all over Europe – would have perished. No one can know, though Wilson and his Russian colleagues were convinced that their view was the right one.

Understandably Wilson is no more popular with French historians than with those of the Soviet Union. After the fight at Malo-Yaroslavets, Wilson and the rest begged Kutusov, whose whole formidable force had now come up, to attack the next day. The Comte de Ségur, Aide de-Campe General to Napoleon, wrote that on seeing Kutusov's position, 'the Englishman smiled at the prospect of a decisive battle. Whether it proved fatal to the French or disastrous to the Russians, it would be bloody and England would have everything to gain by it. When night fell Wilson, still uneasy, wandered through the ranks. He was delighted to hear Kutusov swear at last that he intended to fight, and exulted in the sight of the generals preparing for a violent encounter . . . He went to bed finally believing that their position would not allow them to fall back any further. He was sleeping soundly when, at three o'clock in the morning, he was awakened by a general order to retreat. All his efforts proved fruitless, as Kutusov had made up his mind to flee towards the south.'

According to Wilson's account of that night, Kutusov first told his generals that 'he had made up his mind to resist the advance of Napoleon, and that he was prepared to decide the fate of the enemy by a general action.' Wilson 'congratulated him on the decision as one worthy of the Marshal's character and the great cause confided to his charge: at the same time he begged that all former misunderstanding might be obliterated, and in the transactions of the ensuing day he hoped for opportunity to render him useful service.' Kutusov replied that 'he had determined to finish the war on the spot.' Three hours later at two o'clock in the morning the generals were again summoned by Kutusov and told 'that he had received information which had induced him to relinquish the intention of defending the ground in front of Malo-Yaroslavets.' To Wilson he said, 'I don't care for your objections . . . I am by no means sure that the total destruction of the

Emperor Napoleon and his army would be such a benefit to the world; his succession would not fall to Russia or any other continental power, but to that which already commands the sea, and whose domination would then be intolerable.'

So the Russian army began to fall back to the south while Napoleon, though Kutusov did not know it, turned northwards to regain the Smolensk road. He had concluded that he could not break through to the south and would have to go back the way he had come, deserted and devastated though it was. Briefly the two great armies marched away from each other, back to back, until Kutusov realised what had happened and sent Platov's Cossacks and a powerful advance guard to harry the enemy. East of Vyazma these forces got behind a French corps, but again Kutusov failed to support them in time, and the French got away, though with heavy loss. Wilson tells us that he was so sure that the way was open for the Russians to reach Vyazma before the retreating French, that he borrowed five hundred Cossacks and led them into the town without meeting any opposition. But it was several hours before Kutusov could be induced to move. At Krasnyi the Russians again established themselves across the line of retreat, this time at a point which nearly cut Napoleon's army in two. According to Wilson, Kutusov declared that he would 'no longer act the part of Fabius' but his resolution lasted only until he learnt that Napoleon was leading the French troops in person. His own troops begged to be allowed to attack and to avenge Moscow, and Wilson told him that if he would give the single order 'March' the war would be won in an hour. Kutusov replied, 'You had my answer at Malo-Yaroslavets,' and waited several more hours before giving the order. Wilson commented, 'Every drop of Russian blood subsequently shed – every Russian life lost in the pursuit from the severity of the climate – every soldier wasted in subsequent toils and privations – every rouble spent in the protracted contest – all Russian property afterwards destroyed – every injury inflicted by the flying enemy on a Russian inhabitant forms an item in the accusatory charge against Kutusov.'

The horrors of the Grand Army's retreat have been described by many of those who were there, and Wilson's narrative and Journal are both well sprinkled with horrible scenes. 'Thousands of horses,' he wrote, 'soon lay groaning on the route, with great pieces of flesh cut off their necks and most fleshy parts by the passing soldiery for food. Sergeant Bourgogne complained of the difficulty of hacking meat from the frozen carcasses of horses, even with an axe, but he found that the blood of one newly slaughtered, mixed with snow, made a nourishing soup. 'All prisoners were immediately and invariably stripped stark naked and marched in columns in that state, or turned adrift to be the sport and the victims of the peasantry.' The peasants refused to shoot them outright because they 'thought that this mitigation of torture would be an offence against the avenging God of Russia and deprive them of His further protection.' In one village Wilson saw, 'sixty dying naked men, whose necks were laid upon a felled tree while Russian men and women with large faggot-sticks, singing in chorus and hopping round, with repeated blows struck out their brains in succession.' In the ashes of a cottage he saw a group of wounded 'sitting and lying over the body of a comrade which they had roasted and the flesh of which they were beginning to eat.' Later he came upon 'a Frenchwoman naked to her chemise, with long black dishevelled hair, sitting on the snow where she had . . . been delivered of a child which had afterwards been stolen from her.' He did what he could: he saved the woman, and shared his bread with the starving, but, as he said, he probably prolonged their lives for only a very short time. He used his privilege of writing direct to the Tsar, not only to complain about Kutusov, but also to urge that something should be done about the barbaric behaviour of the Russian peasants. He claims that Alexander did indeed issue orders on the subject and directed that the peasants should be induced to hand over their prisonc.. 'n return for a cash payment. Wilson thought that this had some effect.

Among the prisoners whom Wilson saved was Elliot Clarke, the nephew of General Clarke, a French officer of English descent who, after an undistinguished career in the field, became Napoleon's War Minster and a Duke. General Clarke had been a friend of Hutchinson's and Wilson heard that he had been 'very civil' to English prisoners, so he had his nephew's wounds dressed, gave him a good dinner, money and a cloak, and sent him on his way with a letter of recommendation to his Russian captors. He did much the same for two Würtembergers captured at Dorogobouche, and his excuse for doing good this time was 'respect for our Princess Royal' – the daughter of George III who had married Frederick of Würtemberg. To Talleyrand's nephew, wounded and taken at Pulutsk, Wilson gave two shirts, two waistcoats and two hundred and fifty roubles on the ground that Talleyrand himself was out of favour with Napoleon and had been a friend of Mr Bosville. Clothes and a good dinner must have been hard for the French to come by in Russia in the winter of 1812. Wilson offers no excuse for giving £7 to seventeen Spanish prisoners and having them sent to St Petersburg, except that they were naked. He still believed, as he had in the Peninsula, that Napoleon's non-French troops could be induced to change sides, and he naturally had great hopes of the Spaniards. There was another high-ranking officer on the Russian side who was unable to resist an appeal to his humanity: when a young French officer prisoner said that if he could not be released he would prefer to die, the Russian obligingly drew his sabre and, despite Wilson's horrified pleas, cut off the young man's head. The Russian was the Grand Duke Constantine, the brother of the Tsar.

Wilson himself did not go through the winter unscathed. In spite of his compulsion to gallop to the most dangerous spot in any battle or skirmish, he was never hit by the enemy's fire in Russia, but outside Moscow his droshky overturned and crushed his leg. The wound was painful and took longer to heal than it need have because Wilson, after the first few days, refused to rest it, he simply dressed it with vinegar and water and carried on as before. Far worse was the danger from frost-bite. His Journal gives the impression that towards the end of the campaign he never passed a group of peasants or entered a mess without someone rushing forward to rub his nose with snow to restore the circulation. Others had the same trouble, and on one journey beyond Minsk in December, Wilson and his driver had to examine each others faces every five minutes. Even so, their noses were frozen several times. At the end of this drive Wilson's face was so unpleasant to look at that he was 'frightened and disgusted.' He decided that glory without a nose was not attractive and that the service on which he was engaged was 'rude beyond all parallel.' He also found that glory shone dimly in the Polish hovels where he was lucky to get shelter: 'squalling brats, cockroaches and earwigs in millions' tormented him nightly. So awful were the children that he began to think more charitably of King Herod. Yet his extraordinary toughness carried him through without any permanent disability, even though he wore no special clothing other than his greatcoat. Once when this was being repaired, he walked about with the thermometer at nineteen degrees, in his jacket without a waistcoat and remarked in his Journal, 'The vanity of the act, I believe, kept me warm.' He did not expect everyone to be as tough as he, for he obtained sheepskin coats for his dragoons.

As on his other campaigns, including the ones in the St Petersburg salons, he seems to have needed only a few hours sleep. Not only must he see everything for himself, he was also a compulsive writer; the Tsar and Cathcart in St Petersburg had to be kept regularly informed, and so had Liston in Constantinople; the Journal had to be written up for Jemima and his friends in England; his Whig friend, the Duke of Gloucester, and others had to be given the latest information from the scene of the most important action then taking place in Europe; and there were many other letters that Wilson felt compelled to write. The work was done after a round of other activities under appalling conditions: the night after Malo-Yaroslavets, when Kutusov ordered the retreat, Wilson wrote to the Tsar and to Cathcart 'from the drum-head of one of the battalions of Guards.' On another occasion he wrote, 'Although sitting close to the stove my feet are as ice and my hand can scarcely hold the pen. I have, however, much to write, and must write the greater part of this night again to be ready for the courier.' Young Francis Werry had recently been appointed to the British Embassy in St Petersburg, and in a letter to the Foreign Office in November, 1812, he wrote, 'Wilson, the Russians tell me, is in the hottest part of every action; he charges with the Cossacks, who call him brother. He gets into mêlés, scours the country; and at night, I verily believe, he never sleeps, for he writes folios of despatches, in which he introduces all kinds of matter. He is an astonishing fellow. The parties, jealousies and intrigues in the army are too numerous for him to escape their vortices; he reconciles the Russian generals, but gets himself into hot water.' Werry also says that Wilson was 'incalculably useful', adding, perhaps less accurately, that Lord Cathcart kept him in order by lecturing him. Werry thus confirms from Russian sources the picture that emerges from Wilson's own Journal. Wilson was given to exaggerated language, and sometimes to making exaggerated claims, but by no means always.

The River Beresina should have been Napoleon's Waterloo. Wilson's friend, Admiral Chichagov, had made his way northwards from Moldavia with a sizeable army, and Wittgenstein, who had been covering St Petersburg, was coming south with another. Kutusov, with the main Russian army, was in slow pursuit. A sudden thaw had melted the ice on the Beresina, and the northern and southern arms of the Russian pincers should have prevented Napoleon from crossing while Kutusov destroyed him on the eastern bank. But Napoleon displayed all his military genius, and his marshals, Ney in particular, their astonishing gallantry and dash. Napoleon feinted towards one possible crossing and deceived Chichagov, who in any case was bound by too rigid orders from Kutusov. Meanwhile four miles away out of sight of the Russians the French engineers, up to their shoulders in icy water, were building two bridges. Although between twenty and thirty thousand men were killed, captured or left behind on the eastern bank, by 28th November some twenty thousand of the Grand Army had crossed the Beresina, and were straggling towards the Polish frontier. Wilson was bitterly critical of Kutusov. Acknowledging Napoleon's skill and Ney's courage, he pointed out that if Kutusov had been always at the heels of the retreating French, as he could and should have been, instead of four marches behind, as he was, Napoleon's feint could not have succeeded, nor could the two bridges have been built. This may not be fair: by Wilson's own account the Russian army too was suffering, and it may have been in no condition for swift marches and lightening strikes. However, the Grand Army had ceased to exist. On 5th December, Napoleon handed over command of the now unarmed and ragged columns to Murat and took sledge for France: if his empire was to survive, its leader must be in Paris and not floundering in the snows of Eastern Europe. Nine days later what was left of half a million men crossed the frontier at Kovno; they numbered about a thousand men fit to fight and a few thousand stragglers.

So much has been written of the miseries and the tragedy of the Grand Army that it is easy to forget the price that the Russians paid for their deliverance. Wilson, who so deeply admired the Russian fighting men, did not forget. In December he wrote,

> During these last marches, the Russian troops, who were moving through a country devasted by the enemy, suffered nearly as much as they did, for want of food, fuel and clothing. The soldier had no additional covering for the night bivouacs on the frozen snow; and to sleep longer than half an hour at a time was probable death . . . Firing could scarcely ever be obtained; and when obtained the fire could only be approached with great caution, as it caused gangrene of the frozen parts; but as water itself froze at only three feet from the largest bivouac fires, it was almost necessary to burn before the sensation of heat could be felt. Above ninety thousand perished; and out of ten thousand recruits who afterwards marched on Vilna, only fifteen hundred reached that city; the greater part of these were conveyed to the hospitals as sick or mutilated. One of the chief causes of their losses was that trowsers, becoming worn, by the the continued marches, in the inner part of the thighs, exposed the flesh, so that the frost struck into it when chafed, and irritated it with virulent activity.

Contemplating the hospital at Vilna Wilson felt that in the last two months he had seen more dead than living. 'Seven thousand five hundred bodies were piled like pigs of lead in the corridors, and limbs and heads were stuffed into the holes in the walls to keep out draughts. All over the town were mountains of human bodies and carcasses of beasts, frozen stiff.' Wilson wondered what would happen in the spring, if the wolves had not solved the problem before then. In spite of the horrors there was entertainment of a kind, though Wilson did not much enjoy it, and it is nearly inconceivable that anyone else did. At Minsk there was 'a dance which was attended by about twenty Polish ladies, two or three of them very pretty.' At Vilna Kutusov gave a banquet at which Wilson was present, and he even went to the theatre but 'was almost frozen. As it was a state occasion I was obliged to remain till the conclusion. There was not one lady in the house, which added to the wretchedness.' At Vilna he at last received letters from home, one of which informed him of the birth of the thirteenth child to him and blind Jemima. There was also a 'very satisfying' letter from Cathcart, one from Castlereagh which was 'not quite so liberal in spirit,' and some from Lord Grey and the Duke of Gloucester. We know from Werry that he was 'greatly mortified' by Castlereagh's failure either to recognise his services or understand the financial difficulties of his position. Wilson was evidently more open in his letters to Werry than he was in his Journal, for Werry several times reports him as being 'in very low spirits' at this time. Even Wilson could not go through such a campaign unaffected, but no doubt he did not wish to alarm Jemima by mentioning such a thing in the Journal.

A few days before Christmas the Tsar himself arrived at Vilna and, despite the disgusting piles of frozen bodies and twenty-five degrees of frost, there were parades and dinners, levees and balls. Kutusov was decorated with the Order of St George of the First Class, an event for which the Tsar felt that he had to apologise to the English Commissioner. 'General,' he began, according to Wilson's account,

> I have called you into my cabinet to make a painful confession; but I rely on your honour and prudence. I wished to have avoided it, but I could not bear to appear inconsistent in your estimate of my proceedings; which I must be thought, if my motives were not explained . . . You have always told me the *truth* – truth that I could not obtain through any other channel. I know that the Marshal has done nothing that he ought to have done – nothing against the enemy that he could avoid; all his successes have been forced upon him . . . but the nobility of Moscow support him and insist on him presiding over the national glory of this war. In half an hour I must therefore . . . decorate this man with the great Order of St George, and by so doing commit a trespass against its institution; for it is the highest honour, and hitherto the purest, of the Empire. The Tsar ended by asking Wilson to show the old man 'suitable courtesies' and urging 'an end to every appearance of ill will.'

This is an astonishing speech for a foreign representative to hear from an Emperor about the commander-in-chief of the Emperor's victorious army. So astonishing indeed that its accuracy has been doubted. But that is what Wilson reported and there is no other evidence.

Two entries in Wilson's Journal (here slightly condensed) dated 10th and 17th January 1813, from the small Polish towns in which he stopped after leaving Vilna, give a picture of his life in this part of the campaign and illustrate his characteristic views on several of his favourite subjects. 'In the evening of the 8th,' he wrote,

> after having visited my Spaniards in the hospital; after having passed masses of dead, dying and filth that horrify me by recollection; after having given two hundred ducats to Colonel O'Donnell for a detachment of three hundred Spaniards and one hundred ducats to twenty Piedmontese officers for their clothing and maintenance to Memel, whither the Emperor at my request, had ordered them; after having made arrangements for the protection of a nephew of Mrs Robert Adair [she was French-born] who was here in extreme misery; after having saved him and clothed him, and done the same by an English sailor whom the French had marched from Königsberg; after having obtained Desgenettes' release [the French Army surgeon who did not poison the sick at Jaffa] and advanced him two hundred ducats; after having taken leave of my Polish friends, with whom I hope not to have diminished the opinion previously held of the English; after having adjusted a mass of public business, and cleared all official correspondence to the day of departure; after having had a long conversation with the Prussian General Kleist; after having looked at the spot where my long-to-be-regretted friend [Lord Tyrconnel] reposes in peace – I mounted my horse very near dusk and rode forty versts (30 miles). The next morning at daybreak we rode the same distance. All other generals and almost all other officers perform their journeys in traineaux, covered with furs and furbelows, but since Moscow I have always ridden without a rag of additional covering other than my blue greatcoat, except in heavy snow, when I have put on my Cossack bourka. I confess that there is some vanity in this deviation from general practice, but it is, in its effect, beneficial.

A week later he records the dispositions of the various Russian corps, and continues.

> The total force makes about a hundred thousand men. The wreck is powerful from moral energy, but it is only a wreck. How many thousands would have been saved by the opportune sacrifice of a few hundreds at Vyazma and Krasnya. Had I commanded ten thousand, or I might almost say five thousand, men, Bonaparte would never again have sat on the throne of France. This is not a fanfaronade. I do not mean by the monosyllable *I* to place myself in undue prominence, but to examplify the frequent and facile power of concluding the revolutionary war, which was offered to anyone who should have been authorised to act. There was only one Russian officer who did not feel ambitious to accomplish the achievement. There were various ways of attaining this successful issue — there was only one way of avoiding it — and that one was selected by the Agamemnon of the host.

CHAPTER TEN

The Bitter Victories

The Russian advance brought Wilson to Warsaw. The Poles had supported Napoleon in the hope that he would undo the partition of their country by Russia, Prussia and Austria, and restore its national identity. However, their hostility to the Russians did not extend to the English Commissioner with their armies, and indeed he found in Warsaw that same admiration for the British which seemed to manifest itself wherever he looked for it. 'I was not only received, but sent for by all who were worth knowing, and again had to be proud of British estimation. To be an Englishman is a letter of credit which no rank, no introduction can procure a foreigner. An Englishman is at once admitted, on the faith of his national character, to the regard and confidence which others must prove themselves worthy of possessing . . . woe to him who trespasses to the prejudice of his country.'

Wilson returned the hospitality he had received by giving a grand party attended by sixteen generals. After he had proposed a toast to the beautiful Countess Potocka, his friend Novosiltzov insisted on proposing the same lady, and this apparently gave Wilson the right of naming the drink in which the toast should be drunk. 'I used my privilege,' he wrote, 'and required that the draught should be salt and water, and I drank off a magnum. Novosiltzov shrunk from the contest ignobly.' Lest is should be thought, as it often is, that Wilson was exaggerating, there are in the British Library three letters from this lady referring to the incident and bearing out his claim that the British were much admired by the Poles; though the third, which was written after the Congress of Vienna had failed to satisfy the Poles' aspirations, says that this admiration 'has been somewhat diminished by your conduct at the Congress . . . you are a bad people *en masse* and to love you it is necessary to take you one by one, leaving aside

Commerce and Politics.' It is clear, however, that the Countess had not lost her admiration for Wilson.

Letters also survive from Wilson's publisher: on 11th December John Murray told him that he was the only person able to give the public the history of the campaign, and that he, Murray, would be happy if Wilson would do him the honour of mentioning any arrangements, pecuniary or otherwise, by which he could be so fortunate as to be entrusted with giving Wilson's valuable papers to the world. Longman's, either less delicate or aware that Murray had written a month before them, came straight out with an offer of £1,250 for the copyright of a quarto volume. Curiously, on this occasion Wilson felt inhibited from publishing, and directed that the *Narrative* which he prepared in 1825 should not be published in his lifetime, and it did not appear until 1860, though several of his friends read it soon after it was written. The eventual publisher, appropriately, was Murray.

Before the end of 1812 the Prussians, coerced and reluctant allies of Napoleon, were edging over to the winning side. In February, 1813, they went over officially and the armies of Russia and Prussia pressed westwards in the still bitter weather. Meanwhile Napoleon, now back in Paris, was doing with all his ruthless skill and resource exactly what Wilson feared that he would – he was repairing the damage and preparing to fall once again on the enemies he had beaten so often. He was still master of France, the Low Countries, Italy, Illyria and much of Germany; his garrisons still occupied fortresses along the Vistula, the Oder and the Elbe; and Wellington, despite his victory at Salamanca in July, 1812, and his capture of Madrid, had once again had to retreat and by November was back in Portugal. Incredible though it may seem after his losses in Russia (though less than half of them were French) Napoleon succeeded in three months in getting together an army of over half a million men. True, they were raw and many of them were unwilling – the hills and forests were said to be full of fugitives from the conscription – but the potential was there and Napoleon had the genius to transform these reluctant boys into a fighting force capable of again beating the best that the rest of Europe could offer.

At allied headquarters there was intense diplomatic activity aimed at winning Austria over, and both the Tsar and King Frederick William were there. In these circumstances Cathcart could not remain in St Petersburg, so Wilson found himself once again under the close supervision of a superior. He was particularly offended when Cathcart told him that his status was that of 'volunteer', and promptly took himself off on a tour of the fortresses still in French hands, inspecting their defences so closely that he was frequently shot at. The tour, besides getting him away from Cathcart, enabled him to visit those of his Russian friends who were in command of outlying units, and to call on minor, indeed some major, German royalty. He came away very uneasy at the weakness of the Allied armies and thought that the positions they occupied were too advanced. For once he was in agreement with Kutosov, who was as reluctant as ever to go forward and said, 'We can cross the Elbe all right, but before long we shall re-cross it with a bloody nose.' This time he was quite right, but on 20th March he died, being succeeded first by Wittgenstein and then by Barclay.

Napoleon left Paris in mid-April with 145,000 men and 400 guns, and less than three weeks later he beat the Russians and Prussians at Lützen. Wilson was there, of course, and gave his usual performance. 'It was my good fortune,' he wrote,

> to rally the Prussians as they were flying from Glogau and extending panic through the Russians; to enter with them, sword in hand, and carry the village . . . I then rode to acquaint Count Wittgenstein. The Emperor met me and asked me tidings, and with his and the Count's orders I took a Prussian reserve, put myself at their head and, uniting with the Russians still disputing the skirts, again drove the enemy back upon Lützen . . . It was a severe day, but I never felt more equal to the need. Such is the effect of moral excitement; for as to food I had none, not even one drop of water for thirty hours. I was quite unhappy to see the poor Prussians slaughtered from mismanagement. They are fine material, but they require exactly what has been done with the Portuguese – the loan of British officers to train their own.

He was slightly wounded in the leg by a shell-splinter when leading the counter attack, and he failed to rest it either then or during the Allied retreat across the Elbe. The result was a good deal of pain, but he was confident – justifiably, it seems – that the vinegar and water treatment would 'soon conquer its anger.'

A few days after the battle of Lützen, the British officers at allied headquarters were joined by General Sir Charles Stewart, Castlereagh's half-brother. Wellington had refused him a command in Spain because he laboured 'under two bodily defects the want of sight and hearing:' but evidently these senses were not considered necessary for a diplomat and he was now appointed Minister to the Prussian Court. Sir John Moore had thought him 'a very silly fellow' but George Jackson, who was on his staff at this time, described him as a 'dashing officer and, socially, a most pleasant and excellent fellow.' Jackson also thought that the fact he was the Foreign Secretary's half-brother made up for his deficiencies as a diplomat. Wilson liked him, not only for his good company and popularity with the Prussians and Russians, but also because he was an ally against Cathcart. He also shared Wilson's love of battle. Together they played a distinguished part in the action at Bautzen at the end of May. Seeing a Russian battalion withdrawing from some important ground, the two diplomats, on horseback and 'in glittering kits' (Wilson's phrase) led them in repeated charges and counter-charges for two hours, waving their caps and cheering loudly. Eventually help arrived and the ground was held, but even Wilson wondered how they had survived: he regarded it as a further proof of his conviction that every bullet had its billet.

A few days later, while accompanying the Tsar on an inspection of the Imperial Guard, Wilson enjoyed what must have been one of the most satisfying moments of his life. The Tsar put his hand on his shoulder and asked him to accept the Order of St George for his courage, zeal, talent and fidelity. Then, turning to Stewart, Alexander said, 'General, I give this to Sir Robert Wilson for a long series of distinguished services throughout the campaign – throughout the war.' The Guards crowded round to congratulate him, Stewart 'behaved most generously and kindly,' and everyone assured him that he thoroughly deserved the honour. He was delighted: the Order itself, the place – the head of the Imperial Guard in the field – and the Tsar's manner, were all that even he, who was so avid for glory, could have desired. Afterwards Stewart wrote a suitable despatch to Cathcart with a copy to Castlereagh, and both Jackson and Werry recorded the event with evident approval. Wilson thought that it might convince even his own government that he had done well. 'Perhaps if enquiry were deigned, it would be found that while I was thought an agitator and an encroacher on authority – while my acts were censured, my credit unsustained, and my power of doing good restricted as much as possible – I was promoting the best interests of my country and maintaining its professional honour.' His hopes were disappointed, partly because of his own actions, but he may have derived some satisfaction from the award to both Cathcart and Stewart later in the campaign of Russian and Prussian Orders which he said were of a lower class than he had been given.

In June 1813 the diplomatic pressures and the weakness of his military position – for neither Lützen nor Bautzen had been decisive – induced Napoleon to agree to an armistice. At allied headquarters this was a signal for an intensification of the dinners and galas and balls, so that Wilson, who was by no means averse to such functions, found 'the diplomatic campaign' more terrible than any other, and, tough and abstemious though he was, he went in great fear of gout. An English visitor noted that the atmosphere was not happy as Cathcart was not on good terms with either Stewart or Wilson, and everyone was bored. Wilson relieved the tedium by harnessing four horses to his britzska and driving about in it, resplendent in full uniform with decorations. He was often in the company of the Tsar, and much of a visit with him to Landeck seems to have been spent in a curious form of bathing. 'Czartorysky, Radziwill and myself,' he wrote, 'went off to the bath. the Emperor and about twenty gentlemen and ladies were already chin-deep in water, and their nodding heads reminded me of the dancing angelic group who wanted the 'de quoi' to repose themselves. The spectators, however, in the upper gallery pierced with their eyes to the planks below, and could frame no incorporeal illusions.' This is not the only place in his Journal where Wilson sacrifices clarity to archness, but the next day's water sport is more directly reported. 'The Emperor afterwards challenged me to a combat on the condition that I should not respect him more than I had done Czartorysky etc., for every man's hand had become a scoop against me. I soon drove His Majesty from the field, which enabled me to say with truth, 'Your enemies, Sire, are more formidable when they throw water than when they throw fire against you.'

On 12th August, Austria joined the Allies and the war was resumed. Wilson, recently promoted to Major-General, asked to be attached to the Austrian army: he was, after all, a Knight of the Order of Maria Theresa and well known to the Austrian Commander, Schwarzenberg; with the Russians he was officially no more than a volunteer and the move would not only give him a more official position, but would also get him away from the tiresome supervision of Cathcart. He soon proved his worth to his new comrades, for the Allied assault on Dresden – which he had advised against – was the scene of yet another dazzling exploit. 'At the instant of the huzza,' he reported,

> Prince Leichtenstein and I could no longer restrain ourselves: we galloped down to the redoubt and animated the men to mount. Some by their bayonets had already loosened the cement in one or two places and reached the crest, but did not like to pass over the parapet, as the fire from the town wall, distant only fifty paces was too heavy. I remembered what I owed to Austria, to England and myself. I dismounted, climbed over the palisades, with extreme difficulty reached the crest of the parapet, sprang on it, took off my cap and gave three cheers . . . and then leaped into the battery. My cheers had been answered by all around me of all ranks, and instantly hundreds mounted and joined the redoubt. This being accomplished, I descended. Count Collaredo came up to me, gave me his hand, said various handsome things, and so did all the other generals. It was a satisfactory moment.

Stewart then arrived with his staff and all the offices bent their energies towards consolidating the Austrian gains. But the French made a sally and began to work round the Austrian flank. In the failing light, Wilson, Stewart, Liechtenstein and the rest of their party rode up to a body of troops in order to dispose them in the manner best calculated to protect the retreat that had now become unavoidable. The troops seemed to be facing the wrong way but it was not until Wilson and his companions were in the middle of them that they realised that they were French. They galloped towards the Austrian lines, shouting peremptorily at anyone in their way and, in Wilson's words, 'happily rejoined our own, after having been in the midst of Bonaparte's guards for a quarter of an hour.'

In the confused and bitter fighting in September and October 1813, Wilson exerted in Schwarzenberg's service all his skill and zeal as a fighting staff officer. He rounded up troops and guns, and lead them personally to threatened points, he led Austrian cavalry charges, he persuaded quarrelsome Allied commanders to agree to Schwarzenberg's plans, and he busied himself with reconciling Schwarzenberg and the King of Prussia, who had quarrelled. He also got very wet, for the weather was as rough and rainy as an English December, and his oilskin cloak, holed by a musket-ball, blew into shreds as he galloped in the wind. 'The roads were knee-deep in mud,' he wrote early in September, and went on to describe the misery and confusion of the Allied advance. 'Waggons with dying horses – waggons without horses – waggons without wheels – waggons with waggoners imploring the thunder of Jove to smite all men including themselves, and also all beasts also themselves included; guns which had been spiked by the fugitive French, and which were being withdrawn to be made capable of redeeming their honour; Hungarians without boots – Austrians without shoes – men without energy – women without spirits (in the barrels which they carried on their backs) – and Cossacks without mercy – covered the road. It was a scene of utter devastation.'

But at least the Allies were advancing. Napoleon was now faced in central Germany by Russia, Prussia, Austria and Sweden; by another Austrian force in Italy; and by the gathering menace of Wellington's advance to the Pyrenees. On 19th October, after three days of bloody fighting in which Wilson played a distinguished – indeed, according to Schwarzenberg, a decisive – part, the Allies entered Leipzig and threw Napoleon's army in full retreat to the Rhine. It was time for the Allies to plan the peace that they would impose or accept, and the autumn of 1813 was a period of great diplomatic activity as well as intense fighting. Britain was officially represented by Cathcart and Stewart, and to supplement their efforts Castlereagh sent a new ambassador, Lord Aberdeen, to Vienna. It was an odd appointment, for Aberdeen was young and ignorant of the affairs of Central Europe. He made a bad start, embarrassing everyone by his manner and his ignorance of French. He also appeared to succumb at once to the charm of Metternich, the Austrian Minister. George Jackson's view of the strength of British diplomacy at this crucial time and place was, 'Of the two Ambassadors we now have, one is cajoled and bamboozled, the other laughed at and neglected. Sir Charles Stewart has not sufficient weight to counteract this . . . He is not, as he says, "an adept in difficult diplomacy"'. In the light of this professional comment, it is perhaps not surprising that Wilson should have felt more than usually frustrated. Worse – for him – was to come, for eventually Castlereagh decided that he would have to go out himself and he left England at the end of the year. But before doing so he had decided on another change in British representation: he replaced Wilson by Lord Burghersh.

Wilson was outraged. He simply could not understand how anyone so deep in the councils of two Emperors and a King, to say nothing of innumerable generals and diplomats, could be dispensed with. It seemed an act of irresponsible favouritism to send in his stead a mere colonel who, so far from being on imtimate terms with the allied leaders, did not know them at all. Determined not to surrender his place without a fight, he wrote to Aberdeen, 'I am sure that my presence at this important crisis is of advantage to the public interest: that no one but myself can be *au fait* of what is passing, and no other person instantly, if ever, enjoy that confidence which I have from all.' In his Journal he added, 'Nothing is done militarily or politically that I am not told instanter; nothing is discussed that I do not hear.'

Aberdeen, who succumbed to Wilson's charm as readily as to Metternich's, did his best, as did all Wilson's friends: the most illustrious names of the age, Alexander of Russia, Schwarzenberg, Metternich, Blücher, Radetzky and the King of Prussia, all inteceded for him. 'Schwarzenberg and Metternich have frequently spoken to me on the subject,' Aberdeen wrote to Castlereagh.

> the first has written to me in the most pressing manner; the latter has told me that he has it in command from the Emperor [of

Austria] to express his wishes that he should continue with the army. Schwarzenberg told me that he would as soon part with Radetzky, the Quartermaster-General; that Wilson was admitted to all their councils; that they had the most entire confidence in his zeal and talents. His services in the field have been most conspicuous. On the 16th at Leipzig – which day was saved by the brilliant conduct of the Austrian cavalry under Nostitz – Schwarzenberg declares the success to be chiefly owing to the intelligence and able dispositions of Wilson. In short, to enumerate his military services would be endless. Great as they are, however, they fall short, in Schwarzenberg's estimation, of those which he has rendered out of the field. From his intimate knowledge of the Russian and Prussian armies and the great respect invariably shown him by the Emperor of Russia and the King of Prussia, he is able to do a thousand things that no one else could do. He was the means of making up a difference between the King and Schwarzenberg which was of the utmost importance. In short, I cannot possibly be deceived; I hear it from morning to night, from all nations; and I am perfectly persuaded there is no man in existence who unites in the fourth part of the degree, the love and admiration of the three armies. What Stewart is with the Prussians, Wilson is with all.

A few days later Aberdeen wrote again.

The Emperor of Russia has flatly declared that he will take on himself the responsibility of *making* him stay; and that he will write to the Prince Regent accordingly. The King [of Prussia] has been equally kind; and old Blücher has pressed him to come and share his quarters for the rest of the campaign, where he shall be treated as his son. But in the Austrian army, from the first to the last the feeling is the same and as strongly expressed. Schwarzenberg . . . says that in the disagreeable sort of command that he has over Russians and Prussians, if it were not for Wilson there are many things which he should never venture to propose. In the field it has frequently happened that he has sent Wilson to *persuade* Russian officers – nay! even the Emperor himself – to do what he would not otherwise have thought of.

It is strange that such praise can have been given by such men at such a crucial moment in the history of Western Europe to a mere Major-General, a foreigner, a man whose official position was roughly that of a military attaché. It should be remembered to his credit by his own countrymen, whatever their verdict on his subsequent career. At the time it did him no good at all. Stewart put it about that the change was being made because Castlereagh wished to find a job for Burghersh who, though he may not have known many foreign monarchs, had all the right connections at home: his father was a member of the government, he himself sat on the government side in the House of Commons, he had been Wellington's ADC in Spain and had married his niece. However, it seems certain that Wilson's own activities were the cause. Castlereagh knew that he was in regular correspondence with the leaders of the Opposition and regarded him, justifiably as a Whig spy. Wilson might have replied that as Cathcart had for long denied him any official position, he was entitled to write to anyone he liked. He might also have argued, had he known it, that a similar situation had arisen in the Peninsula in 1812 when Colonel Gordon, Aberdeen's brother, was, as Creevey reported to his wife, 'in constant correspondence with both Grey and Whitbread . . . his accounts are of the most desponding cast. He considers our ultimate discomfiture as a question purely of time.'

Castlereagh may have felt that Wilson's correspondence with the Whigs was no great matter when the main problems were military and British troops were not present, but no Foreign Minister could feel easy if his confidential diplomatic negotiations were liable to be revealed to the Opposition and perhaps made the subject of public debate. Nor do Foreign Ministers – or at any rate British ones – look favourably on representatives who become too closely identified with the interests of those to whom they are accredited, and Wilson was becoming decidedly Austrian. Metternich was reluctant to press Napoleon to the extremity of defeat, which he feared would destroy the balance of power on the Continent, and he regarded a negotiated peace, which would settle matters in central Europe, as more desirable, and more readily attainable, than one which would satisfy the British as well. Castlereagh was firmly against such a settlement, but Wilson obviously had much sympathy with the idea. The Whigs too were in favour of a negotiated peace. In the circumstances Castlereagh was justified in thinking that Wilson's continued presence with the Austrian leaders would be more likely to promote Austrian policies in London that British policies at allied headquarters.

So Castlereagh's comment on Aberdeen's letters was that if Wilson had the confidence of all other Governments, he lacked that of his own; and he regarded the intervention of the allied leaders on Wilson's behalf as an unwarranted interference. However, he evidently felt that it would not matter much if there was a Whig spy attached to the Austrian armies in Italy, and the appointment was offered to Wilson. His first reaction was to refuse and go home, but after hearing from Jemima that if he did, he would 'be shipped off to some remote settlement,' he changed his mind and accepted. There was a somewhat embarrassing interlude when he and Burghersh were both on the scene at the same time. Though they dined together and Wilson was convinced that he was behaving with dignity, Lady Burghersh wrote home that he was treating her husband badly, and Burghersh himself told George Jackson that his place was being 'usurped by anticipation'.

The farewell interviews with his illustrious friends in January 1814, were both painful and gratifying – he collected another high decoration from Alexander – and he was particularly pleased with a phrase used by Schwarzenberg in a letter to Marshal Bellegarde, to whose headquarters in Italy Wilson was now to be attached. Schwarzenberg recommended Wilson to the Marshal as an Englishman who was proud enough to regard the whole of Europe as his own Fatherland and who did not regard the happiness of his own island as the sole objective of a true English patriot.

The scene of Wilson's new operations would have been uncomplicated but for the activities of two of his old acquaintances, Lord William Bentinck, still British Minister and Commander-in-Chief in Sicily, and Joachim Murat, still King of Naples in spite of having deserted Napoleon's armies. For some years Northern Italy had been one of Napoleon's vassal kingdoms with Eugène de Beauharnais, Josephine's son by her first marriage, as Viceroy. At the beginning of

1814 an Austrian army under Bellegarde was trying to drive Eugène out, the intention being that this Austrian force should eventually form the left wing of the main allied thrust across the Rhine and into France. Murat in January 1813, had taken French leave of the beaten troops which his brother-in-law had entrusted to his command, and hurried home to try to ensure that whatever the outcome of the great struggles that were impending, he would retain his Kingdom. He made overtures to Austria and they were not rebuffed by Metternich, for the Austrians needed to secure their left flank as they advanced westwards across the north Italian plain against Eugène's troops. There were, of course, those who said that Metternich was glad to be of service to Caroline Murat, Napoleon's sister, because she had once been his mistress.

Napoleon was well aware of his brother-in-law's intrigues and summoned him to French headquarters at Dresden. Murat obeyed and arrived in time to take a brilliant part in the battles at Leipzig, only to desert again some weeks later. At last, in January 1814, he signed a treaty with Austria which guaranteed him the throne of Naples in return for an undertaking to put 30,000 men at the disposal of the Allies. Although the British Government was prepared to tolerate Murat for so long as he could be useful in the struggle against Napoleon, Bentinck, the man on the spot, was accredited to Ferdinand, the rightful King of the Two Sicilies, which included Naples. Moreover Bentinck not only wished to see the Neapolitan Bourbons regain Naples, but he did not believe that Murat had any intention of fighting Eugène. He therefore landed a British force at Leghorn where they threatened Murat's flank. This caused Murat to re-open communications with Eugène and if the two old comrades-in-arms joined forces, Bellegarde's situation would become precarious. Bentinck and Bellegarde both looked to Wilson to get them out of their difficulties, and in March 1814, he set off on another delicate mission which he describes with another toot on his trumpet. He had already learnt, to his gratification, that Murat had been talking about him. 'Wherever I am,' Murat was reported to have said, 'in all the great battles, I have seen General Wilson. He is certainly one of the most distinguished officers, and if it had not been for him, we should in various instances in Russia have got through much better. He has done us infinite harm, but it is a fatality that he should always be opposed to me.' Wilson respected Murat's superb leadership of cavalry and, though he regarded his desertion of Napoleon as treachery and the Allies' duplicity towards him as justified, he was unhappy about it. At their meeting in Bologna the two cavalrymen fought their battles over again and recalled the moment in Russia when Wilson could not pull the trigger of his pistol. Though Bentinck nearly ruined the negotiations with another of his rude letters, Wilson apparently succeeded in convincing Murat that the British troops at Leghorn would not attack him, and in persuading him to resume his co-operation with the Allies.

While in Bolgna he added yet another monarch to his collection, for he called on the Pope and had 'a conversation of some interest.' There were other diversions as well, concerts and balls, with Murat in red pantaloons and with his hair in ringlets down to his shoulders playing the gracious host. Wilson found the ladies lacking in beauty, a deficiency which he blamed on the Cardinals, who did not, he wrote, 'seem to have attended to the quality of the fair sex in their establishments'.

The fighting in Northern Italy was desultory compared with that in Germany, but Wilson made himslef as useful to Bellegarde as he had to more illustrious commanders. He particularly distinguished himself in the action at Valeggio where Bentinck believed that Wilson had saved the Austrian army by walking calmly backwards and forwards between the ranks of the Hungarian guards at a moment when they were wavering.

But his heart was no longer in his task. He could not fail to see that he had been relegated to a side-show. His Journal for this period is dismal with regret for the position he had lost, and the carping, over-pessimistic note is all too frequent. There were military reasons for his gloom as well. He knew that the Russian regiments were far below strength, having suffered terribly in 1812, and that their generals, second-rate at the best, were quarrelling incessantly among themselves and with their allies; he knew that many of the Russian officers and men were war-weary and wanted to go home, that the Russian military machine had lost its impetus. He could not believe that the Prussians had recovered from their earlier disasters, and he underestimated Blücher. He foresaw that the Swedes would do as little as possible. Only the Austrians seemed to him strong, but as they advanced to the Rhine their communications lengthened and their flanks were exposed. The Commander-in-chief, Schwarzenberg, was handicapped by having no direct control over the armies of his allies. Napoleon, on the other hand, had personal control over all his armies and the closer he came to France, the stronger he became: if he could recover from the disaster of 1812, he could, Wilson reasoned, recover from Leipzig: once across the Rhine and into France, the Allies could, and probably would, meet with disaster. In his letters home he harped on these themes despite warnings from his friends that he was acquiring the reputation of being 'an incorrigible croaker,' and despite the fact that the Allied armies, though checked from time to time by Napoleon at his most brilliant, advanced relentlessly towards Paris.

It was not only his contemporary reputation that he was damaging; historians have held him partly to blame for the Whigs' policy of pressing for a negotiated peace with Napoleon. Sir Charles Webster, in a passage of almost Regency vehemence, thus denounces Grey and his friends:

> Above all the Whigs lacked both deep conviction and reliable information. They dreaded the might of Napoleon as much as those they opposed, and their cowardly opportunism did not do justice to themselves or their country . . . It is . . . almost incredible that he [Grey] should have relied so much on the inaccurate and unfair reports of Sir Robert Wilson . . . Brave and energetic as Wilson undoubtedly was, his stupid vanity and itch for fame led him into the most ridiculous criticisms of the Government he was serving. Yet Grey seems to have accepted him as a reliable authority even after his information and his confident prophecies had repeatedly been proved false.

Certainly Wilson's forecasts proved wrong, but they sprang not so much from vanity: as from close – indeed too close for one who was supposed to be a detached diplomatic observer – involvement in the camps and the battles, and also from his political convictions. These factors blinded him to the true significance of the three days fighting at Leipzig; he failed to see that it was a turning point and not just another check from which Napoleon would recover. Immediately after the battle he wrote a revealing letter to Aberdeen.

> It will be said by some that Buonoparte had no further means of resistance and that he is annihilated. Do not let these gasconnades lead you into error. Depend upon it he has the force and intention to fight again. He has been discomforted and distressed, but not ruined . . . Providence has given us success in spite of our distractions: but unless you can secure the command of the army to one chief – unless you can make the war popular to the Russians – unless you can supply the Prussian losses – unless you can render the Crown Prince [of Sweden] more efficient – unless you can do many more things so as to render the impossible possible, I give my counsel for peace . . . if you neglect the golden opportunity, France will probably show that she may be pressed, but only to rise with elastic bound: if she is prostrated, depend upon it you will have discord, war . . . I am anti-Buonopartist and a soldier, but I regard general welfare more than personal passions and interests.

When in mid-February 1814, Napoleon turned and inflicted two sharp defeats on his pursuers, it seemed that Wilson's gloomy predictions were coming true. Sir Harold Nicolson thus describes the scene at Russian headquarters:

> It was then that the news of Napoleon's victories at Montmirail and Montereau reached Troyes. Something like panic supervened. 'We are uncertain', wrote Lady Burghersh, 'dilatory and (entre nous) frightened.' 'The Tsar,' recalled Hardenberg, 'has gone to pieces and the King [Frederick William] talks all the time like Cassandra'. Aberdeen, writing from Chatillon on February 28, expressed the fear lest the delegation might be captured by the local population who were forming armed bands. Prince Schwarzenberg advised the Allied Sovereigns to ask for an armistice and urged a general retreat. Metternich himself was alarmed.

When such great personages, so close to events, were so pessimistic, it is not surprising that Wilson should have expressed similar sentiments. Unfortunately for Wilson's reputation, but fortunately for his country, the man who kept his head, who was sure that the Allies' position was basically strong, and who rallied them at the conference table as Wilson had so often rallied them on the battlefield, was Castlereagh.

It was not only for military reasons that Wilson believed that the Allies intention of dictating peace from Paris would end in tears; he had strong political reasons as well. 'The invasion of France,' he wrote at this time, 'for the dethronement of Buonaparte is unwise, unjust and indecent.' 'Unwise, unjust and indecent' were words which Grey would surely have endorsed, and not because they came from Wilson, but because they reflected Whig principles and his own temperament: they reflected in fact the principles of Charles James Fox, the mentor of Wilson and Grey and all true Whigs. The Whigs had no wish to see the ideals of the French Revolution extinguished in France and all Europe engulfed in a wave of reaction and absolutism. In May 1814, after Napoleon's abdication, Wilson wrote, 'With all his faults, crimes and misrule, Buonaparte did more for the advantage of mankind than can ever be effected by the repeal of his acts and the abolition of his establishments.' Grey's attitude at this time is ascribed by Sir George Trevelyan to his dislike of imposing the Bourbons on the French people, his distrust of Britain's allies, the absolutist regimes of Austria, Russia and Prussia, and his temperamental pessimism about the outcome of military operations. This last was undoubtedly strengthened by Wilson's reports, but it would be unjust to both men to put down their advocacy of a negotiated peace to vanity on the one side and gullibility on the other.

As he rode homewards from Northern Italy after Napoleon's fall, Wilson was able to observe at leisure some of the political effects of the wars in which he had played so considerable a military part. The French had ruled Italy well and had awakened a feeling of Italian national unity. Now the French were withdrawing and the Austrians taking over. The Italian people were being treated as pawns – for the general good of Europe, of course, for Austria had to be compensated in Italy for the losses that she would have to accept in the Low Countries and possibly also in Poland: without such sweeteners there might be no peace, and continued war would have been much worse. But the Italians were pawns nevertheless. They might have accepted this before the Revolution, but it was hardly to be expected that a people whose aspirations had been encouraged in the name of 'Liberty, Equality and Fraternity' would cheerfully pass under Austrian rule to make up for Austria's loss elsewhere of an equally alien dominion. Whereas Wilson and other British officers were cheered in the opera – which he visited as often as he could – Bellegarde and the Austrians were not, though the controlled press said they were; and Italian soldiers refused to join the Austrian army. In passages which are strikingly modern and prophetic – correctly so, this time – Wilson reveals an understanding of the situation that was not shared by men far abler than he was. He perceived that neither men nor nations could for ever be humiliated without rising in fury. He acknowledged the dignity of ordinary people, applying his feelings for private soldiers and Hottentots to international politics. Though Italy was uppermost in his thoughts he felt equally strongly the danger of humiliating France. 'The Cossack pike which presented the constitutional charter,' he wrote of the new dispensation there, 'and the bayonets of Russia raising the throne of Louis, are images which will sooner or later fret the people to madness:' and again, 'Napoleon in the Isle of Elba has in this case only to be patient. His enemies will be his best champions.' He was indignant at the Allies' refusal to recognise Poland's right to national existence, and at their transfer of Norway to Sweden as a reward for her none too effective assistance. His Journal is full of comments on the theme of human and national rights. 'The good old cause, as it is called, triumphs. Its insignia of victory are the fetters of tyranny and superstition. If Austria refuses to recognise the political existence of this kingdom [Italy] . . . she will rue and justly suffer the penalty of her avaricious rage. It is impossible to extinguish the national spirit. Those who attempt it are enemies to mankind. It is dangerous in these times to force the *feelings of nations*. The day is passed for the contempt of public opinion.' When an Italian deputation told Castlereagh of the pro-Italian views held by Bentinck, Wilson and another British general, Castlereagh replied, according to Wilson, that Britain's honour was best maintained by attending to the general interests; that the government of Austria had always been paternal;

and that he could do nothing in opposition to Austria. Wilson commented, 'Lord Castlereagh . . . will find that man in this part of the world requires some consideration of his moral dignity.' The essential conflict in international affairs between those who seek and accept settlements which satisfy the majority – Castlereagh's 'general interests' – but leave minorities with a deep sense of injustice, and those on the other hand who try to satisfy everyone at the risk of settling nothing, has never been resolved. Castlereagh and Wilson (and, of course, his fellow Whigs, for his views were shared by most of his party) both had right on their side: Castlereagh's general settlement prevented a major war for generations, though revolts and unrest were incessant and bloody: but Wilson's prophecies all came true: after more than fifty years of conflict and bloodshed Italy freed herself from the Austrians, the Popes and the Bourbons, owing much in the process to another Napoleon; Norway's freedom took longer and came peacefully; Poland's took longer still, indeed has still not been achieved, and may prove to have been the bloodiest of all; the humiliations of France exploded less than a year later.

CHAPTER ELEVEN

General Pimpernel

As Wilson made his way homewards through France, another strand of his political thinking, indeed of his character, was revealed in his Journal. His sojourn in Italy had shown him that there was more to Napoleon's Empire than tyranny and aggressive war, that the French had not everywhere forgotten the principles of the Revolution. Indeed in Italy it was his erstwhile friends the Austrians who were playing the tyrant. The Whig principles of his youth were now applied to the rulers who were replacing Napoleon and they were found to be establishing not national constitutional monarchies but absolutism and foreign domination. Napoleon himself was deposed and humiliated, and Wilson did not like seeing anyone humiliated; it was indecent. He was glad that the British warship which took the fallen Emperor to Elba had saluted his flag, thereby acknowledging his sovereignty, and that he was still styled 'Emperor'. 'The recognition of his title,' he wrote, 'gives him consideration.' Wilson set great store by 'consideration', but in his view all men were entitled to it, and not only the upper classes – not the same consideration for everybody, of course, but the consideration that was due. He still felt strongly that he himself was entitled to a good deal more consideration from his own government than he had received. After reaching England in July, 1814, he had interviews with both the Prime Minister, Lord Liverpool, and the Prince Regent, but no recognition of his services and no new appointment was offered him. He appealed to the Duke of York but without result, for the New Years Honours List did not contain his name.

Relapsing all too easily into the mood which had possessed him after his return from the Peninsula four years before, he resumed his position as military adviser to the Whigs at Brooks's and as Grey's London correspondent, feeding him with information from the

Congress of Vienna which he got mostly from Czartoryski. The mood of the Whigs can be seen from a letter from Lady Holland to Creevey written in October: after saying that the peace satisfied no class, she went on, 'Those who hate France think enough has not been done to reduce her power of mischief, and those who feel some sympathy with her from a recollection of the original cause in which she engaged . . . lament her humiliation, and resent yet more the triumph of her enemies.' When Napoleon escaped from Elba in the spring of 1815, many of the Whigs, including Wilson and Grey, were in favour of making peace with him, and Wilson was so impressed by Napoleon's generalship at the beginning of the Waterloo campaign – did not the great Duke himself say that he h..d been humbugged? – that he made a public fool of himself. Henry Bennet described the scene to Creevey. 'Nothing could be more droll than the discomfiture of our politicians at Brooks's. The night the news of the battle of Waterloo arrived, Sir Rt. Wilson and Grey demonstrated satisfactorily to a crowded audience that Boney had 200,000 men across the Sambre, and that he must then be at Brussels. Wilson read a letter announcing that the English were defiling out of the town by the Antwerp gate; when the shouts in the street drew us to the window, and we saw the chaise and Eagles. To be sure, we are a good people, but sorry prophets.'

After the war the outlook was bleak for Wilson and his fellow Whigs. Wellington was the greatest man in Europe, and Liverpool and Castlereagh seemed unshakeably in power in Britain. The Prince Regent now supported the Tories and no preferment was likely from that quarter. The advent of peace was not the best moment for a dashing cavalry general whose stock was not high with either the military or the political establishment. Rejected and frustrated at home, and believing that in the present state of the country parliamentary discussion was 'a pernicious fallacy,' he decided to go and live in Paris. Knowing that Grey was as depressed as he was, he suggested that he should give up politics and join him there.

After installing their eldest daughter in the Ursuline Convent at Rouen, Wilson and Jemima took lodgings in the Rue de la Paix in Paris. He told everyone that he intended to live a quiet life, but his friends did not believe that with his 'activity of limb and nimbleness of tongue' he would keep out of mischief. The idea was, of course ridiculous. Instead of the glorious and victorious Empire, founded, if not always conducted, on liberal principles, France was now ruled by a dull, reactionary and vindictive regime, presided over by a fat and gouty Bourbon who could mount his horse only with the aid of a crane. Louis XVIII certainly did not inspire the reverence which Wilson normally felt for monarchs, and when his government arrested Marshal Ney, Wilson and many others, including Grey and Holland, took up the cause of his old opponent. Ney had undertaken to serve the restored Bourbon regime after the fall of Napoleon, and when the Emperor escaped from Elba, Ney told Louis that he would bring him back to Paris in a cage. Instead he went over to Napoleon and led the French cavalry at Waterloo. When Paris capitulated to the Allies, it was on condition that those inside, who included Ney, should not be molested. However, on the return of the Bourbon government for the second time, Ney was arrested, tried for treason and, six hours after the inevitable verdict, taken out and shot. Wellington was appealed to but on a number of grounds declined to intervene: he held that the capitulation was a military one which did not cover French political problems, and that it was not his duty to interfere: he could, of course, have asked the King as a personal favour to spare Ney, but he was unwilling to do this because the King had been rude to him. His latest biographer, Lady Longford, says that he sacrificed the major virtue of magnanimity on the minor, though respectable, altars of personal honour and public duty. Wilson's judgement was not so charitable.

Ney was not the only victim of the repression that followed the Bourbon's second coming, a repression which was provoked by fears of a resurgence of Bonapartism, for it was widely believed that Napoleon's return from Elba was the result of a grand conspiracy, and that if the leading conspirators were not eliminated they would once again plunge the country into turmoil and war. Count Lavallette, the Imperial Postmaster-General, was high on the list of those proscribed. He had been one of General Bonaparte's aides-de-camp in Italy and Egypt, and was a member, albeit a distant one, of what became the Imperial family. His wife was a Beauharnais, a niece of Josephine, and it was Bonaparte himself who had arranged the match. Lavallette was a captain on his staff at the time but there were political difficulties in the way of promoting him, so the General had to find another way of rewarding him. According to Lavallette's account the following conversation took place in a coach. 'I cannot make you a Major,' General Bonaparte told him, 'I must therefore give you a wife. You shall marry Emilie de Beauharnais. She is very handsome and very well educated. Do you know her?'

'I have met her twice. But, General, I have no fortune. We are going to Africa. I may be killed. If that happens what will become of my poor widow? Besides, I do not particularly want to get married.'

'Men must marry to have children: that is the chief aim in life. Of course you may be killed. In that case she will be the widow of one of my aides-de-camp – a defender of his country. She will have a pension and may marry again advantageously. As it is she is the daughter of an emigré and no one will have her: my wife cannot present her in society. The poor girl deserves a better fate. Come, this business must be settled quickly. Talk to Madame Bonaparte about it in the morning. The mother has already given her consent. The wedding will take place in a week's time. I will allow you a fortnight for your honeymoon.'

'I will do whatever you please, but will the girl have me? I do not want to go against her wishes.'

'She is tired of her boarding-school and she would be unhappy if she were to go to her mother's. During your absence she will live with her grandfather at Fontainbleau. You will not be killed. You will find her when you come back. Come, the thing is settled. Tell the coachman to drive home.'

The wedding took place, Lavallette was not killed in Egypt, though four of his seven colleagues were, and the marriage was a great success. Indeed Captain Lavallette had the best possible reason some years later to be thankful that he had taken his General's niece in lieu of promotion.

After Napoleon's abdication in the spring of 1814, Lavallette took no part in public life nor – according to his own account – in the hare-brained Bonapartist plots that were hatched and of which, as he said, everyone seemed to know except the government. But on 20th March 1815, after hearing that the King and his government had fled, he again took over the Posts. After Waterloo he stayed in Paris and wrote to Talleyrand justifying his conduct and asking to be put on trial. The government quickly obliged him, but he was charged not only with the usurpation of public authority, of which he was certainly guilty, but also with conspiracy against the State, a crime which carried the death penalty. This reflected the government's belief that Napoleon's return had been engineered by a network of plotters whose communications had been arranged by Lavallette. He was found guilty of this charge and condemned to die by the guillotine. Great efforts were made to save his life, particularly by his wife. She succeeded in reaching the King, in spite of the order that she should not be admitted, but all he said was that he must do his duty. Next she worked out a plan for him to change clothes with her and walk out of the prison in her place. At first Lavallette would have none of it. He thought that there was no chance of success and he recoiled from the idea of being recaptured in women's clothes; least of all could he bear the idea of leaving his wife in the hands of his goalers. But Emilie was adamant and she had already made all the arrangements.

At five o'clock in the evening of the day which they judged was to be his last, Emilie arrived at the prison accompanied, to Lavallette's surprise, by their fifteen year old daughter, Josephine. She told him that he was to leave at seven o'clock precisely, with Josephine on his arm; he must walk very slowly, wear gloves and hide his face in his handkerchief. As the doorways were low he must take care to bow his head in order not to break the feathers in his bonnet. The goaler would hand him into a sedan chair and he would be taken to a waiting carriage. At a quarter to seven Emilie took her husband behind a screen and helped him to dress. After reminding him to stoop when going through doors and walk as if bowed down with grief, she took him back into the room and he pulled the bell. Emilie slipped behind the screen as the turnkey opened the door.

Followed by Josephine, Lavallette negotiated the first door without breaking any feathers in his bonnet, but when he straightened up he found himself in the presence of no less than five turnkeys. He dabbed his eyes with his handkerchief as the goaler came up, full of sympathy, and said, 'You are leaving early, Madame.' Lavallette and Josephine sighed. At the far end of the room there were two more doors and another turnkey, but they passed through safely into the guardroom where an officer and twenty men stood waiting to see the tragic Madame Lavallette. Forcing himself to walk slowly, Lavallette went down the room, out of the door and into the sedan chair. But there were no chairmen in sight and no servant to lead the way, only a sentry six paces away who stared at Lavallette and fingered his musket. At last the servant appeared with the chairmen, and Lavallette was borne away. Soon he was in the carriage being driven to, of all places, the house of the Duc de Richelieu, the Minister of Foreign Affairs, where a sympathiser hid him in the attic.

He had exchanged one prison for another, for the authorities, readily convinced that the escape was the result of yet another great Bonapartist plot, were searching the houses of all his friends and even distant acquaintances, and had shut the barriers on the roads leading out of Paris. His friends made a plan to disguise him as a woman once more, take him to a port, and find a band of smugglers who would run him across to England with the brandy. Another idea was to hide him in the back of a carriage belonging to a Russian general who badly needed eight thousand francs to clear his debts. The money was ready, but when the general heard the name of the fugitive, he had visions of Siberia and drew back. A more promising plan was to march him out with a battalion of Bavarian troops who were due to leave France. But the police had thought of this possibility and were closely watching the troops and making contact with their officers dangerous. At last after nearly three weeks Lavallette was told, 'Some Englishmen have offered to serve you.'

Two women friends of the Lavallettes had made the acquaintance of the romantic Michael Bruce. He had been the lover of Lady Hester Stanhope in the Levant and his current mistress, it was said, was Madame Ney. He had taken a prominent part in the attempts to save the Marshal and was an admirer of Napoleon. On being asked if he would help Lavallette, he agreed enthusiastically, but he realised that with France under military occupation and Paris ringed with barriers, he would need military help.

Wilson was the obvious person to turn to: he was a general, a dashing character and was by now known – to the French authorities as well as to everyone else – as an ardent Bonapartist. Wilson, in his own words, 'did not hesitate,' though of course he seldom did. He enlisted the help of two officers of the Guards, Hutchinson, the nephew of his former chief in Egypt and East Prussia, and Ellister. The plan was a straightforward Scarlet Pimpernel operation, though it was made more difficult by the fact that the authorities were looking for a man whose features were well known, particularly to postmasters.

Lavallette was given careful instructions about how to turn himself into an English Guards Colonel: he was not to wear moustachios, his beard ws to be shaved very clean, and his wig was to be of the English pattern. It would not do simply to sew the right regimental buttons on any greatcoat – one would have to be made by the regimental tailor. Wilson procured passports from the British Ambassador, in the names of his brother-in-law and another officer, and with these Ellister obtained post-horses for the supposed colonel's carriage. Lavallette and Wilson, both in uniform, were to pass the barrier at Clichy in Bruce's English cabriolet, with Hutchinson and Wilson's servant riding beside them, as if they were going to inspect troops. If anything untoward occurred, Wilson and Lavallette would try to get away on the two riding-horses. Wilson would have preferred to ride through the barriers, but he thought than an open and confident drive at a leisurely pace and in broad daylight would avert suspicion. A relay horse was to be ready at La Chapelle, and at Compiègne they would change to Wilson's carriage which Ellister would bring from Paris. From there they would make for the Belgian frontier via Cambrai and Valenciennes.

The night before the journey Lavallette was brought by his friends to Hutchinson's apartment. All four Englishmen were there, having let it be known that they were going to a punch-drinking evening. Lavallette says that he saw before him a gentleman of tall stature and noble features – this was Wilson – and he evidently tried to express his gratitude. Nothing, of course, could have been more embarrassing to the Englishman, and Wilson later wrote, 'We did not permit him to give vent to all his sentiments of gratitude.' Lavallette did not think that his rescuers seemed at all uneasy, but Wilson at least was, for he said afterwards that he was 'not without anxiety,' particularly on account of Jemima, to whom he had not revealed very much but who had obviously guessed that he was about to do something rash. He and Ellister left after about an hour, having instructed Lavallette to be ready in his Guards Officer's coat at eight o'clock the next morning. Bruce also left, believing no doubt that his part in the affair was now over. His thoughts were already turning to other diversions: 'I am going,' he said as he took his leave, 'to spend three days at the country seat of the Princesse de la Moskwa' – that is, Madame Ney.

On the following morning, Lavallette, Wilson and Hutchinson set off in beautiful weather, but they were not on a joy ride. Wilson judged that his position in the world – by which he set such store – was at stake, and perhaps his liberty; Lavallette knew that if he were taken he would not a second time escape the guillotine. Hutchinson too was taking a grave risk. Even before they reached the first barrier they were in danger, for two British officers showed marked surprise at seeing a senior officer of the Guards who was unknown to them, and Hutchinson had to engage them in conversation to divert their attention. At the barrier itself Lavallette was closely scrutinised, but as the troops presented arms he was able to hide his face in his salute. At La Chapelle four gendarmes were standing in front of the door of the inn where they were to collect a fresh horse. Wilson walked haughtily through them like a general ignoring the existence of the common soldiers, but he did not fail to see that they had in their hands leaflets giving a description of Lavallette. Again it was Hutchinson who diverted their attention, and when the horse had been changed the gendarmes saluted the departing quarry. On the way to Compiègne Wilson saw that some of Lavallette's grey hairs were showing under his brown wig. Why a major-general in full regimentals should carry a pair of scissors is not explained; characteristically Wilson did, and the offending hairs were quickly snipped away.

At Compiègne Ellister joined them with Wilson's carriage and then returned to Paris with Hutchinson. Wilson and Lavallette set off alone in the carriage with the lamps lit and only three horses and one postillion: this was to show that they were innocent travellers in no hurry. But they were well armed, Lavallette keeping his hand on his pistol, determined to blow his brains out rather than be taken. At Cambrai they lost three maddening hours when the sentry refused to call the gate-keeper because he had not had orders to do so. There was another hitch at Valenciennes, but eventually they crossed the frontier. After dining together at Mons they separated, Wilson returning to Paris and Lavallette making for Bavaria. Wilson reached Paris after only sixty hours absence and immediately wrote an account of the journey to Grey. In it he expressed confidence that he would have 'no very bad consequences to fear from my undertaking . . . I do not wish,' he went on, 'either to be put in prison or to lose my rank in life, but I had made up my mind to both before I embarked on this enterprise: however, it does not seem that I shall have reason to regret an attempt that has so completely succeeded.'

In fact, not completely. Lavallette got clean away and was given sanctuary in Bavaria, being allowed to return to France six years later. But one of the police spies saw Wilson's carriage in the courtyard of his hotel and noticed that it was covered with mud. The concièrge told him that the General had just returned from a journey that had lasted three days. As Wilson was a known Bonapartist, this would at once have aroused suspicion. Under police questioning his servant said that his master had been to Mons with a Guards officer who, curiously, could not speak English. The description fitted Lavallette. The same servant was in the habit of taking Wilson's correspondence to the British Embassy, and the police bribed him to show it to them first and so intercepted the letter to Grey.

At a quarter past seven in the morning of 13th January, 1816, the police burst into Wilson's bedroom and showed him an order for his arrest and the seizure of his papers. If they thought that he would be impressed and go quietly, they had mistaken their man: Wilson was not one to help the police. He declared that as the order had not been countersigned by the British Ambassador, he would yield only to force, and he stayed firmly in his bed. A commissioner arrived, searched Wilson's room and Jemima's, and removed every scrap of paper. He then drew up a protocol. Wilson refused either to listen to it or to sign it. But he did get up and dress and was taken to the Prefecture. There he refused even to give his age and was put in 'a loathsome cell.'

At two in the afternoon a magistrate sent for him but he refused to go, so the magistrate went to him; but all the poor man could extract from Wilson was a claim for 'protection under the law of nations' and a demand for his linen, clothes, books and dressing-case. These were not provided, but a note arrived from the Ambassador and Wilson agreed to answer questions – that is, he divulged his name and his age, but would say nothing which could incriminate himself and nothing about his accomplices. Nor would he discuss whether or not he had wished to prevent the execution of Marshal Ney. At this point, for the first time, the exact charge was read out to him: it was simply one of removing Lavallette, who had been condemned to death, from France. Eventually his clothes arrived, accompanied by a note from Jemima saying that she was not allowed to see him because he would not answer questions.

On 17th January he was moved to the prison of La Force and put into a cell which measured 10 feet by 9 feet and contained a bed, a chair, a table and a stove; the walls were filthy, the floor damp and the window barred. However Wilson decided to make the best of it and to exert his charm. He made friends with the chief warder, whom he found an 'intelligent and good man,' and engaged a fellow prisoner as a servant. No doubt as a result of this new spirit of co-operation he was allowed to shave and to take half-an-hour's exercise. Many of the warders had been prisoners of war in England and confined in the infamous hulks. They spoke of them with horror, as a diabolical invention, but they do not seem to have borne any resentment against Wilson. No doubt he agreed with them.

The next day the Ambassador's representative called, and the day after Jemima, Lord Buckingham and a French lawyer. Wilson explained that his refusal to answer questions was based on an Englishman's right to refuse to say anything which might incriminate him. He was wise to be careful on this point because, as he no doubt realised, Lavallette's escape had aroused all the old fears of a Bonapartist plot: he was himself suspect on account of his support for Ney and even he must have been uneasy about what might be read into the papers that had been taken from his room. In fact the authorities were indeed contemplating charging him with a much more serious offence. However, he was a convinced believer in attack as an effective means of defence, and, when faced with his own pro-Bonapartist letters to his brother and Grey, he declared that governments should protect the people and safeguard their morals, not commit the crime of bribing servants and violating what he called the 'sanctuary' of families. In any case, though it was indiscreet of him to write such letters, it was not an offence: phrases like 'the Bourbons will be overthrown,' and references to 'counter-revolutionary activities' were opinions to which he was entitled, not facts, and they did not amount to conspiracy against the State. The magistrate said that he was prepared to accept Wilson's statement that he had no motive in helping Lavallette other than to respond to an appeal 'not only to Personal Humanity but to Natural Generosity;' and he admitted that the offence with which Wilson was originally charged was no more than 'délit correctionel' and that the political overtones were for the benefit of the public.

In spite of this, however, the Tribunal of First Instance formally added a second charge, that of conspiring to overthrow not only the government of France, but the political system of Europe as well. This introduced an altogether new dimension into the affair, for the additional charges carried the death penalty. At this juncture Jemima, despite her blindness and her precarious health, set off across the Channel for help. She saw the Duke of York, the Prime Minister and Castlereagh. Most important of all, in spite of attempts to refuse her an audience, she saw the Prince Regent in Brighton. He treated her with the consideration that her journey and her gesture deserved, and he offered to take two of her children under his care. Wilson wished to refuse this offer, feeling that it would be humiliating to accept, but Grey persuaded him that it would not.

In London Grey and Grenville told the Prime Minister, Lord Liverpool, that the execution of the three men – for Bruce and Hutchinson, but not Ellister, had also been arrested and charged – would have serious consequences in Britain, and they urged that the French government should be prevailed upon to drop the new charge. In reporting this to Wellington, Bathurst, the War Secretary, said that he and Liverpool were 'convinced that nothing would be so prejudicial to the cause of the Bourbons in this country as the execution of these three men,' but stressed that Wilson should not be told of any efforts by the British government on his behalf, lest he should so conduct his defence as to humiliate the French government. Wellington replied that he had already spoken to Richelieu and had been assured that the papers found were not sufficient to convict the defendants of the offence of conspiracy, and that even if they were convicted, the King would pardon them: it had been necessary to prefer the charge in order to enable the authorities to reveal Wilson's intrigues. Wellington added that he accepted this but would speak to Richelieu again, and to the King himself if necessary. So far as Wilson was concerned, the Duke said that 'excepting a perpetual intrigue, [he has] apparently been guilty of no act of treason; and the correspondence in the possession of the French government . . . tends only to show his wishes and the objects and designs of those intrigues.' But the intrigue tended, in the Duke's view, to subversion of the French government and to war and confusion in Europe. This of course was the Tory description of Wilson's political activities: the Whigs would have described the same activities as opposing both the forced restoration of the Bourbons and the reactionary settlement at Vienna. However legitimate this may seem to-day, Wilson had behaved with great recklessness in taking so active a part in the opposition politics of the country in which he was living as a foreigner, and then, by helping Lavallette, giving the authorities the chance that they needed to do him mischief. He should also have been more careful about his communications – but he was a compulsive communicator, quite unable to refrain from imparting information that came his way.

Though Buckingham told him that 'the [British] Government would have put you up to the Guillotine had the French Court demanded it,' the sensible and humane views of Wellington, Liverpool and Bathurst would doubtless have prevailed. In any case Richelieu proved right about the French intentions and the capital charge was dropped before the trial began on 22nd April. With two such romantic figures as Wilson and Bruce in the dock, the trial attracted enormous interest, especially among women. Miss Berry greatly looked forward to it, particularly when it seemed that the men would be on trial for their lives. 'I shall certainly be in the audience,' she wrote in her Journal, 'He [Wilson] is to be tried for high treason, which makes his case worse than was expected.' The day before the hearing began she wrote, laying aside her knitting, 'They will be acquitted of everything except extreme folly.' She thought that at first they made a poor impression, speaking too much bad French, yet even so, she 'would not have missed the trial on any account,' in spite of having to be there soon after eight in order to get a good place. She spent eight to ten hours there on each of the three days. As the prosecution had in their hands Wilson's own account of the escape, M. Dupin, the defending lawyer, had an interesting task which he performed with great address. Having no straw with which to make defensive bricks, he spoke with eloquence of ancient Athens, St Louis, St Vincent de Paul and Wilson's humanitarian acts towards French prisoners in Oporto and Russia; he referred to Wilson's decorations as 'hieroglyphics of honour,' and read out testimonials from the Emperor of Russia, the King of Prussia and Metternich – which might have been relevant if the charge of subverting the political system of Europe had been retained. Such purely legal arguments as M. Dupin was able to adduce were described by the *Annual Register* as sophisms.

Then Wilson, wearing full uniform and the stars of the seven or eight European Orders, rose and addressed the court. His dignity and confidence produced a strong impression. Speaking in French, with what Miss Berry described as an 'extra bad pronunciation', he acknowledged that he had been interested in the fate of Lavallette on political grounds, but maintained that this had little effect on his actions. 'The appeal,' he said,

> made to our humanity, to our personal character, to our natural generosity; the responsibility thrown upon us of instantly deciding on the life or death of an unfortunate man, and, above all, of an unfortunate stranger – this appeal was imperative, and did not permit us to calculate his other claims to our goodwill. At its voice we should have done so much for an obscure, unknown individual, or even for an enemy who had fallen into misfortune. Perhaps we were imprudent; but we would rather incur that reproach than the one we should have merited by basely abandoning him who, full of confidence, threw himself into our arms; and these very men who have calumniated us without knowing either the motives or the details of our conduct – these very men, I say, would have been the first to stigmatise us as heartless cowards if, by our refusal to save Monsieur Lavallette, we had abandoned him to certain death. We resign ourselves with confidence to the decision of the jury; and if you should condemn us for having contravened your laws, we shall not, at

least, have to reproach ourselves for having violated the eternal laws of morality and humanity.

Miss Berry thought the speech 'manly, soldier-like, to the point, temperate' – perhaps the only time that adjective was applied to Wilson. But the jury found all three men guilty, nevertheless. Their crime carried a minimum penalty of three months imprisonment and a maximum of two years. Wilson and his friends each received the minimum. But this could not be the only penalty for the serving officers. Wellington, with the difficult task of supporting the authority of the French government and with his own deep sense of a soldier's duty to obey, strongly disapproved of Wilson's escapade. Bathurst had previously written to Wellington, 'I trust there is no doubt of the English officers now on trial in Paris being dismissed the army if they be found guilty.' Others were shocked at the deception Wilson had practised in procuring British passports from the Ambassador, who was a close friend, under false pretences. But once again he was lucky: instead of being cashiered, he was formally censured in a General Order issued by the Duke of York and expressing the Prince Regent's high displeasure.

Though he can hardly have expected less, Wilson was very upset and contemplated resigning his commission, but Grey dissuaded him. His imprisonment, on the other hand, was not hard to bear, as Captain Gronow reported after visiting him in gaol accompanied by Lady Oxford's dog. In June Wilson was even allowed back to his lodging on parole to look after Jemima, whose health had broken down again. A Mr Smith has left us a glimpse of him in the prison at La Force which shows him well in control of the situation and in typical form. Although the authorities had been persuaded that they had no right to detain Mr. Smith, they were not willing to let him go without inflicting on him as much unpleasantness as they could, so he was to be deported from Calais and sent there in chains. Mr. Smith, anticipating the sit-in technique by a century and a half – and in a prison too – declined to leave until these arrangements were changed. Wilson also had advanced ideas on demonstrating dissatisfaction: announcing that he would not see an Englishman, nor indeed any human being, treated with such brutality, he and his companions succeeded in preventing the warders from entering the prison yard, and in the end they won their point.

Captain Gronow also reported that Wilson's exploit made him a popular hero for his life. Away in St Helena, Napoleon, with whom the Jaffa accusations still rankled, thought that the Lavallette incident showed that Wilson had seen the light. In England the Whigs were naturally delighted with the performance of their man: Grey and Lambton – the future Earl of Durham who was also known as Radical Jack – Grenville, Holland and many others, praised his generous and humane conduct, and commiserated with him over the censure. Many who had no sympathy for Bonapartism or Lavallette, or even for flouting authority, were won over, as Miss Berry was, by Wilson's bearing. Others were no doubt delighted to see a gallant British officer making the foreigner look silly. What is rather more surprising is to find among Wilson's papers several letters from Dupuy, the examining magistrate, which show that the two men were on terms of warm friendship.

CHAPTER TWELVE

Southwark Mountaineer

On Wilson's return to England it may have been this wave of popularity and support that caused his attitude to Westminster politics to change: whereas in 1815 Parliamentary discussion had seemed to him to be a pernicious fallacy, by October of the following year he was writing to Grey about the possibility of finding a seat. He may have remembered his father's wish that he should enter Parliament, and he would certainly have agreed with his friend Creevey, who in 1822 wrote, 'I became a member of the House of Commons in 1802, and the moment a man became such, then if he attached himself to one of the great parties in the House – Whigs or Tories – he became at once a publick man, and had a place in society that nothing else could give him. I advert particularly to such persons as myself, who came from the ranks, without either opulence or connections to procure for them admission into the company of their betters.' Hitherto Wilson had gained for himself a great deal of consideration, thanks to his involvement in great matters and his friendships with the greatest men of his day. In 1813 he had written, 'I have had the good fortune to force my progress through formidable impediments. When I think on all my difficulties, I can scarcely believe the success I have realised. Children ought to be very grateful to parents who give them hereditary consideration. It levels many obstructions and ensures many a helping hand; it makes those payments in gold which abstract merit would receive in baser metal.'

He had achieved his success with his sabre and his pen, and there were to be opportunities for the further employment of both these weapons, opportunities which he seized, but his strong Whig connections and his concern for the distress and danger into which the country was sinking were impelling him towards a parliamentary career. This did not deter him from starting another book, nor from being tempted to accept offers from Chile and Mexico of a command in their struggle to free themselves from Spanish rule. 'Parliament or Mexico are the only two fields which afford any interest and I will keep both strings to my bow,' he told Grey in 1816; and six months later, referring to South America, he wrote that if he could not rescue his own country from slavery, he would willingly assist the redemption of others. Hutchinson, now Lord Donoughmore, was as ready as ever with the cold water to pour on Wilson's enthusiasms. 'The war in South America,' he wrote, 'does not appear to me to be a war of soldiers, but of plunderers and Banditti, affording no hope of glory or any opportunity of showing those military talents which you possess.' He added a strong reminder that Wilson was too old for such capers – he was 40. He never went to South America though he corresponded with Bolívar and his eldest son, Belford, became Bolívar's aide-de-camp. The cause of the struggling colonies was for many years close to his heart and he did his best to help them. In 1812, at Bolívar's request, he attempted to mediate between Spain and Colombia, but nothing came of it.

One circumstance which helped to keep him from South America was Jemima's health. The strain of his trial and imprisonment, and of her own efforts on his behalf, had seriously affected her. The doctors obviously had no idea what was wrong with her or what to do about it. They thought variously that her trouble was in 'the vessels of the head' and that she had a tumour on the brain and an incurable disease of the liver. Wilson told Grey that she bore her suffering, which was 'continued and severe' with great courage and resignation. In October 1817, he wrote that he would accept the command in Chile, if Jemima did not get worse, but she did and he did not go.

So for the time being Wilson's sabre remained in its scabbard, and while he continued to look for a seat in Parliament he worked on his book. It appeared in 1817 under the title *A Sketch of the Military and Political Power of Russia*, and was promptly sold out. Wilson's argument was that the Allies had fought against Napoleon in the name of liberty, but as soon as they had won they imposed upon France and on the nations they claimed to have liberated, despotic governments which were hated by those over whom they ruled; that Russia had emerged from the struggle so much stronger than her allies that she was a menace to them; and that England was hated by the people everywhere for her support for the despots. Some of this is tenable, but Wilson's picture of Napoleon omitted all his crimes, and the account of the campaigns of 1814 and 1815 was strongly pro-Napoleon, claiming that he was defeated by treachery and bad luck, and that the Allies had behaved so stupidly that they should have been beaten – indeed in reading this part of the book it is difficult to resist the impression that the author wished that they had been. The victory at Waterloo was dismissed in a brief phrase and Wellington was not mentioned.

Wilson's remedy for the wrongs of Europe was that France should be 're-united to Europe' by placing Napoleon's son and his Austrian-born mother on the French throne: Austria and France would then combine with an England which would have withdrawn her troops from the Continent, expanded her Navy, paid her debts and harnessed the energies of her people by restoring their freedom: such a combination would keep the Russians out and give liberty to Europe.

Unfortunately, such validity as there is in this view is obscured by exaggeration, by arguments that are illogical or, at best, two-edged, by inconsistency and by examples that are irrelevant or do not support the proposition. The Tory *Quarterly* was not the sort of publication to miss such a chance of wounding a Whig or ridiculing a Whig view of the world. In a review of over twenty thousand words the critic began in the best traditions of his magazine by attacking the man and his motives, suggesting that it was the failure of ministers to give Wilson the recognition that he wanted that had caused him to attack their policies: and he went on to make the accusation that Wilson had falsely reported his action at Baños as a victory. Turning to more serious criticism the reviewer makes the most of Wilson's inaccuracies and bias, and particularly of his disparagement of his own country; the review defends the Tories' post-war settlement and argues sensibly that Russia was not as powerful as she looked. The book showed Wilson in his worst mood, the mood in which his deep liberal principals and concern for human dignity spilt over into resentment against those on his own side who did not agree with his views or remedies.

At the beginning of 1818 he was urged to stand for Southwark, but Jemima was seriously ill again and for once the propsect of action failed to rouse him from a mood of dejection. 'In the uncomfortable situation in which I am from Lady W's doubtful state I am by no means so eager as I was on the subject [i.e. of standing for Southwark]. It is possible I may be ordered to another climate with her and a thousand things may arise which would require my being unshackled. It is also most true that I am very much disgusted with publick affairs and that upon the present system I could without much regret relinquish all attention to them.

The public affairs with which he was so disgusted seemed in sober fact to be moving towards a tragic dénouement. The problems created by the Industrial Revolution had been exacerbated by the sudden change from war to peace. Soldiers and sailors had been discharged in large numbers and thrown upon the labour market to compete for work with men discharged by the ironworks and factories whose production was no longer needed. Agriculture also slumped, and there was unemployment and distress in the countryside as well as the towns. Though taxes were high, ordinary people had no say in the government of the country, for the franchise had not changed with the altered pattern of life and activity: villages with a handful of electors whose votes were controlled by the magnates returned two members to the House of Commons, while the great manufacturing towns had no representation at all. In the years following Waterloo sober people thought revolution was all too likely.

Though Mr Creevey spoke of the two great political parties, the Whigs and the Tories, the parties at this period were not the disciplined and cohesive bodies that party leaders hope that their followers are to-day. Men like Pitt, Addington and Liverpool, with their loyalty to the King and the Anglican Church, and their support for, and from, the country gentry, were, of course, Tories: Fox and his followers, who supported the principles of the French Revolution and disliked and distrusted George III and George IV were clearly Whigs. But within these groupings, members of Parliament, including peers, tended to gather round a commanding figure – Pitt, Fox, Canning, Grenville, etc. – who became for them the leaders of parties within parties, and who sometimes operated very close to the ill-defined border between the two main parties. Forming and maintaining an administration depended on ensuring that these leaders did not cross that border and take their followers with them. The other requirements were the support of Parliament and – for persons as well as policies – that of the King.

After the war political power remained in the hands of the Tories, who believed that greater representation for the people would lead to revolt. When the war began on the Continent, repressive laws had been passed in Britain to prevent revolutionary ideas spreading from France, and Fox complained that a man could be sent to Botany Bay for arguing that Manchester should have as many members of Parliament as Old Sarum. Faced with unrest at the end of the war – machinery was smashed and food-shops were looted in the towns, and ricks were burned in the country – the Tories continued the policy of repression and reinforced it with spies, informers and agents provocateurs. The Whigs were in a most difficult political position, for the Tories could claim to have won the war and saved the country; and nothing was easier for them than to brand any who opposed them, as traitors and revolutionaries – the latter category included, of course, anyone who called seriously for reform. In 1820 Wilson found that two figures of men in rags with the words Radical and Reformer painted on them were being used by the 31st Foot as musketry targets.

By no means all the Whigs were calling for reform or even, wanted it, for the party in which Wilson was about to play a bright, though spluttering part was split into what in modern parlance would be called a right, a left and a centre. The right-wingers, led by Lord Grenville, were reactionary and ineffective, but they possessed great influence by virtue of the boroughs that they had in their pockets. The centre were not much livelier, for their leader was Grey who felt helpless in the face of the Tories' entrenched position, and who was himself afraid of revolution: he had been strong for reform in his youth, and was to become so again, but now he preferred his country house at Howick to hopeless argument in the House of Lords. It was the left wing of the party, known as the 'Mountain', which supplied what drive there was in the party and it was to them that Wilson attached himself, despite his continuing friendship with Grey. Creevey, Lambton and Brougham were his close political associates.

Though the basic assumptions of most of the Whigs did not differ substantially from those of the moderate Tories, at any rate in domestic politics, and the main battle was for power, the Whigs, except perhaps for the Grenvillites, could legitimately claim a greater commitment to 'liberal' and humane causes, such as the abolition of slavery, the grant of full civic rights to the Catholics – 'Catholic emancipation' – the reform of the brutal penal system and the reduction of extravagance and corruption in government. The trouble was that, anxious as they were to ameliorate the harsh lot of the poor, they too were an aristocratic party at heart who not only feared revolution but were inclined to regard the people's distress as the unavoidable aftermath of twenty years of war and blockade. Some of them would probably have agreed with Lord Liverpool's statement in the House of Lords that the 'evils inseparable from the state of things should not be charged on any government; and, on enquiry, it would be found that by far the greater part of the miseries of which human nature complained were in all times and in all countries, beyond the control of human legislation.' Even on parliamentary reform, that is the extension of the franchise and the abolition of the pocket boroughs, the Whigs were divided: the Grenvillites were, of course, entirely against it; Grey was for the time being lukewarm; and only the Mountain were wholly for it. In February, 1817, Wilson wrote to Grey, 'Reform, I take it, is absolutely necessary for the Salvation of this country, both in Parliament and out of it. The majority of the people are of that opinion, but they differ as to the quantum and the mode . . . A more equal representation of the people and the doing away with the rotten boroughs would tend very much to the prosperity of my country.' But he was for law and order too – 'if the nation is left to run wild in its distresses and without the needed direction, formidable consequences are inevitable' – and he thought that reform, so far from leading to revolution, was the only way of preventing it. 'Ministers,' he wrote to Grey, 'and not the Reformists are the real revolutionists,' for they were 'advancing to the crisis where complete Despotism must be attempted as the last security against general anarchy.' In short, Wilson and his friends at this time were for freedom, better government, more humane treatment and more equitable representation, but all under a system of constitutional monarchy which maintained law and order and, as the *Edinburgh Review* put it some years later, 'the natural and wholesome influence of wealth and rank, and the veneration which belongs to old institutions.' Liberty and fraternity they saw as desirable and perhaps attainable; equality they seem to have realised was neither.

The Mountain were not the only reformers, for to their left stood the Radicals. Not numerous in Parliament, they were vociferous and influential outside it. Reform was one of their main planks in their platform, and they were regarded as near-revolutionaries by even the middle-of-the-road Whigs. Wilson flirted with them and so did Brougham, but it was as a Whig, though of the advanced sort, that he was urged to stand for Southwark in 1818. His black mood was beginning to give way before his more usual optimism and the process may have been hastened, as had happened in East Prussia eleven years before, by prophecies of certain defeat from Donoughmore. To one of these the Earl, writing from his seat at Knocklofty in Tipperary, added, 'Your legs are long, your activity is immeasurable, your time is of no value to you, you have no longer any character for discretion to forfeit, you never can stand worse with the government than you do at present, therefore I give you my permission to make use of any quantity of words but of no quantity of money.' This was an important consideration, for 'the Maidstone constitutents,' Wilson told Grey, 'wanted 4000 l. to vote as *Independent* men. The Boro of Southwark, independents have more handsomely offered to bring me in gratis.' Southwark was no pocket borough, for there were several thousand voters and the contests were genuine.

So in the spring of 1818 Wilson decided to stand for Southwark. He had joined a political society called the 'Rota' whose members were pledged to Reform; Bruce was also a member, as was John Cam Hobhouse, Byron's friend. Byron himself wrote from Italy that he would like to join. In later life Hobhouse wrote that the members of the Rota 'read essays, concocted plans for reform, framed resolutions to be made in Parliament and drew up addresses for Parliamentary candidates. We were all Parliamentary reformers but were by no means agreed on the extent or general character of the change that ought to be made in the representative system . . . The member of our society who in those days seemed to be determined to be satisfied with nothing short of Radical Reform was that one of our associates who afterwards became member for Southwark. The address of that gentleman to his constituency was concocted at our Rota.'

Thus supported, and assuring Grey that he intended to be moderate, Wilson faced the mob★ – for elections in Southwark were notorious for their turbulence – as well as the wealth and beer of his opponent, Mr Barclay, the brewer. Thanks to the *Quarterly's* smear about his action at Baños, he was able to put his entire military record before the electors without incurring the charge of boasting – his skill as a publicist has been in evidence before – and the mob loved him: he was a reformer and, if not a radical, at least an advanced Whig well-known for his humanitarian views, a fine figure of a man, with a glittering war record, spitefully used and still unfairly attacked by the stuffy Tories. Those who thought that he had no chance did not undertand the attraction of such a man to people who were as patriotic as any Tory squire but who had had enough, not only of hardship but of the intolerant and overbearing ways of the Tory establishment.

Of course he got in triumphantly. Donoughmore congratulated him handsomely, adding that the metropolis had acknowledged services which the ministry ignored. From Paris came congratulations from the lawyer who had defended him, and from all over Britain people unknown to him sent him their good wishes. He also received much good advice from his friends, some of it distinctly patronising: an old comrade, General Long, wrote suggesting that at the beginning he should bring his ambition and pride down to the level of his capacity; and Donoughmore told him to read and meditate so as 'to acquire some solid knowledge.' For once Wilson took their advice despite the fact, or perhaps because of it, that Jemima was ill again. 'No man,' he told Grey, 'ever applied more diligently to improve himself than I have done these last six months. I have toiled unremittingly with an eye and pen but the result is knowledge of my ignorance and fearful diffidence of my abilities to satisfy my own former pretensions and publick expectation . . . my ambition is now reduced

---

★Lavallette was present at a subsequent election at Southwark and left an account of the precedings in his memoirs. Since there are probably not many accounts of English elections by one of Napoleon's ministers, the excerpt from the English version of Lavallette's memoirs is reprinted in Appendix 1.

never to say a silly thing and thus avoid disgrace until observation and practice permit me to soar on a bolder pinion.'

For Wilson to appear diffident was unusual, perhaps unprecedented, and it suggests that embedded in his normally sanguine temperament lay a grain of unsureness and instability which it was one of the objects of his life to overcome. To his great credit he did not let this deflect him from supporting, in and out of Parliament, the causes in which he believed even though, as he realised, he would have been more likely to achieve the consideration for which he craved if he had been a Tory or a less advanced Whig. Just how sensitive he could be, became apparent when Parliament assembled in January, 1819. He had intended to wait a while before making his maiden speech, as Grey had advised, but his friends rallied him so much that a few days after the session opened he told Grey that he did not think that he could wait even a fortnight because of 'the questions and wit' of his friends. 'If I do fail,' he went on, 'I shall ascribe it entirely to the feelings which the rallies have excited, for everyday I find my confidence diminish.' He could easily endure the fire of his enemies but not the teasing of his friends.

He did fail. He made his maiden speech on 20th January, only twelve days after he first took his seat, and even his fellow Whigs thought it a failure. He himself described it to Grey as 'a check'. He had spoken, he said, 'at an inauspicious moment for my success in the House. I am now, however, at comparative ease and can patiently endeavour to regain consideration.' Realising that his speech had been over-elaborate – for Grey had given him excellent advice about speaking in the House of Commons – he resolved to simplify his style and he hoped that the damage would not be permanent. In fact he was never entirely successful in the difficult art of pleasing the House: his speeches were too long, too frequent and too elaborate. He was also inclined to give members the benefit of little-known facts about the many countries in which he had travelled, and to put them right on military matters: on one such occasion he referred to 'the learned civilian opposite'. He also tended to blow up every cause he supported into an issue of the highest national importance, which no doubt irritated those with a better sense of proportion. He was, in fact, a bit of a bore in Parliament.

He claimed in his letters to Grey that his constituents were well pleased with his work on their behalf, and as they re-elected him time after time, his parliamentary abilities were evidently more appreciated in Southwark than on the other side of the river. But this did not console him for his failure to achieve consideration among his peers and his betters, for Hobhouse reported that Wilson found that 'the aristocratic system here prevents any equality between men of very unequal influence,' and that he was, 'disgusted with the figure he had made.' This seems somewhat exaggerated, but no doubt Hobhouse caught his colleage in one of his moods of dejection which, though deep at the time, seldom lasted long. The causes which he advocated in the House were worthy ones, but some were likely to bore those who did not believe that anything could, or perhaps should, be done about the hardship of the poor. His maiden speech was a protest against government extravagance and complacency – he spoke of 'that aggregate catalogue of distress, crime and discontent which pervades this country, notwithstanding this House has been assured by Ministers that the country is 'enjoying a repose of calm and peaceful joy and gladness,'' language which must be felt by the community to be the language of mockery.' The country, he said, was bankrupt and no more sacrifices should be imposed until the people had 'the security of a reformed Parliament.' His next intervention concerned an impost on cod, to which the electors of Southwark objected; and his third was in favour of an Irishman who had been dismissed from his minor office in circumstances which suggested that a member had tried and failed to buy the man's vote.

In the course of the session many of the great questions of the day came up for debate and Wilson put forward views which would be accepted by almost everyone in the country to-day, or else would be regarded as not liberal enough; but at the time they seemed to many sensible people to be outrageous. He attacked those who thought that any change meant destruction and who refused to admit that the revolution in France had been caused by the 'profligacy, corruption and imbecility of the French government. The Government of this country,' he continued, 'must always depend in a great measure on the authority of opinion, and that authority cannot be maintained without showing a respect for popular rights.' On the details of reform, he repudiated the advanced Radicals' demands for annual parliaments and universal suffrage, advocating instead triennial parliaments (in place of seven-year ones) and a property qualification for voting which should be 'the amount of property which could easily be obtained by industry.' He did not believe in the secret ballot, finding

> something in the concealment and muffling up, which the system of ballot proposed, repulsive to my feelings, contrary to the English character, and to the publicity which every elector ought to be desirous of seeking . . . The circumstances of France and America are different from ours; but I have conversed with North Americans . . . who declared that the ballot system was productive of so many evils in their country that they wished it could be got rid of . . . I am the representative of 5000 or 6000 who came openly and boldly and good humouredly to the hustings to give their vote, and I never will give a vote which will deprive them of the pleasure they feel at publicly displaying their sentiments.

As regards Catholic Emancipation, he thought it 'preposterous . . . after this country had restored or subsidised all the Popish powers of Europe . . . that we should turn round on our own countrymen who co-operated in all our exertions, partook of all our sacrifices . . . and deny them the participation of those constitutional securities which they so patriotically defended.' These sentiments are markedly different from those which he confided to his Journal in East Prussia in 1807, for he then said that, though he had no prejudices against any man because of his faith, he would 'not ever support the measure of Roman Catholic Emancipation in the British Empire' for fear that it would 'revolutionise the British Constitution, put a Romish King on the throne and re-light the faggots of Smithfield'.

He naturally took an early opportunity to denounce corporal punishment in the Army, only to be followed by a member who argued that the victories in the Peninsula were due in part to flogging. Some years later two Tory members actually claimed that flogging made the soldier happy.

In the summer of 1819 he was called away to deal with another illness in the family: this time it was his sister, who was living in Paris. With some qualms, for his friends warned him that for one with his record it would be easier to get into France than to get out again, he set off in July. He met with no trouble and was soon writing enthusiastically to Grey that France was 'the Eden of Europe' and the 'seat of European liberty', referring evidently to his Bonapartist friends rather than to the Bourbon government. There is no doubt that France under any ruler fascinated him. At home in London his Bonapartism took the form of meeting and helping any former associate of the fallen Emperor, pleading their cases in the House of Commons when necessary.

Shortly before he returned to England in September, what came to be called 'the massacre at Peterloo' darkened the political and social scene. A meeting in St Peter's Fields in Manchester was broken up by a charge of Yeomanry, and the speakers, the chief of whom was 'Orator' Hunt, a Radical and an associate of Wilson's, were arrested. After the charge eleven people, including two women, lay dead, and several hundred were wounded. The Radicals believed that the government, the magistrates and the Yeomanry had planned and ordered the operation and so were guilty of murder. Many Whigs shared this view and their anger was increased when the government sent a letter of approval to the Lords-Lieutenant of Lancashire and Cheshire and asked them to convey the Prince Regent's thanks to the magistrates and the Yeomanry. Wilson went so far as to undertake to prove that the action of the authorities amounted to murder, but he never fulfilled the undertaking, though he ardently espoused the cause of Hunt who was tried and imprisoned for his part in the affair. In a well known letter Grey warned Wilson against the extreme Radical company he was keeping. 'Is there one among them,' Grey asked,

> with whom you would trust yourself in the dark? Can you have, I will not say any confidence in their opinions and principles, but any doubt of the wickedness of their intentions? Look at the Men, at their characters, at their conduct. What is there more base, more detestable, more at variance with all taste and decency, as well as all morality, truth and honour? A cause so supported

cannot be a good cause. They may use Burdett for their instrument
for a time, and you also if you place yourself in their trammels,
but depend upon it, if a convulsion follows, I shall not precede
you many months on the scaffold, which you will have assisted
in preparing for us both.

The fears and the aristocratic outlook of the moderate Whigs are
clearly reflected in this letter, and Wilson's reply sums up equally
clearly his own political views at this time. 'The difference between
us seems to be,' he wrote,

> that you entertain more apprehension of the *radicals* than the
> *terrorists* [that is, those who used the weapon of terror against the
> people.] I have very little for the former if the law be not outraged
> to check them and if reasonable concessions be granted to the
> spirit of reform which is abroad, but I have the greatest alarm of
> the latter for they can, and are prepared to, execute what they
> propose without any regard to public freedom, feeling or distress.
> They are desperate, ignorant and merciless. They care for nothing
> but the preservation of their own authority and I firmly believe
> they would rather rule over a ruined empire than see the empire
> saved by the hands of others. The Radicals are ill-fed and misled.
> The terrorists are tyrants in Nature, Education and Habits. Think
> of their approving letter [after Peterloo] – can there be any more
> flagrant proof of their vicious designs against the Constitution
> and Humanity. That letter ought to be expiated and a judicial
> enquiry granted. I speak no more of the Manchester subject but
> I hope to see Parlt[y] reform become a question during the Sessions
> in such a shape as to secure the support of the Whigs and establish
> a point of reunion between them and the sober part of the
> Publick, which is the vast majority.

Only the left wing of the Whig party agreed with Wilson's plea that
the party should put itself at the head of the movement for reform.
The others were demoralised and falling apart; Grey almost despaired
of keeping them together and for fear of a split he dare not commit
the party or himself openly to reform. Nevertheless he remained in

close contact with Brougham and Wilson, who were frequent visitors to Howick at this time, and with Lambton, who had married his daughter. Grey asked Wilson to find out for him what views the rank and file of the Whig party held about reform, how a Whig administration could obtain the people's confidence, and other delicate questions which were important for the formation of Whig policy. As the advanced Whigs were the only section of the party with drive and vision in these difficult days, it was as well for the cause of reform that their links with Grey held. The rest of the Whig party regarded them as unreliable and dangerous. Indeed it must have been difficult to remain on good terms with both the Whig aristocrats and the electors of Southwark, but Wilson not only kept trying, but even had a fair measure of success. This was partly due, no doubt, to his personal charm, partly to his friendship with Grey and partly because, though his support for men like Hunt looked dangerous, his actual speeches in the House of Commons were moderate.

Another link with Grey was their common interest in liberal causes on the Continent, causes of which Wilson often had first-hand knowledge. Since his experience in Italy in 1814, he had watched with indignation the advance of what he regarded as oppression and reaction. This had already provoked, or was soon to provoke, outbreaks of violence in several German states, Portugal, Spain, Naples, Piedmont and Greece. Wilson had been right in predicting that the peoples of Europe would no longer accept passively what their betters thought was good for them, and besides drawing attention in his book on Russia to the dangers of this situation for Britain, he also did what he could in Parliament to further the cause of freedom. He intervened powerfully in support of the Neapolitans, who were in revolt against the Bourbons whom he had been so anxious to see restored in 1812, and drew from Castlereagh the retort that he was not prepared 'to feel all the animation with which the gallant general appears invariably to contemplate every possible species of revolution,' and was 'against the principle that the British government were bound to rush forward and acknowledge every change in a foreign government without the least deliberation as to its nature'. This was fair comment on Wilson's view of the Euopean scene which was, as Canning told him, essentially romantic. 'Let us not,' Canning said in the debate on Naples, 'in the foolish spirit of romance, suppose that we can regenerate Europe.'

Even Canning, for whom he had much affection and regard, could not cure Wilson of romantic flights, and at this juncture – 1820-21 – there were not only captive peoples to be rescued abroad, but a fair lady, though the description could be challenged, to be protected at home. Wilson was more than ready for both adventures.

CHAPTER THIRTEEN

Two Scrapes

In January, 1820, George III at last died and the Prince Regent came to the throne as George IV. This immediately raised the problem of his wife, Caroline of Brunswick. In fact the problem had been with him ever since April 1796, when he had married her. He was deeply in debt at the time and agreed to marry on condition that his debts were paid and his income doubled: in other words he married for the taxpayer's money. When he first set eyes on his future wife he felt so ill that he had to be revived with brandy, and he is said to have spent his wedding night lying drunk in the fire-place. Caroline seems to have taken an equally strong dislike to him, but nevertheless the couple dutifully produced a child, Princess Charlotte, and then parted, mutual revulsion prevailing over the need for a more assured succession. George retired to Brighton and Mrs Fitzherbert, and Caroline to Bayswater, where her undignified habits and vulgar exhibitionism suggested that she was not entirely right in the head. For some years before 1820 she had been living abroad, mostly in Italy, and lurid stories floated back to England about her scandalous dress and behaviour. She was constantly in the company of an Italian of dashing appearance named Bartolomeo Bergami or Pergami, who, after being first her courier and then her chamberlain, was widely believed to have been promoted to her bed. Now, unless something was done, this 'half-mad slut, ' as many people thought of her, was to be Queen and be prayed for in the Litany.

As far back as 1806 the Regent had caused the Whig administration to enquire officially into her conduct in the hope that evidence would be found to enable him to get a divorce. The Tories had, of course, defended her at the time and accused the Whigs of making a base attack on a woman's honour. When the Regeant deserted his Whig friends and the Tories were in office, the Tories were obliged to take over the attack on a woman's honour and the Whigs her defence. At an early stage Brougham had seen the political and personal possibilities in the situation, and when the old King died he urged Caroline to come to England at once to demand her rights as Queen. This would precipitate a conflict with the government, in the course of which he hoped that the Tories would be ousted and he himself achieve office. Caroline reached England in June 1820, and was greeted with frenzied enthusiasm by a populace determined to show their dislike for the King and the Tories by acclaiming this unlikely heroine. Meanwhile the new King ordered that, despite her obvious need for all the prayers that she could get, the Queen's name should be omitted from the Litany, and asked his Ministers to institute proceedings for a divorce. They strongly advised against this, but agreed to introduce a Bill of Pains and Penalties into the House of Lords which, if passed, would have ended her marriage and deprived her of the title of Queen. The long debate on the Bill was a most unsavory affair, for it amounted to a public investigation into whether the Queen had or had not slept with her chamberlain in her jaunts round Italy and the Levant.

Though Brougham led for the defence, the moderate Whigs hoped to remain neutral in the matter, for many of them regarded Caroline with aristocratic disapproval and believed her guilty. Wilson himself was lukewarm at first. The government, obliged to follow an unpopular and undignified course with no certainty of success, seemed very weak, and Canning, its brightest star, was known to have been friendly to the Queen in the past and was contemplating resignation. This, coupled with Brougham's brilliant advocacy, encouraged the bolder spirits among the Whigs, Wilson of course included, to take up the Queen's cause, mainly in the hope of turning out the Tories. When the Bill of Pains and Penalties passed the Lords by so small a majority that the Prime Minister decided to drop it altogether, the Whigs were jubilant: at last there seemed a possibility that they might achieve office, despite the fact that the king hated them. As early as May, 1820, before the Queen had even arrived, some Whigs, Wilson and Brougham among them, had begun to believe in the possibility of a coalition between the Whigs and the moderate Tories. So ill-defined were the lines which divided the parties that some Tories evidently had similar views, for Arbuthnot, the Treasury Secretary, suggested to the Prime Minister, Liverpool, that he should try to recruit members of the Opposition in order to strengthen his position in Parliament. On 19th May, Wilson wrote to Grey, '*Party* on all sides [is] adverse to take the initiative. My own belief, however, is that a strong independent body is forming which will be eventually the commanding force.' As sometimes happened with Wilson's forecasts, he was right, but some years in advance of the event. When, after the hearings, Canning did resign, Wilson and Brougham again hoped for a coalition, but were again disappointed.

Caroline regarded the dropping of the Bill of Pains and Penalties as a triumph and duly gave thanks in St Paul's, attended by a cheering mob. Wilson was by now enthusiastic in her cause and one of his sons had become her equerry. While the Bill was still before the Lords, he had declared – as if it was the beautiful Queen of Prussia who was. being traduced – that 'there was no resistance – no obstacle – no impediment – which the wit of man could devise or perserverance apply, that he would not make use of to stop its progress'. At the beginning of 1821 he presented to the House of Commons a number of petitions for the inclusion of the Queen's name it the Litany: the petitions came from his constituents in Southwark, from 2,097 morocco leather-dressers, from 1,300 London coopers and from 1,184 braziers. It is mildly surprisingly that there were so many morocco leather dressers in the country and that they all cared so much about praying for Caroline.

This activity naturally did not endear Wilson to the Tories, and *Blackwoods Magazine*, the Tory quarterly, which was evidently not averse to a few blows below the belt, depicted him as he must indeed have appeared to the more reactionary of his political opponents and, no doubt, to some of his military superiors. 'Who', the magazine asked,

> are at this moment the most vehement and active of the Queen's friends? There is Sir Robert Wilson, the gallant but spurious knight, of whose equestrian dignity the sharpest questioning had not been able to elicit the authentication: a person so enamoured of sedition that after making his first essay of service in foreign lands, he has returned to his native country to head the legions

of tumult – a thorough renegade who, from the most abusive libeller of the 'child and champion of Jacobinism,' has crept into the meanness, not only of panegyrizing, but of protecting and serving, its vilest slaves. The member for Southwark is, indeed, a sad example of the fortunes of radicalism, and a brief, but touching, epitome of the instability of the human will.

However, for everyone except Wilson the farce or tragedy of Queen Caroline was nearly over. After one last undignified exhibition, when she tried to force her way into Westmnster Abbey during the King's coronation, Caroline of Brunswick died. It was in August and Wilson was in Paris. As soon as he heard the news he set out for London anxious, as he put it, 'to pay a last tribute of respect to Her Majesty'. This was somewhat disingenuous, and one of his close political associates, Henry Bennet, was more candid: he himself was present, he later told the House of Commons 'to do honour to the character of the illustrious deceased and to mark my hatred of her inveterate persecutors'. Since the most inveterate of these was the King himself, it is hardly surprising that he should have perceived the political motives of the mourners and profited by an incident which occurred during the funeral procession to take his revenge on one of them.

The procession set out from Hammersmith on 14th August – a vile and rainy day – bound for Harwich, whence the body was to be taken to Germany for burial. A number of Opposition personalities were present besides Wilson and Bennet, notably Brougham. The route was lined with people whose motives for being present were evidently the same as those of Wilson and his friends, and they were determined that the procession should pass through the City, which was strongly radical. The authorities naturally wished to avoid that, and intended that the route should be from Kensington Church northwards towards Bayswater Road and the Edgware Road. All went well from Hammersmith to Kensington Church, where there was a long halt and reports came back to Wilson and his companions, who were riding behind the mourning coaches, that 'soldiers were cutting down the people'. Wilson rode forward and found that the crowd had held up a military supply wagon loaded with rations and soldier's wives on its way to Windsor, and that it was blocking the road. He remonstrated with the people and pointed out how wet the wives were getting, and the wagon was allowed to go on its way. The procession moved forward once more, but at Hyde Park Corner, instead of continuing eastwards towards the City, it was turned north into the Park, to the fury of the crowd. By the time it reached Cumberland Gate, where Marble Arch now stands, the situation looked serious and a troop of Life Guards was sent for. Again reports came back to Wilson that the 'soldiers were cutting down the people', and soon afterwards he heard shots. He went forward again, remarking to Joseph Hume, the Radical M.P., that it was his duty to preserve or restore the peace if he could. At Cumberland Gate he found that the hearse was stopped in the road by some obstruction and that the Edgware Road was sealed off by the mob, but that the escort of the Blues was formed round the hearse in good order. The Life Guards, however, were being stoned by the mob and some were knocked off their horses. They were, said Wilson, in considerable confusion and they told him that they had no orders and were being 'ill treated' by the people. He tried to find an officer or a magistrate, and then a pistol shot whizzed past his head. Turning round he saw the men re-loading their pistols and told them that it was disgraceful to fire on unarmed people, adding, according to his own account, that they were soldiers of Waterloo who had had cannon shot at their heads and should not lose the honour they had won there on account of a few stones. The firing stopped but two civilians had been killed. Wilson then found both magistrate and the officer commanding the detachment, who had been arranging the removal of the obstruction. The officer, Major Oakes, said he had given no order to fire, and now proposed to withdraw, the obstruction having been removed. Wilson suggested that the troops should retire down a side street which would take them away from the crowd and prevent either side provoking the other.

The procession then moved off towards Marylebone, with Wilson once more in the rear, but in the end the people had their way and it was turned south again into the City by way of Tottenham Court Road. At Ilford Wilson left it and returned to his own house. He rode out again the next day and accompanied the hearse to Harwich. On returning to London he was warned by a friend that he was being accused of having organised the obstruction. Soon all kinds of rumours were abroad: it was being said that when the news of the Queen's death had been brought to him in Paris, he had been drinking in the company of thirty French officers and had immediately proposed the toast, 'God damn the King'. In fact he had been dining with Count Orloff and had been given the news by the British Ambassador. Another story was that he had arranged the obstructions at a meeting in a Hammersmith tavern, though he would not have had time to have gone there. It was also reported that he had offered free beer to the mob if they would pull up paving stones in order to stop the procession. Grey at Howick heard that his words to the officer commanding had been of a more serious nature than he had admitted. Whether or not they believed these stories, the government and the military authorities realised that by apparently helping to divert the procession through the City and by giving orders to troops not under his command, Wilson had put himself at their mercy, and they were not disposed to show him any. He himself realised his danger and characteristically went straight to the Horse Guards to ask the Duke of York, who was still Commander-in-chief, whether he was in any way influenced by the reports that were being spread, and to refute them if necessary. The Duke was away in Brighton but his military secretary said that he had received no instructions in the matter, so Wilson returned on 5th September to his family in Paris.

While this was happening in London, George IV had been in Ireland. That his views on his wife had not changed since he first saw her may be judged from the fact that when earlier in the year they brought him the news of Napoleon's death in St Helena with the words, 'Sire, your worst enemy is dead,' and he replied, 'Is she, by Gad?' Now when they told him in Dublin that the Queen was really dead, he said that it was the happiest day of his life. Wilson was therefore wise to take the precaution of asking Donoughmore to call on the King and present his side of the story. With some trepidation, for he knew the King's mind, Donoughmore did as he was asked, but the King's ominous reply was. 'Why was Sir Robert Wilson there at all?' That, Donoughmore reported, was the strength of the case against him. The King was not a fool and knew perfectly well why Wilson and the other members of the Opposition were there, and so did the government. On 19th September the British Ambassador in Paris asked Wilson to call, and when he did so the next day he handed him a letter from the Duke of York which read, 'Sir – I have it in command from his majesty to inform you that he no longer requires your services. I am, Sir, Frederick, Commander-in-Chief.' The King, in consultation with his ministers, had used the royal perogative to dismiss Wilson from the Army without trial and without specifying his offence.

Wilson replied to the letter the same day, asking what the charges against him were and for a court of inquiry at which he might vindicate his conduct. The request was peremptorily refused, as was a subsequent request for a court-martial. He returned to London early in October to try to obtain a hearing, but in vain. His friends of course rallied round him; Hobhouse and Bennet, Bruce and the Concentric Society, another political group of which he was a member, wrote letters encouraging him and approving his conduct, and Lavallette offered his services. Grey advised Wilson not to solicit justice from his enemies but to show them 'a proud and dignified defiance'. A subscription was opened to compensate him for the loss of his commssion, which was a saleable commodity, and of his half-pay; but it was not a success as few of Wilson's Whig friends subscribed. His family also stood by him though they were seriously affected. He told Grey, 'The person most to be admired throughout is Lady W. She has never for a moment entertained an unsuitable regret but most nobly prepared to encounter all the threatened inconveniences without complaint. I must add my children have behaved with most gratifying spirit tho' Henry has lost his commission in the Guards and Belford his commission in the army by removal from Sandhurst. I shall send the one to Bavaria, the other to Portugal . . . Thank God I have health and energy enough left to put myself in the career of fortune whenever suitable opportunity offers.' People were seldom angry with Wilson for long, and the Duke of York later gave Henry an ensign's commission, without purchase, in a line regiment.

Though all Wilson's efforts to obtain a hearing from his military superiors were rebuffed, he still had the ear of Parliament, and in February 1822, he stated his case in one of his better speeches.

Maintaining that the use of the royal perogative in such a case was incompatible with the honour of the army or the freedom of the people, he accused the government of making use of an incident in which he had acted properly and moderately to preserve order and prevent further bloodshed, in order to revenge themselves on a political opponent. After again demanding a trial, he gave the House a detailed account of his actions on 14th August, adducing proof that he could not have been guilty of the conduct with which the rumour-mongers had charged him. His account was not challenged in the subsequent debate and was borne out by Hume and Bennet. He then addressed himself to the argument that it was improper for him to have been at the funeral at all. Besides his wish to pay his respects, he said, he owed it to his constituents, who had shown a deep interest in the Queen's cause; and ministers themselves had paid their respects by providing a guard of honour. If he had not been dismissed for 'being there at all,' was it, he asked, for intervening to prevent bloodshed? He denied that his language had been improper and observed that he had the satisfaction that his words 'made no windows or orphans, but had probably averted that calamity from many of the assembled multitudes.' Lord Holland, who had not seen much to admire in Wilson since the days of the Loyal Lusitanian Legion, described the speech as a 'complete, spirited and judicious refutation of calumny,' and Grey and Brougham, among others, regarded it as an excellent defence.

The Government's case was put by Palmerston, then a Tory and Secretary-at-War. He claimed that the right of the Crown to dismiss an officer without cause assigned was 'necessary not only for the maintenance of discipline in the army, but also for the maintenance of the integrity of the constitution', and he instanced the execution of Charles I in support of this curious argument. He refuted rather more convincingly Wilson's claim that his dismissal was an act of political revenge, but went on to assert that it was gross insubordination for him to have addressed the troops at all. Palmerston was followed by Lambton, who stressed the humanity of Wilson's action. 'It was neither more nor less,' Lambton said, 'than an act of humanity; it was one of the brightest points of my gallant friend's character that, during the most horrible carnage in his professional career . . . he had found means to devote time to the aid even of suffering enemies. It was disgraceful to England that such a man should be dismissed for saying a few harsh words to soldiers who were returning from the murder of their fellow-citizens.' Castlereagh, in one of the last speeches he made in the House of Commons, argued that Wilson had been guilty of interfering with troops in the execution of their duty and had, in effect, condoned the actions of the mob in stoning the soldiers and diverting the procession. The Opposition's motion in Wilson's favour was, of course, lost, but the ninety-seven votes that it secured represented a considerable achievment.

In the year that elapsed between the defence of his actions at the Queen's funeral and his departure for his next escapade, Wilson continued to be as busy as ever in Parliament over international, national and purely parochial affairs; and as concerned as before over Jemima's health and the education of his daughters in Paris. During the summer recess he and his family were expelled from France, not, so the authorities said, for any specific misdemeanour, but simply because he could not help becoming an attraction for malcontents, by which they meant Bonapartists.

In the House of Commons his interventions covered the policy of the Holy Alliance of Russia, Austria and Prussia in Europe, and the policy of the brewers in England, and he was strongly opposed to both. He maintained that licences should not be granted to public houses which were owned by brewers because he was sure that the practice would lead to a deterioration in the quality of the beer – another example of his being prematurely right. He spoke in favour of a man who had been fined 'for selling Roasted Wheat, not with intent to defraud the revenue, but bona fide as a breakfast beverage', and in a debate on the Irish Insurrection Bill he asked prophetically, 'Is it not in the course of nature that grievances should produce hatred; that neglect should produce lawlessness; that intolerance should produce impatience and insurrection?' He pleaded for better conditions in Ilchester goal for Hunt, and kept up his agitation for reform and against high taxation, the proceeds of which, he said, went towards maintaining a government majority in the House of Commons by corrupt methods. On the Poor Relief Bill he argued in favour of a poor man's right to relief if he was unemployed, and would have none of the argument that relief encouraged idleness. He opposed both the Aliens Bill, which gave the government powers of deportation which were used against some of his Bonapartist friends; and the renewal of the Foreign Enlistment Act, which was intended to prevent British subjects from enlisting in foreign armies, though it was seldom enforced: he had, of course, a personal interest in this measure.

In international affairs Wilson and his friends continued to voice their detestation of the Holy Alliance and particularly of what they regarded as the Alliance's determination to crush the liberals in Spain. In 1820 the Spaniards had risen in revolt and obliged King Ferdinand to accept a constitution. Alexander of Russia and Metternich were now in the frame of mind to regard any revolt as the precursor of another Jacobin revolution, but for two years Castlereagh, who was not nearly so reactionary as Wilson – and the poet Byron – thought, succeeded in preventing any intervention in Spain. But in April, 1823, the French government, afraid that revolutionary ideas might cross the Pyrenees, and not averse to the increase in power, prestige and glory that would follow a successful military intervention in favour of Ferdinand, sent an army into Spain to restore Ferdinand to what his fellow Bourbons in Paris considered to be his rights.

The indignation in Britain was far from being confined to romantics like Wilson: ten years after their expulsion by Wellington, French troops were back in Spain in support not only of absolutism but of the right of one country to intervene by force in the affairs of another. Nobody, of course, was more indignant than Wilson, and nobody more eager for action. Portugal was also threatened by the French and a few months before the invasion Wilson believed that he had been offered the command of the Portuguese army — 'Beresford's post' as he pointed out to Grey – and had been told by the Spanish authorities that in the event of war they hoped that he would raise and lead five thousand British troops in their support. It must have seemed to him that at last the fates were smiling on him: denied by his own country the recognition for which he craved, dismissed from his own army and apparently deprived of any further chance of achieving military glory, he was now to receive a command which had brought a peerage to Beresford, to lead the troops of two countries for which he had much affection and respect against an enemy he knew well, and to do this in a war for liberty against despotism. He accepted the Portuguese offer as soon as it was made and expected confirmation of his appointment by the middle of February. When war broke out in April he had still heard nothing, but he found an outlet for his impatience in helping to organise the 'Patriotic Dinners' which were held at the London Tavern to demonstrate 'Patriotic Zeal in the cause of Spanish Liberty'. But even the strains of the song 'Spain awakened from slavery's trance' sung to the tune of 'Scots wha hae' were a poor substitute for the clash of arms, particularly when his old comrade General Long wrote him a scornful letter after one such dinner, declaring that what Spain wanted was swords, not knives and forks. Although Jemima was again very ill, she begged him not to let that stand in his way and on 26th April he could wait no longer and sailed for Spain. Arriving at Vigo on 1st May, he enlisted in the local militia as a grenadier.

Though the Spanish Constitutionalists soon abandoned Madrid to the advancing French and appeared stangely unlike the people who had resisted so heroically fifteen years before, the province of Galicia seemed likely to put up a fight and Wilson was received with enthusiasm and festivities. Once more the streets of a Spanish city rang with cheers for 'El generoso Wilson', and poems were addressed to 'El ilustre y valiente General Britano Sir Roberto Wilson, filósofo amable, generoso amigo de los pueblos libres'. He replied with fervent speeches and bombastic proclamations, one of which, after listing all his titles from Member of Parliament to First Grenadier of the Vigo Militia, called upon the peoples and soldiers of Europe not to intervene in Spain.

The instruments available for the defence of Galicia were two bodies of troops under Generals Quiroga and Morillo, Wilson, two other British officers, and Wilson's hope that he would be able to raise a force of volunteers in England. On the strength of this hope the Spaniards promoted him from grenadier to lieutenant-general. A trickle of supplies was sent by a committee of sympathisers in London, for although the British government had proclaimed its neutrality, Canning, who had succeeded Castlereagh at the Foreign Office, had not concealed his hope that the French would be repulsed and had lifted the ban on the sale of arms to Spain. The arrival of the first consignment was celebrated by another proclamation from Wilson, addressed this time to the 'Grenadier Company of the Vigo Militia', and beginning, 'Brave companions in arms! The freemen of England, animated by respect for your patriotism and desirous to confirm the assurances I gave when I had the honour to enrol myself in your ranks, amongst other supplies, transmitted four officers' swords and 120 stand of arms with the request that they be placed in the hands of the Grenadier Company of Vigo.' He told Grey, 'If England assists but very little we can maintain the war without danger of being forced in this province and Asturias . . . If I could but get over 5000 B^{sh} volunteers . . . we should very soon change the defensive into an offensive war with assurance of success.'

After a visit of inspection to Corunna and other ports, he crossed into Portugal, reaching Oporto on 1st June. Any idea that he may have had of repeating his former successes in that city were promptly dispelled by a counter-revolutionary outbreak aimed at restoring absolute power to the King. Wilson judged it prudent to leave, but at Braga he found himself in some danger from a mob because be refused to shout for the absolute monarchy. He was rescued by former members of the Loyal Lusitanian Legion and sent back to Oporto under escort. He was kept under surveillance by the new junta and treated in a manner which was scarcely fitting for one who a few months before had been offered command of the Portuguese army. Eventually he was ignominiously expelled from the country.

Back in Vigo by the middle of June, he fretted at the failure of any volunteers to arrive from England. Although at first he tried to conceal from himself that the counter-revolution in Portugal and the inability of the Galicians to co-ordinate their action or cease quarrelling made a successful resistance unlikely, he was soon obliged to accept that the outlook was bleak unless more help, and particularly more men, arrived from England. His Whig friends were doing what they could, but it amounted to little more than getting up a subscription. Spanish resistance was very different from what it had been in 1808 in July Morillo made his peace with the French. This left them free to attack Corunna where Wilson was. Once again he found himself facing French guns, but this time they were better directed, for in this obscure and unsuccessful action the man who had fought almost unharmed through some of the greatest battles in history, received his only serious wound, a musket-ball through the thigh. He was carried back into the city and a great fuss was made of him, particularly by the women. Luckily no bone was broken and his sound constitution ensured him an easy convalescence. A week after he was hit he wrote to Grey that his fever had gone and that he had every prospect of a rapid cure, even if cloth had got into the wound. When Long heard the news, he wrote to Wilson to say that he was glad he had been wounded because it had done his reputation good and helped to counter adverse publicity: the allegation that he was nothing but a 'fanfaron' or 'playboy' had been effectively refuted and truth 'had been obliged to admit that practice and profession have been most consistent and that you have acted up to the point you have aimed at with energy, honour, and effect – they begin to praise you and this is a great sacrifice for envy to make.' Referring to the lack of reliable information, Long added. 'The news (of you) has been as wild and incomprehensible as your natural self.' He reports that Jemima's health is the same and mentions the efforts being made to recruit volunteers. The letter ends, 'Lady Donegall was making kind enquiries after you to-day and Mrs Massey did the same to me by letter – anxious probably to be assured that the *vital member* was intact.'

Incapacitated as he was, Wilson felt that he could be of no more use at Corunna and left for Vigo, but not before he had characteristically secured the release of nine French prisoners whose prospects did not look pleasant. One of them was the brother-in-law of the French Prime Minister, Villèle, and Wilson said that he had acted as he did in order to 'show M. de Villelle (sic) how to defend principles without personal hostility'. He always liked to give a high-sounding explanation for his inability to contemplate unnecessary suffering. Villèle later showed his appreciation,

Corunna fell soon after Wilson left and Vigo was threatened, so the invalid embarked for Gibraltar on a British schooner. In the Tagus the ship was boarded and searched by the Portuguese, who ordered the British flag to be hauled down and behave rudely to Wilson. There and then he wrote a furious letter to the Portuguese authorities protesting against 'the ungenerous, vindictive and lawless treatment' that he had received 'under circumstances that would have secured one protection and hospitality from all but the most barbarous nations', and renouncing the Portuguese Order of the Tower and Sword.

In Algeciras Wilson met Sir William A'Court, the British envoy to the Spanish government, and discussed with him an idea that had been in his mind ever since he had been obliged to admit that the Spanish cause was unlikely to prosper, namely that the British government should mediate between the Constitutionalists and their opponents. In fact his idea was more ambitious, for he proposed not only a British meditation but a British guarantee of the subsequent settlement. He realised that a guarantee would be unenforcable without a base of operations, so he also advocated the raising of the British flag over a Spanish town. Worse still, one of the chief attractions, in his eyes, of this ridiculous scheme, was that the British once in occupation of Spanish territory, would be unable to avoid involvement in any conflict that might ensue. No doubt A'Court was sympathetic to the idea of preventing Spain from slipping back into tyranny and of ensuring that Ferdinand did not massacre those who had favoured the liberal constitution; but it is inconceivable that a British diplomat, and a Tory at that, should have authorised Wilson to tell the Spanish government that Britain was willing to guarantee that a representative system of government would be maintained in Spain, that there would be a general amnesty and that negotiation could take place on a British frigate. Yet that is what Wilson believed, and he informed the Spanish authorities accordingly. A'Court, of course, indignantly repudiated the communication, denied that he had promised any guarantee, and accused Wilson of making use of a private conversation for public purposes. An acrimonious correspondence ensued in which Wilson vigorously maintained that A'Court had authorised him to act as he did, and A'Court as vigorously denied it.

This is perhaps the most discreditable episode in Wilson's career. Even if he did not deliberately misrepresent what A'Court had said in the course of a private conversation, the whole plan of involving Britain in Spanish affairs in such a way that no withdrawal would be possible was thoroughly irresponsible. It would be charitable, and might be justified, to ascribe these painful proceedings to the effect of Wilson's wound. His bad, or silly, behaviour often occurred after a period of great physical strain.

It was not the last disaster that was to afflict him on this regrettable escapade. The French were approaching Cadiz, where the Constitutionalists still held out. It was the city that Wilson had inspected in 1812 and it was where the decisive action would take place. He therefore went north from Gibraltar, his wound completely healed, and on 12th September was entrusted with the command of the forces defending the city. On the same day he learnt that, three weeks before, Jemima had died. He was desolate and went about his new task at Cadiz 'without repose for body or mind', for he reproached himself for having left his sick wife. It was more than he could bear, and after securing some sort of undertaking that there would be an amnesty for the Constitutionalists, he resigned his command and left Cadiz. From Gibraltar he took ship for home and landed at Falmouth in November, 1823.

His homecoming would have been desolate enough without his fear that he might be imprisoned for contravening the Foreign Enlistment Act. Friends warned him that the goverment intended to prosecute him, but after two weeks at home he was able to tell Grey that the Attorney-General had left him alone, and to add, with a flash of his old spirit, that he was nevertheless prepared for the worst and would transfer his abode to Newgate if ordered to do so.

But if his own government did not molest him, his erstwhile friends, the monarchs of Russia, Austria and Prussia, did: as a punishment for having fought for freedom in Spain, they stripped him of the decorations that they had given him. Strictly speaking, though nobody, not even the *Quarterly*, seems to have been unkind enough to mention it, this must have meant that he was no longer entitled to call himself 'Sir' Robert Wilson. In less than two years he had lost his job, his wife and his decorations.

CHAPTER FOURTEEN

Right About Turn

For some months Wilson went little into society, occupying himself with family matters. He was, he told Grey, 'most constantly harassed by the most melancholy images and time has not as yet ministered the relief which is usual, because the more I think, the more I am dissatisfied with myself'. In January 1824, he decided to bring home his two daughters from their school in Paris, and he was distressed and indignant when they were prevented by the French police from boarding the packet at Calais. They were marched like criminals to the police station, he heard, and their baggage and persons searched. He dashed off demands to Canning that the British Ambassador should intervene, but nothing incriminating was found on the girls and they were allowed to leave. No doubt the action of the police was unfeeling and unnecessary, but in the light of the language that Wilson had used about the Bourbons in his last book, his ardent Bonapartism and his ceaseless struggle against what was, however regrettably, the lawful government of France, it is not surprising that the French authorities should have taken exaggerated precautions against him. But as he himself was able 'to defend principles without personal hostility', their attitude was incomprehensible to him.

In Parliament Wilson's interventions were fewer than usual and shorter, but his impatience with humbug was as strong as ever. After a member had said that foreign potentates should not be abused in the House because they could not reply, Wilson, who was unlikely to be feeling partial to foreign potentates at the time, observed, 'If those sovereigns are tyrants, no gentleman can be wrong in designating them accordingly.' His most notable intervention in this session was his defence of his conduct in Spain. After speaking sensibly about the need to get the French army out of Spain, and deploring Britain's declaration of neutrality, which he maintained had given the French the signal to invade, he said he must refute the slanders and repel charges that had been made against him by the monarchs of the Holy Alliance: it was, of course, unpleasant to have to speak about himself, but he would undertake the task fearlessly. He then used the loss of his decorations as an opportunity to remind the House of how he had won them, and sought to show that nothing he had done in Spain justified his being deprived of them. Of course the monarchs could have replied, as his own King had done eighteen months before, by asking what Sir Robert was doing there at all. But they were not there to defend themselves and the speech was well received on both sides of the House. The Tory who followed – the speech does not read as though irony was intended – began with the words, 'As it must have been painful for the gallant officer to state his own personal circumstances to the House, I seize the first moment to assure him that no change which has been affected, either by the caprice of others or from any indiscretion of his own, could induce me to view the gallant officer in any other light than as one of the brightest examples of chivalric courage and generosity to be found in the history of modern time.' It is significant, how often, in English, French and Spanish, the word 'generous' was used of Wilson.

Canning's reply to Wilson's speech was politically important and no less friendly. He had perceived Wilson's good qualities as well as his weaknesses in the Tilsit affair in 1807. Now he defended the government's decision to remain neutral when the French attacked Spain, and chided Wilson with having made difficulties for him by taking part in the war. But he did so gently and, although they were on opposite sides, he referred to Wilson as 'My honourable and gallant★ friend' because 'although the forms of discussion might exclude [such usage] I could have no wish to disavow the sentiments of kindness and regard which I have always entertained for him.' Two months after this debate, the Tory, J. W. Croker, wrote of differences between Canning and his colleagues in the government, and of his politeness to the Opposition, particularly 'his uncalled for eulogy of Sir Robert Wilson in his speech on the Spanish question'. He wondered whether a coalition was in the wind. Donoughmore too read the signs. 'I think

★Presumably Canning was alluding to the fact that, having been dismissed from the army, Wilson was no longer entitled to be referred to as 'gallant'.

that on the whole,' he wrote, to Wilson, 'you have got off very well
. . . Canning is a very extraordinary kind of tumbler, nevertheless
he is getting considerable Parliamentary faction about him.' In fact
Liverpool's Tory government had been moving for a year or so
towards a more liberal line. At the Foreign Office Canning made no
secret of his disapproval of the ideas of the Holy Alliance; and at the
Home Office Peel was dismantling the apparatus of repression and
espionage with which his predecessor, Sidmouth, had kept his fellow-
citizens in subjection. Huskisson had begun to tackle the country's
economic problems and times were getting better. John Edward
Taylor, the founder of the *Manchester Guardian*, noted that 'the whole
spirit and conduct of government' had improved and that the Tories
had become 'much less intolerant and overbearing'. Of course, not all
the Tories had moved with the times, and the Whigs, under the
forceful leadership of Brougham, exploited the situation by praising
Canning and his associates whenever they could and claiming them as
allies against the obscurantism of the 'ultra'-Tories. Croker was not
the only one who saw that the Canningite Tories were moving
towards the moderate Whigs.

Before the new session of Parliament Wilson was twice more
offered the chance of military glory, but he now found it easier to
resist such temptations. First Bolívar wrote that the Mexicans had
asked him to be their 'military protector', but that he had declined,
and had recommended Wilson. The latter regarded the proposal as
'very flattering' but assumed that, as the Mexicans had now succeeded
in freeing themselves from Spain, they would not need his services.
Then he was offered the command of the Greek forces which were
still trying to eject the Turks. Wisely – for Greece was as fatal to
reputations as it was to health – he refused, on the grounds that he
did not want a second time to put his himself in jeopardy under the
Foreign Enlistment Act, particularly as the government had been so
tolerant on the previous occasion. Hobhouse's unkind comment on
his friend's suitability for the task was: 'A brave heart and a weak
head, but better than nobody.'

The rejection of these offers seem to mark a certain descent from
the romantic heights in which he normally moved. He was now forty-
seven, and some sobering up, some inclination to the political right

and to a more constructive role, would not be surprising at such a time even in a Wilson. The loss of Jemima no doubt had its effect. In the session which began in February, 1825, he spoke sensibly in favour of Catholic Emancipation and against the Corn Laws – two other problems over which party differences were narrowing, for Liverpool too was in favour of reducing the duties on corn (which had been imposed for the benefit of Tory landowners) and although he was against Catholic Emancipation, his Governments' official line was one of virtual neutrality. Wilson continued his support for measures which were of practical help to ordinary people, such as those which made it possible for wounded officers' pensions to be paid quarterly instead of half-yearly, and which provided a grant for Mr Macadam in recognition of his services to road-making. But he also played his part in driving the wedge of Whig goodwill between the Canningite Tories and the ultras. He supported Peel over the army estimates, and Peel acknowledged the weight of support from 'such a competent judge'. Some time before he had helped to smooth over a potentially dangerous quarrel between Brougham and Canning – indeed his peace-making powers had been in evidence several times in the House and had apparently not deteriorated since the Leipzig campaign – and so was well placed to further the rapprochement between the two men and their followers. Neither was the titular leader of his party, for Liverpool was, of course, the Tory leader and though Grey had virtually resigned the leadership of the Whigs, his official successor was Lord Lansdowne. But Canning and Brougham were the brightest stars of their parties and the House of Commons, not the Lords, was the place to shine.

In February, 1827, Liverpool had a stroke and later died. Though Canning was his obvious successor, there were serious obstacles in his way. One was the King, who at that time had the power to refuse to accept a man whom he did not like, and he did not like Canning. This was due partly to Canning's supposed partiality for Queen Caroline and partly to his commitment to the cause of Catholic Emancipation, to which the King was deeply opposed. In any case there was probably no majority in Parliament or in the country for relieving the Catholics. Another obstacle was the attitude of Wellington and the ultra-Tories, who distrusted Canning for his liberal policies and his humble origins. Canning got over the Catholic difficulty by letting it be known that, though he was determined eventually to bring about their relief, he would not try to do so until there was some chance of success. He also dealt firmly with his two rivals, Wellington and Peel, by refusing to serve under them: since they knew that no Tory government was possible without him, they had no choice but to leave the field to him and hope that he would fail for lack of support.

That he did not fail was mainly due to Brougham: his energy and drive, and his influence over both Lord Lansdowne and the Press, enabled him to overcome the hesitations and aristocratic prejudices of his colleagues. In the critical days he was able to rely on the loyalty, enthusiasm and – surprising though it may have seemed to his detractors – the good sense of Wilson.

The Whigs had decided before the end of February that they could support a government lead by Canning, and they conveyed that information to him. Early in March Brougham left London for the Northern Circuit, authorising Wilson to look after his interests. However, on 18th March, impatient and uneasy at the lack of news, he wrote to Wilson re-affirming his support for Canning, but expressing his fears that he might yet take office with the ultras: if he did, Brougham went on, the Whigs would have to act against him. He then added a message for Bolívar in South America, to be transmitted through Wilson's son Belford. Because of the threat of hostility at the end of the letter, Wilson did not send it to Canning, but forwarded it straight on to Belford, though he had the message of support conveyed to Canning. Canning asked to see the original, but as this was impossible, Wilson wrote himself, giving what he knew to be Brougham's views and clearing the letter first with Lansdowne. At the same time he asked Brougham to send him another letter, which could be shown to Canning. This Brougham did and his letter of 16th March was duly passed to Canning. A week later Brougham wrote yet another letter to Wilson, but as this too contained a threat of vigorous Whig opposition if Canning should fail to form a sufficiently liberal government, Wilson, again showing good judgement, decided not to pass it on.

On 10th April the King overcame his reluctance and asked

Canning to form a government, but he urged him to invite all the outgoing minsters to remain. Brougham's anxiety lest the ultras should manage to stay in power was therefore not groundless, though there was never really much chance that Wellington and Peel would serve under Canning. But the value of Whig support, indeed its necessity, became apparent when not only Wellington and Peel, but half the former cabinet and over forty other office-holders refused to join Canning. Thereupon negotiations began between Canning and the Whigs, but broke down almost immediately.

Brougham, who had returned to London on 15th April, was furious: in his eyes the Whig Lords, meeting in Lansdowne House and out of touch with the rank and file of the party, were wrecking the whole future of liberalism, and of their own party, 'on subordinate points and punctilios of honour'. Wilson, who kept notes of the proceedings in these critical days, described what happened next.

> Brougham and myself resolved to make an appeal at Brooks's against the decision of the Lansdowne House council. I convoked the meeting for 10 o'clock at night . . . Brougham and myself then stated to different groups the terms proposed by Mr Canning and the answer, which threatened the perpetual exclusion of the Whigs from power, and the return of the intolerant oligarchy. The address was calculated with a tact 'to make the very stones mutiny.' The sedition being established and shaped to action, deputation after deputation was despatched to Lord Lansdowne imploring – requiring – insisting on his renewal of the negotiations.

The rebellion, for it was a rebellion, succeeded, and the renewed negotiations led to the formation of Canning's coalition cabinet, in which the Whigs had three seats. The credit was Brougham's, for without his decisive action the chance would have been missed or muffed. But he was well served and supported by Wilson. Neither of them achieved office, Brougham by his own wish, but they did achieve not only a better and more liberal government, in which their own party had a say, but also, thanks to the rebellion at Brooks's, a loosening of the grip which the Whig lords had on the party, and a broadening of the base of party consultation. It was a development which both men earnestly wished for, and one on which Lords Holland, Dungannon and Essex commented in shocked tones.

Lord Grey too was shocked by the whole proceeding. He was opposed to the Whigs entering a Canningite administration so long as the question of Catholic Emancipation was shelved, and he regarded Canning as unfit to be Prime Minister because his mother had been an actress. But even though he was no longer the active leader of the party, his colleagues should not have kept him completely in the dark about what they were doing. Wilson says that Grey had told Lansdowne not to prejudice the party by refusing office, and therefore should not have objected to the negotiations; but Wilson admits that it was because he was aware of Grey's feelings about Canning that he himself did not tell him what was afoot lest he should tell others who might try to frustrate the plan. However that may be, it was the end of their long friendship. Grey's daughter complained to Hobhouse of Wilson's baseness and ingratitude, while Wilson took to referring to Grey as an old woman. Grey also became estranged from Holland, Lansdowne and Brougham, for the Whig groups were now as mobile as those of the Tories, and many besides Grey believed that the party had been destroyed. Donoughmore was one, and he told Wilson, 'You may panegyrize your own virtues and those of your coadjutator Brougham as much as you please, but I still think that when you dissolved the great Whig party you were two most mischievous individuals.' He added in his best style, 'Your principle supporters now appear to be the Court and two pot-houses in Southwark. An odd mixture but worthy of you.'

Wilson felt at home with the new ministry: it was reasonably liberal; it had been formed, not by, but in spite of, the great lords of both parties; and yet it was entirely constitutional and had the blessing of the King. His policy was, as he put it, to make himself 'eminently useful, particularly in allaying heats and correcting misunderstandings'. In his first speech from the ministerial side of the House, he said that he had got there 'not by the circuitous path which gentlemen usually follow when moving from one side to the other, but boldly and unblushingly, at once, because I have come with the colours of liberal principles flying, to support a ministry formed for the purposes of uniting the prerogative of the King with the liberty of the people'. A few months later he underlined his views by remarking in a debate on froeign affairs that the South American states had 'released themselves from those aristocratic pretensions which, however respected and respectable, are more frequently accompanied by injury than benefit'. Outside the House he made himself useful by getting Canning's son-in-law out of a nasty scrape.

This politically happy state of affairs lasted only a few months, for in August Canning died. An attempt was made to carry on a Canning government without Canning, but it soon broke up and the King sent for Wellington. At first it seemed that the Tory factions had re-united, for the new cabinet contained not only Wellington and Peel, but the Canningites as well. Indeed it looked as though the ultimate effect of the rebellion at Brooks's had been to revive the Tories and dish the Whigs. But a coalition between Wellington and the Canningites was inherently unstable: after two months they fell out over the disenfranchisement of two rotten boroughs and the Canningites left the Tory fold, never to return. Meanwhile events in Ireland had convinced Wellington that unless something was done for the Catholics, there would be civil war. With great difficulty and skill he won over the King, and in the spring of 1829 the Bill emancipating the Catholic was passed. The ultra-Tories were, of course, furious at what they regarded as a betrayal, and Wellington had thus lost – as he never had in battle – both his left wing and his right.

In June, 1830, George IV died and was succeeded by his brother William. A month after his accession the new King, on the advice of Wellington, reinstated Wilson in the army and promoted him to the rank of Leiutenant-General. In the general election which in those days had to be held on the accession of a new monarch, Wilson was re-elected for Southwark on his usual platform and to the strains of:

> He is a noble Briton and a patriot most firm.
> In our cause his zeal we've tried, 'tis to him we must return.
> He is a gallant general, from his post he will not fly,
> And nobly fight in freedom's cause, or in it he will die.
> 'Twas in the cause of virtue his honours they were lost
> And for the sake of Caroline his fortune it was crossed.

But now brave William our King and Adelaide both reign.
They've given him great honours and returned his sword again,
That sword which does him honour and which he'll never stain,
But to defend an injured Queen he'd draw that sword again.
And the ladies wish him back again, they'll do the best they
can.
For although a gallant general, he is a ladies' man.

Although the reformers made substantial gains at the polls, the
Tories still had a working majority and Wellington carried on. In the
new House of Commons Wilson's inclination to the right was again
apparent and on one occasion he even told Peel that the government
possessed 'more power to do good and were less likely to be
counteracted in their endeavors to do so, than any other government
that could be found in the present state of the parties'. This was hardly
the sort of sentiment to be expected from the idol of the Southwark
mob, but political loyalties were more than ever in a state of flux: the
liberal Canning had formed a ministry without insisting on Catholic
Emancipation and three Whigs had joined it; two years later emancipation was actually achieved by the arch-Tory Wellington, who had
refused to serve under Canning. Having recently sat on the ministerial
side of the House, Wilson was obviously uncomfortable at finding
himself in opposition to so reasonable a Tory as Peel. However, his
unease did not last long – or should not have lasted long – for it was
becoming clear that, as Lady Longford has said, 'the country wanted
reform more than they wanted Wellington.' Three months after their
election victory the Tory government fell and Lord Grey, at last,
became Prime Minister.

Donoughmore heard that Wilson was trying for office and
advised him against it, suggesting instead, 'Avail yourself of the present
occasion and get a regiment. That will be your reward.' But Grey
had more important things to attend to than the claims of an erstwhile
friend. Prepared in great secrecy, lest the fainter hearts should hear of
its sweeping provisions and rat, the Reform Bill was introduced into
the Commons by Lord John Russell on 1st March, 1831. It proposed
the complete disenfranchisement of sixty English rotten boroughs and
the partial disenfranchisement of forty-seven others, and the vote was

to be given to householders rated at £10. The Bill was acclaimed in the country and on 22nd March the House of Commons gave it a second reading, but by a majority of only one. Wilson, of course, voted for a measure which represented everything he had fought for politically since he had entered the House thirteen years before, and which omitted just those provisions which he feared would lead to anarchy, such as annual parliaments, universal suffrage and the ballot. In fact it left the working class still without the vote and was certainly no recipe for revolution.

One result of the Bill as introduced would have been to reduce the total number of members in the House of Commons by 62, from 658 to 596, the greatest reduction being in the seats allotted to English constituencies. The Tories objected to this because their greatest strength lay in the English seats; and others objected because they feared that a disproportionate number of Irish catholics would be elected and exercise a bad influence. General Gascoyne, a Tory who sat for Liverpool, therefore proposed that the proportion of members from England and Wales, from Scotland, and from Ireland should remain the same as it had been at the time of the Acts of Union. This put the government in a serious difficulty: with a majority of only one for the Bill, they could not risk losing a single vote; but if they accepted the proposal they would lose some Irish and Scottish support, and if they refused it they would offend those who feared an Irish influx. They tried to get rid of the difficulty by letting it be understood that they would not object to retaining the existing number of seats, namely 658. Gascoyne thereupon amended his proposal so that it provided that the number of representatives from England and Wales should remain the same. As the government could not accept that either, it was, or should have been, clear to everyone that it was a wrecking move designed to prevent the Bill being passed at all.

In the early stages of the debate there may have been confusion in some members' minds about what the government would accept if pressed, and Gascoyne accused Lord John Russell of saying one thing one night and another thing the next. But later, when it became apparent that the amendment was attracting all the anti-reformers – Gascoyne himself was an ultra – the government came out clearly and strongly against it, describing those who professed to support both the Bill and the amendment as 'dupes and gulls'.

Wilson, alas, was one of them. On 19th April he made a speech which Stanley, who followed him, and no doubt many others, heard 'with no ordinary amazement'. After saying that his objection to reducing the number of members for England and Wales was 'insuperable', Wilson told the House that he would rather give up his seat than support a bill containing such a proposal, but he failed to make it clear what his insuperable objections were. He went on to say that in view of those insuperable objections he had sought and obtained assurances from the government that they did not regard the reductions as essential to the Bill. He added that Gascoyne had assured him that his motion was not intended to be hostile to the Bill. On the strength of these assurances he had promised Gascoyne that he would support his motion. Ministers had subsequently repeated that the reductions were not essential until suddenly, two nights before, they had declared that the motion was hostile. So now, because of the vacillations of the government, he found himself in an embarrassing dilemma: because of his duty to his constituents he could not vote for a measure which the government said would endanger the Bill; but, equally, he could not vote against a measure which he had promised to support; in fact he 'had been inveigled into his present dubious position by his mistaken confidence in the assertions of ministers'. This is nonsense. What ministers could have accepted was a motion opposing any reduction in the total number of seats: what they decided was hostile was a motion opposing a reduction in the number of seats for England and Wales. Despite the confusion that the different proposals may have caused (there were three in all: that the proportion of seats in the three countries of the United Kingdom should not be changed; that the total number of seats in the House should not be changed; and that the number for England and Wales should not be changed) it is difficult to believe that Wilson did not understand that the assurances he had received did not relate to the motion that was actually debated. It may also have been the case that the motion that he had undertaken to support was not the one that was debated. It is much easier to believe that he simply did not want to understand these things. Nor was this the only flaw or jarring note in his speech. In the circumstances his claim to be a Reformer, 'but not the Reformer who could change his opinions on the subject of Reform every week . . . not a flightly Reformer . . . not the Reformer who put on and cast off his principles with as much readiness as his garments', sounds hollow and silly. As Stanley remarked, he was about to do the very mischief to the cause of Reform that he was sent into the House to prevent, and it was not good enough to say that, having done that mischief, he would resign. For Wilson saw what his conduct would entail and faced it honourably, though with too much protestation about his willingness to sacrifice everything for what he thought right.

The House divided at 4.30 a.m. on 20th April and Wilson abstained. Gascoyne's motion was approved by eight votes – the government being thus defeated. Wilson, as Croker reported, was 'assailed by his constituents who call upon him to resign his seat, and call him rat, apostate, etc. If there be a dissolution he will hardly find his way back.' He was bitterly attacked in the radical press and the windows of his house in Chapel Street were broken by an angry mob. 'His pedestal was knocked to pieces and so were his windows,' jeered Lord Grenville.

Wilson did not try to find his way back. In the ensuing General Election, which returned the government with an increased majority, he did not stand. In the following year after much trouble and some strife, the Reform for which Wilson had fought so hard until its success was assured, became a reality.

CHAPTER FIFTEEN

Epilogue

Why did he do it? The reasons that he gave in his speech do not carry conviction any more than those he gave afterwards. Although he had voted for the Second Reading, he says in his Journal that he considered the Bill 'as the initiatory measure of a Republican form of Government', and some time later, after the Bill had become law, he wrote that 'during its progress it brought the country to the extremest verge of rebellion'. This is not only contrary to what he had always maintained but dishonest as well, for it was not the Bill's progress that had caused riots, but the fear that it would not progress. This was exactly what Wilson, in his reforming days, had predicted.

It could be argued that he was motivated by malice. He had fallen out with Grey, whom he regarded as an old woman who had refused to fight when success was so hard to achieve and who was now to be credited with a great victory. He could legitimately claim that Grey had treated him badly: when in 1814 the Tories had failed to include his name in the Honours List, no one had shared his indignation more warmly than Grey. 'Your services,' he had written, 'are too well known and have been too generally acknowledged to leave your character exposed to injury by such an act of partiality and injustice. In truth, the disgrace, if any, must rest upon the military government of the country.' But when he came to power, Grey not only did nothing for Wilson but gave K.C.B's to fourteen officers who were junior to him. Four Colonelcies of cavalry regiments were also vacant, but not one went to Wilson. The Tories, on the other hand, had restored him to the army and promoted him to Lieutenant-General, even back-dating the promotion to the time when he could have expected to get it, and they had done this before the Reform Bill had even been introduced.

Even so, Wilson's capacity for malice, though it existed, was not nearly great enough to account for the step he had taken: his rancour was neither deep nor long-lasting. General Wallas had written in 1818, at the outset of Wilson's parliamentary career, 'It is not in your nature to be severe or bitter – your political opponents will find in you a generous adversary,' and there was much truth in that view. Wallas was Wilson's brother-in-law and it may be noted that he too uses the word 'generous'. Wilson would not have risked wrecking the Reform Bill in order to revenge himself on Grey; and he had not quarrelled with the other Whig leaders.

Perhaps he had turned against reform. This must be part of the explanation. Politicians often move to the right in their maturity, partly, no doubt for reasons of temperament and partly because some of the progress for which they have fought has been achieved. From the middle of the decade Wilson had been finding it less and less congenial to attack the more liberal Tories like Canning and Peel, who were such an improvement in his eyes on Castlereagh and Sidmouth. He was as anxious as ever to put down humbug and to support individual good causes, but he found the new Toryism compatible with his ideas of national freedom and constitutional monarchy – the union of 'the prerogative of the King with the liberty of the people', as he had put it. The emancipation of the Catholics by a Tory government, the replacement of George by William on the throne, not to mention his own re-instatement, would all have strengthened the view that the new dispensation was in far less need of reform than the regime of Peterloo. The parliaments that were sustaining the Canningites and the Peelites were elected under the rotten borough system, so perhaps it was not so bad.

But this cannot be the whole explanation, for he was still proclaiming himself a reformer in April 1831 and he voted for the second reading of the Bill. Yet soon afterwards he could write, 'Anarchy will never find me a partizan . . . I have been, and I am, as eager as any one in the cause of independence and freedom, but I never proposed to riot in the disorganisatin of our political and social system . . . It is not what the world sees and hears that I fear, but an undertide that is sweeping with great violence towards waters of endless agitation.'

Fortunately we do not have to believe that a smaller number of seats for England and Wales was a sign of this violent undertide: the real undertide, and the real reason for his otherwise unexplicable conduct, is clearly marked by the eddies and reverse flows in his career. Over a quarter of a century before, outside a Boer farmhouse in South Africa, he could not bring himself to shoot two men who would escape and reveal the presence of his force: in Russia, where he so often urged Kutusov to move in for the kill and where he longed for a few thousand men with whom to capture Napoleon, he could not pull the trigger on Murat: he was sorry for the Bourbons in exile in their leaky palace on the Baltic, hostile and contemptuous towards them when they returned to the Tuileries: when Napoleon fell, the soldier and propagandist who had fought so hard to bring about that fall became an ardent Bonapartist. Several of his friends perceived his difficulty without discerning its cause. 'Though I may admire,' one of them, a Tory, wrote, 'I do sincerely regret that the several changes in your political opinions have always occurred at the moments most hurtful to your personal interests.' The same correspondent wrote on another occasion, 'It is impossible not to admire the romantic generosity of your nature which led you to commit a splendid error,' but as the letter is undated it is not possible to determine which splendid error is referred to; the important point is that the phrase could be applied to more than one episode in Wilson's life. It was a political enemy, the writer of the hostile review in the *Quarterly*, in 1817 who put his finger on the root cause of Wilson's inconsistencies. 'There are some spirits,' the reviewer began, with Wilson in his sights, 'so strangely constituted that, though zealous and able allies in the hour of danger, they cannot bear to witness the too complete success of the cause in which they have laboured.' In other words, Wilson could not bear to win. In the light of this, his life falls into a rational pattern. Reluctance, even sheer inability, to press home an advantage is not a recipe for worldly success, but it is an engaging characteristic, even to those who are let down as a result, and it no doubt accounts for the personal kindness with which Wilson seems always to have been received by many different kinds of people in many countries.

He was in his mid-fifties when his parliamentary career ended so abruptly, and he had eighteen years still before him. Those years brought him much of what he had always wanted. Already in October,

1831 he was once more dining with his King in the Pavilion at Brighton, and when he was restored to the army he received ·many letters of obviously sincere congratulation from friends and from those who could perhaps not be accurately so described. Cathcart generously went out of his way to say how much he had always admired Wilson's military services; Sydney Smith wrote at length, saying that not only he but everyone was delighted; and Princess Lieven bore him out when she wrote, 'This is generally approved except by a few friends of the late King who think it an insult to his memory.' Lord Grenville also noted that the re-instatement had given 'universal satisfaction', adding that 'though this officer had justly forfeited his position by his conduct at a period of great public excitement, his previous services had been very important, and a deprivation for ten years of the emoluments of military rank was considered a sufficient punishment for that indiscretion'. Among the carefully preserved testimonials in the British Library is one from 'two Italian immigrant officers who had the honour to militate under your orders in Galicia of Spain for the freedom of that country'.

He got his cavalry regiment too. In 1836 he was gazetted Colonel of the regiment which he had joined as a sixteen-year old Cornet over forty years before. Peel described the appointment as a 'very honourable and most justly deserved reward of military service', perhaps making the point that Wilson's political services were less deserving. He still had no K.C.B., for the party he had supported for so long had failed to give it to him, and Peel, when he became Prime Minister, took the view that a violent partisan had no right to expect favour from the government he had opposed. But though he failed to get a star from his own government, he solicited and obtained – with the help from Wellington, it is pleasant to record – the return of his foreign ones. In 1841 the rulers of Austria, Portugal, Prussia and Russia reinstated him in their Orders, and the erstwhile enemy of the Holy Alliance and all its works wrote fulsome letters of thanks to Metternich and the rest.

Whatever his political views at the time of his last speech in parliament, he was soon afterwards a true blue Tory, for he never did things by halves. Having crossed the floor of the House in spirit, he now crossed St James's Street in person, abandoning Brooks's for

White's where he was to be seen in the company of arch-Tories like Arbuthnot and Croker, lamenting the state of the country and prophesying doom. He also found himself acting, as he had formerly for Grey and Brougham, as Arbuthnot's London correspondent, charged with letting him know 'what you hear of the projects of our vile Ministers'. Arbuthnot, of course was close to Wellington and it may have been partly his advocacy which brought about a warm friendship between Wilson and the Duke. For Wilson the relationship was no doubt facilitated by the fact that it was some time since the Duke had won any victories, political or military. He regularly invited Wilson to shoot at Stratfield Saye, and even offered to find him a safe Tory seat in the House of Commons – Cheltenham was the one he had in mind. Croker had the sense to see that he could not expect to succeed there and strongly advised against the idea; and Wilson had the sense to take the advice.

Wilson's friendship with Lambton, now Earl of Durham, remained unimpaired. He called when Durham was ill early in 1833 and received this note: 'I am now able to come downstairs and shall be most happy to see you any day between 1 and 6, as would Lady Durham, who had not been told of your calling. Be assured that no change in my situation makes any difference to my feelings towards you. They were never abated during the time I was in office and one of my greatest annoyances was that I was always thwarted in my attempt to show them otherwise than by words. I have never forgotten and never can forget old friendships.' It would seem from this that at least one of his old friends had tried to get Wilson his K.C.B. and had been deliberately 'thwarted'.

Wilson made a new friend too – Miss Hatfield. This lady enjoyed a considerable vogue at the time as a poetess, though it is difficult to see why. She was so much taken by Wilson that she wrote a poem to him called *The Minstrel Maid to the Warrior* which began:

> Oh I would watch thy tent by night
> And guard thy bosom all day
> Thy shield be in the hour of fight
> Thy Minstrel when 'twas passed away.

Though he may well have preferred the earthier muse of the Southwark mob, Wilson corresponded with Miss Hatfield and expounded his political views to her.

Towards the end of 1841 Wilson, now a full General, Colonel of the 15th Hussars, reinstated in all his continental Orders, and having, in the words of the King's private secretary, 'abandoned that wild and violent course and the extreme opinions which excluded him, very properly, from the favour of the Crown', asked Wellington if he could help him to obtain employment, though he was well over sixty. In January, 1842, he told the Duke that he had had an encouraging interview with Stanley and was confident of employment under the Colonial Office. Soon afterwards he received 'the reward to which his early services entitled him', for Queen Victoria, on Peel's recommendation, appointed him Governor and Commander-in-Chief of Gibraltar.

Though not quite the Tsar of All the Russias, he was a monarch of sorts with troops to command and subjects to rule. He corresponded with his fellow rulers on the North African coast, and was presented by the Emperor of Morocco with a 'fowling piece of Moorish manufacture and a walking-stick made from the horn of a unicorn'. Although the stage on which he was appearing was somewhat restricted in size, at least he was taking the chief part; he was no mere candle-snuffer; he had achieved consideration. He reigned uneventfully for seven years and then, when on a visit home in May, 1849, he collapsed and died in Marshal Thompson's hotel in Oxford Street. A week later he was buried in Westminster Abbey in the north aisle near the west door. The plaque which marks the spot shows him and Jemima as mediaeval figures, with Wilson, appropriately, in knightly armour.

Was he anything more than a 'knight-errant, an Adventurer, a fellow of active head and nimble heel' – the description is, of course, Donoughmore's. Was he as slippery, hot-headed, inconsistent and unreliable as his enemies, and occasionally his friends said? Was the Reverend Mr Gleig (in his *Personal Reminiscences of the Duke of Wellington*) right in portraying him as a 'fine soldier' but consumed with 'morbid self-appreciation' and given to boasting of his victories in the boudoir as well as in the field? Of course there is some truth in some of these charges. Wilson was – morbidly, if Gleig likes – concerned with 'consideration', with gaining the recognition which so many of his friends and acquaintances acquired from birth or influence but for which he had had to fight. When he was denied it the condition got worse. He was certainly partisan; if he espoused a cause, he espoused it passionately, and friends of that cause became friends of his, however unacceptable they might be to his other friends. To the prudent, the calculating and to those with an assured station in society, the actions of such a man would sometimes seem foolish and thrusting. Allowance must also be made for the violence of political passions at the time and for the violence of the language in which they were customarily expressed. Creevey and Brougham were on the same side but that did not prevent Creevey from describing his learned friend as 'a canting, mischievous fellow' and referring to his 'low, lying, dirty, shuffling villainy'. In the light of adjectives like those, some of the remarks made about Wilson lose their sting.

On the other side of the ledger there stand the causes for which Wilson fought, the prophecies which did come true, often long after they were made – as is often the case with radicals – the praises that he won and the distinguished men who were not only his friends but who thought well of his abilities. Grey and the other Opposition leaders relied a good deal on Wilson's views on military and international affairs between 1810 and 1815, and though his military forecasts proved wrong, his appreciation of what was happening below the surface in Europe was accurate. As we have seen, in 1820 Grey was using him to sound the rank and file of the party on important matters of policy, and six years later Brougham used him as a go-between during the formation of Canning's administration. Long before this Wilson had earned the respect, the affection, even the admiration, of some of the greatest men of his day. Alexander of Russia, Schwarzenberg, Metternich, all went out of their way to retain his services and do him honour. Though there was no doubt an element of policy in the wish of the Austrians to have Wilson with them, their respect for his military and diplomatic talents and for his personality was surely genuine. Canning, though aware from their first co-operation of Wilson's weaknesses, held him in most friendly regard – but Canning too had had to make his own way in the world.

The major figures in the early stages of the Peninsular War, Cradock, Wellesley, Beresford and even Cuesta, found much to praise in his military conduct. The French feared both his sword and his spirit. Diplomats like Frere and Liston, Aberdeen, Jackson and Werry all found in Wilson many admirable qualities and 'much sound sense at bottom'. Even when he was at his most irresponsible in the eyes of the Whig and Tory Lords, consorting with men like Hunt, Burdett and Cartwright – dangerous radicals – Grey put the best construction on Wilson's behaviour, assuming that it was due to 'that general good nature, which makes you always so anxious to allay and obliterate enmities', and adding, 'I trust that nothing can happen to diminish our personal regard and affection.' For many years nothing did, not even the equally strong regard and affection which evidently existed between Wilson and his Southwark constituents, and which Lavallette witnessed. When in the end Wilson did fall out with Grey, and when his fatal inability to accept victory caused him to let down his own side, he not only retained many of his old friends, but he passed smoothly into the good graces of the Duke of Wellington and his circle, even if not into those of the Reverend Mr Gleig.

Gleig's charge that Wilson boasted of his success with women is interesting. That he was greatly attracted to them is obvious, for descriptions of women occur in his military appreciations almost as often as descriptions of fortifications; and for their part, women, from the Countess Potocka in Warsaw to Lady Jersey in London, not to mention the beautiful Sally in the rout at Roubaix, were attracted to him: nor did it escape them in Southwark that the gallant general was a ladies man. Happily we do not now have to speculate – or mind – whether in his long absences from home in foreign camps and drawing-rooms his admiration for women ever turned into what he might have called 'ardent passion' or beyond. But we should mind if he boasted about it. Gleig's reminiscences were written when he was in his ninetieth year and his account of Wilson's career is so full of inaccuracies that it would be unwise to rely on anything he says in it which is not supported by other evidence. Though many charges were levelled against Wilson, this one is unique to Gleig and must therefore be considered to be unproven.

That Wilson was devoted to Jemima after his fashion – or rather after the fashion of the age – cannot be doubted: he put his service to his country and his own career first, as was unusual at the time, but in the years of illness which she endured with so much fortitude he was always with her and her health was his constant preoccupation. The night he heard of her death he wrote,

> I saw in an instant all my hopes destroyed, all my dreams vanish . . . A union which has lasted 25 years is broken for ever. Thro' what scenes we have passed since it began. When I first saw Jemima Belford she was the admiration of society. The Face – the mouth – the colour of the lips – the Bust, the Form, the Limbs and Feet were a perfection ... with a manner that commanded homage from all who approached. In the Pink of her Youth and Charms she was stricken with blindness after my return from Egypt. Her Resignation was a Prodigy. Her cheerfulness never deserted her and such was the extraordinary animation of her countenance . . . that no one unless told could discover her misfortune altho' long in her company . . . the agonies of the last eight years were borne with a patience which baffles all description. Indeed Dr Bailey . . . told me she was one of the most extraordinary women who ever lived and that she had in spite of disease preserved life solely by her moral force. Exposed to a thousand Temptations her conduct was always irreproachable and a model for imitation. The truest and most devoted wife, anxious to share every anxiety . . . she in the hour of peril flew from London to Brighton in order to ensure my safety and by her noble, prudent and decorous conduct attained every object she proposed with accumulated benefit to her family. 'My husband does not ask mercy or favour, but Justice' were her words to the Lords Liverpool and Castlereagh and also to the King into whose presence she obtained admission with every possible impediment thrown in her way. Her affection for her children was without bounds but it was an affection which prospered their welfare and tended to their improvement . . . Altho' a woman in grace of manner and expression, she had a masculine power of mind. Few men had quicker perception or more acuteness in argument. She was always . . . against injustice

and oppression. When I went to Spain, so untimely for my own happiness, she sympathised with my feelings in the Cause, and never added to my distress by one remark that might inflict a wound. On the contrary, she approved the spirit and only hoped it might tend to my honour and the interests of her children. She was indeed a marvellous creature and has left I am certain impressions on all who have known her that can never be effaced. I would willingly lay down my life to give her the length of that which in the due course of Nature might be expected. Her life would assuredly be a blessing to her Family – mine has lost its charm and therefore its incentive to action, but how true it is that when we may enjoy we neglect to profit by our opportunity and that we only know the full value of the good we have rejected by its loss. If I survive to days of tranquility I will at last do her memory justice and leave a record of utility as well as Honour to her descendants. She had in very conscience but one fault and that was too much attachment to myself who little merited such a treasure but who never for a moment since he knew her, failed in his heart to her love and affection.

So many different kinds of people, Emperors and Southwark shoemakers, great ladies and Miss Hatfield, distinguished soldiers, diplomats and politicans, radicals and Tories, cannot have been mistaken all the time. Sir Robert Wilson was much more than a wild and inconsistent knight-errant who first misled and then deserted the Whigs. He was a man of achievement and humanity, culture and talent. He produced good books – and bad – at a time when, as Gleig noted, British officers rarely pretended to be capable of writing an ordinary despatch. He was not a major figure on either the military or political scene, but he had the knack of being present at great moments in history and of playing a part in them which might at any moment have tipped the balance. At Leipzig Schwarzenberg, who was in command, said it did: in Northern Portugal in 1808-9 Wilson's part may have been decisive for the future of the Peninsular War. After Tilsit he tried gaily to reserve a decision which had already been reached on the field of Friedland, but the effort was worth making. In 1812 his objectives were admirable, and his activities as a foreigner operating between two commanders-in-chief, their Emperor and a staff of quarrelling generals were well-nigh incredible. His military exploits were remarkable even in a romantic and heroic age. His published attack on Napoleon's conduct at Jaffa stiffened the morale of Europe. In politics he appeared at the end to have failed completely, but for many discouraging years he was one of a stout band of reformers who fought for better treatment for the poor and oppressed in his own country and everywhere else, for a greater regard for human dignity, for softer penalties for criminals, for a lightening of heavy hand of the landed interest, for more enterprise and less corruption, for an end to arbitrary government and for parliamentary reform. He was always in the front line in politics as well as in battle, and he kept up the fight when his betters had given way to despair. His heart was in the right place though his head was often in the clouds. In the end he deserted, but only after his political work was done and victory assured. In this he showed himself a true dissenter, for he dissented from his own sect when it was about to become orthodox. Such consistency is rare indeed, but Francis Werry was right; Sir Robert Wilson was an astonishing fellow.

Lavallette's Account of the Southwark Election in 1826

The first public sitting for the election opened this morning. There are three candidates for the borough of Southwark – Sir Robert Wilson and Mr Calvert, the late members, and Mr Polhill, a candidate to be elected instead of one of them. Each candidate wears his colours: Sir Robert has chosen blue Marie Louise; Mr Calvert sky-blue; and Mr Polhill, orange or yellow. It was agreed that I should be at Sir Robert's at half-past eight or nine o'clock. We stepped into an elegant landau drawn by two beautiful horses; Sir Robert and his eldest daughter, Jemima, sat on the back seat; the youngest and myself on the front one. They were elegantly dressed though with simplicity; their father's colours shone on their bonnets and sashes. The two footmen, the coachman, his whip and the horses, were all covered with those ribands. All went well till we arrived at the entrance of the Borough; but there the crowd entirely filled up the broad street we were going through, and we were soon stopped by an immense number of people bearing the banners of Wilson, and music playing. The horses were taken from the carriage, which dragged along by the people for nearly half a league, with cries of 'Hurrah! – Wilson for ever!' it was a tumult – a confusion which the strongest heads could with difficulty have borne. In front of the people that dragged us along were placed the banners with deafening music, and behind them the carriages of several Frenchmen, such as, Messrs de Stael, Francis and Alexander Delessert, the lady of the latter, young Montebello the son of Duvergier de Hauranne, Daru, Montalevet, and, among others, Sir Robert was standing at the bottom of the open landau, bowing to everybody, offering his bare hand to the dirtiest hands I ever saw. Women of the lowest classes stretched out their children to him, that he might caress them; while the windows and even the roofs of the houses, were literally covered with inhabitants, crying out as loud as they could, and carrying, on the walls and before the shops, large bills fastened to long sticks, with the following words: 'Wilson, the friend of humanity!' – 'Wilson and Liberty!' – 'Wilson and the abolition of slavery!' – 'Wilson and the Protestant Constitution!' – 'Wilson for ever!' We advanced slowly. Sir Robert said: 'We shall soon arrive in the enemy's country.' In fact, a little while afterwards we passed before Mr Polhill's door. Yellow began to show itself on the windows, coaches, and handbills, – but the crowd that accompanied us redoubled their cries of 'Wilson for ever!' Five minutes later, we saw Mr Polhill pass by in a very elegant coach, but a shut one, and all his followers covered with yellow ribands. The mixed cries of 'Wilson!' – 'Polhill!' – the hurrahs, the hissings – the thick crowd made such a confusion, that I certainly thought we were going to be overthrown, and crushed to death. I observed the young ladies growing pale, but they felt so happy at being near their father, that it renewed their courage; and the emotion that was visible in their handsome faces was the only thing that betrayed the anxiety that tormented them. They did not make a motion, nor utter a cry. I endeavoured to tranquillize the eldest, who sat facing me. 'No, no!' she said, 'I am only afraid for the poor people that surround us.' Generous in their hostility the two rivals bowed to one another as they passed, and we arrived at last before the *Hustings* situated in a place where the street divided into two and forms a small square, scarcely wide enough for a battalion of six hundred men to manoeuvre, and where, however, more than four thousand persons were assembled. We stepped out with difficulty before the hustings, at the house of a wealthy tradesman, a zealous partisan of Wilson's, and from a parlour on the first floor we distinctly saw the whole sight of the election. What they call the *Hustings* is a scaffolding large enough to hold two hundred people, and covered with boards as a shelter from the rain – something like what we see in our public ceremonies on our quays and boulevards. Sir Robert left us to get up on the hustings. The High Bailiff, a magistrate delegated by the Lord Mayor or the Sheriff, opened the meeting in presence of all the people, by declaring that the election was about to take place. He read the writ, proclaimed the names of the candidates, and made known the forms that were to be observed in the election. Afterwards, according to custom, a friend of the first candidate made a speech, in which he expatiated on the titles of the candidate to the suffrages of the people, his public conduct, his opinions in regard to Parliamentary Reform and Catholic Emancipation. Then came the friend of Sir Robert. The celebrity of his name, the splendour of his life, rendering it unnecessary for the orator to enter into particulars, he bounded himself with praising his parliamentary conduct, and explaining to his hearers that the attempt made to expel him for the House had been directed by a party that might endanger Liberty. Afterwards, the candidates, presenting themselves in person, were received – the two first, Sir Robert and Calvert, with a great deal of favour; while Mr Polhill could never succeed in obtaining a hearing: the hootings, hissing and cries of all sorts perpetually covered his voice. Wilson, at last, went up to him, took him under his protection, and claimed silence from the mob. Mr Polhill seemed touched by this generous act of his rival, but he did not reap any more assurance from it. He looked embarrassed; and some person who went near the foot of the hustings to listen to what he said, assured me that the House of Commons would not have gained an orator in him if he had been elected. At last, after three hours' speeches, to which the people listened with an attention that proves how fond they are of political discussions, the High Bailiff said that the election was about to take place, and invited the electors to hold up their hands for the candidate they preferred, when they heard his name uttered. Mr Polhill had very few hands for him, the greatest part of the crowd being for the two others. A great number of electors' tickets were thrown among the people. The polling took place on the front of the hustings, with books prepared to receive the votes of the electors. Each voter came with his ticket, and put down the name of one of the candidates: this operation lasted about two hours. At four o'clock the number of voters was counted and proclaimed aloud, as also by means of a bill stuck up. The result was, 175 for Sir Robert Wilson, 170 for Mr Calvert, and 106 for Mr Polhill. The polling will continue tomorrow and probably the day after. The candidates will speak the whole morning, and from two till four o'clock the books will be opened, and the votes taken down: nevertheless, if during the space of an hour not one voter appears, the book is definitely closed, and the majority of the voters decides the nomination. It is probable that Mr Polhill will give up the contest.

THE SOURCES

The main sources for this book are the manuscripts, publications and speeches of Wilson himself, and the writings and speeches of his contemporaries. His son-in-law, the Rev. Herbert Randolph, published a *Life* in 1862 which consists largely of excerpts from Wilson's Journals and letters, but which does not go beyond 1807. Professor Costigan published a biography in 1932, in which he thoroughly explored the contemporary sources, including the newspapers and periodicals, and the Foreign Office and War Office records, thereby leaving all subsequent biographers greatly in his debt. Mr Michael Glover published another 'Life' in 1978 and I have profited greatly from both these works, though I take a more charitable view of Wilson than either of them.

Rather than weary the reader with references on every page, which then have to be looked up at the end of the book, I have generally indicated in the text the sources of the remarks and judgments made about Wilson, and these indications are supplemented by the notes on the sources for each chapter which are given below.

Standard collections, such as the Creevey Papers and Wellington's Despatches, as well as the memoirs and diaries of people like the Hollands, Grenville, Croker, etc., are mentioned in the text and in the chapter notes, but are too well-known to need listing again in the bibliography. The other sources are given their full titles there.

Chapters I and II: are based on Randolph's *Life*, Farington's *Diary* and Bunbury's *Narratives*. Fortescue is invaluable for the military background. Napoleon's forgiveness of Wilson is implicit in Las Cases. *Chapter III*: Wilson's own book on the Egyptian campaign, Randolph's *Life*, Bunbury and Fortescue are the main sources, with Mr Christopher Herold's *Bonaparte in Egypt* as a valuable and entertaining supplement. The personal description of General Hutchinson is Bunbury's.

Chapter IV: Many writers besides Wilson have described the shooting of the Turkish prisoners and the alleged poisoning of the French sick at Jaffa. I have made use particularly of Beyle (Stendhal), Bourienne, Charles-Roux, Lanfrey (who quotes Bertrand) and Las Cases. I am indebted to Mr Laffin for the details of flogging in the British Army, and to Mr White for the information on Dr Keate's prowess with the birch.

Chapter V: Randolph gives Wilson's account of the journey to East Prussia and of the campaign there, and George Jackson, in his diaries and letters, supplies the counterpoint.

Chapter VI: the French historian Vandal's detailed account of the proceedings at Tilsit and St Petersburg is, with Wilson's version in the *Life*, the basis of this chapter. The translations from Vandal, including those of the correspondence between Napoleon and Savary which he quotes, are mine. The letters of Leveson-Gower and Jackson are valuable, and events in England are described in Malmesbury's papers. The identification of the Tilsit spy as D'Antraignes, is Sir John Hall's. Fortescue (and the letters of Napoleon which he quotes) has been my guide through the military scene.

Chapter VII: Wilson's account of his activities in the Peninsula is taken from the manuscript in the British Library, for Randolph's *Life* stops in 1807. Napier, Oman and Fortescue are of much help, as are Professor Costigan and Mr Glover. There are published accounts of the Loyal Lusitanian Legion, by Colonel Mayne and Captain Lillie, who served in it, the latter containing material from the French side. The Portuguese historian quoted, is Texeira Botelho. The affair at Baños is the subject of Wilson's published defence to his constituents at Southwark and figures, of course, in Wellington's despatches. Napoleon's order from Valladolid is taken from Balagny. The tribute from General Foy occurs in a letter from him which is among Wilson's papers in the British Library: the translation is mine.

Chapters VIII and IX: are based on Wilson's diaries for 1812–14 edited and published by Randolph, together with his *Narrative* of the 1812 campaign. Dr Duffy's 'Borodino' gives an invaluable exposition of the military situation.

Chapter X: Wilson's diaries are again the main source. For the military and political background I have relied on Sir H. Nicolson's *Congress of Vienna.* George Jackson re-appears. Alexander Gordon's communication with the Whigs is recorded by Creevey. Wilson's long and copious correspondence with Grey begins to become a major source. There are no published diaries after 1814.

Chapter XI: the account of Lavallette's marriage, his activities in 1815 and his escape are taken from the English version of his memoirs. The account of the journey from Paris to the frontier is compiled from Lavallette and from Wilson's fatal letter to Grey. There is a great deal of material on Wilson's arrest, behaviour and trial among the papers in the British Library. The source of the contemporary comment is indicated in the text. The involvement of British Ministers is noted in Wellington's supplementary despatches. Mr Ian Bruce is the authority for the belief that Michael Bruce was Madame Ney's lover, and Sir Arthur Bryant for Louis XVIII's unusual use of a crane.

Chapters XII to XV: the contemporary sources for these chapters are Wilson's papers (particularly his correspondence with Grey and Donoughmore), Hansard, and the letters, diaries and memoirs of men like Creevey, Croker, Grenville, Brougham, Hobhouse etc. Wilson's own account of his part in the formation of Canning's administration was published. More modern guides through the political tangles have been Trevelyan on Grey, Aspinall on Brougham, Miss Wendy Hinde on Canning, Lady Longford on Wellington, and Mr Norman Gash on Lord Liverpool and the position of the parties.

BIBLIOGRAPHY

Sir Robert Wilson, Additional Mss 30, 095–30, 143 British Library.

History of the British Expedition to Egypt (London, 1802)

An Enquiry into the present State of the Military Force of the British Empire with a view to its reorganisation (London, 1804)

Brief remarks on the Character and Composition of the Russian Army; and a Sketch of the Campaigns in Poland in the Years 1806 and 1807 (London, 1810)

Sketch of the Military and Political Power of Russia in the Year 1817 (London, 1817)

Letter of Sir Robert Wilson to his Constituents in refutation of a charge of despatching a false report of a victory to the Commander-in-Chief of the British Army in the Peninsula in the Year 1809 (London, 1818)

Narrative of Events during the Invasion of Russia by Napoleon Buonaparte, and the Retreat of the French Army, 1812, edited by the Rev. Randolph (London, 1860)

Private Diary of Travels, Personal Services, and Public Events, during Mission and Employment with the European Armies in the Campaigns of 1812, 1813, 1814, from the Invasion of Russia to the Capture of Paris edited by the Rev. H. Randolph (2 Vols, London, 1861)

Life of General Sir Robert Wilson, edited by the Rev. H. Randolph (2 Vols, (London, 1862)

Canning's Administration: Narrative of Formation, with correspondence, 1827, edited by the Rev. H. Randolph (London, 1872)

OTHER WORKS

Aspinall, Arthur, *Lord Brougham and the Whig Party* (Manchester, 1927)

Balagny, *Campagne de l'Empereur Napoléon en Espagne (1808–1809)* Vol. 5 (Paris 1907)

Berry, Miss Mary, *Journals and correspondence, 1763–1852,* edited by Theresa Lewis (London, 1865)

Beyle, Henri (Stendhal), *Vie de Napoléon* (Paris, 1929)

Blackwoods Magazine, Vol. 8 No. XLVII

Bourgogne, Sergent, *Mémoires.* (Paris 1898)

Bourienne, *Mémoires de M. de Bourienne* (Paris, 1829)

Brett-James, Anthony, *General Wilson's Journal 1812–14* (London, 1964)

Brook, Michael, *The Great Reform Act* (London, 1973)

Bruce, Ian, *The Nun of Lebanon* (London, 1951)

Buddle-Atkinson, R.H.M. and Jackson, G.A. *Brougham and his Early Friends* (London, 1908)

Bunbury, Sir Henry Edward, *Narrative of the Campaign in North Holland* (London, 1849)

Bunbury, Sir Henry Edward, *Narrative of some passages in the Great War with France, 1799–1810,* edited by the Hon. Sir John Fortescue (London, 1927)

Bryant, Sir Arthur, *The Age of Elegance* (London, 1950)

Charles-Roux, F, *Bonaparte, Governor of Egypt,* tr. E.E.Dickes (London, 1937)

Cole, Hubert, *The Betrayers. Joachim and Caroline Murat* (London, 1972)

Cornung, C.H., Francis Galton & Eugenics, *History To-day*, Vol. xxiii no. 10

Costigan, Giovanni, *Sir Robert Wilson: A Soldier of Fortune in the Napoleonic Wars* (Madison, 1932)

Cronin, Vincent, *Napoleon* (London, 1971)

Duffy, Christopher, *Borodino* (London, 1972)

Fortescue, the Hon. J.W., *History of the British Army* (London, 1910–1923)

Gash, Norman, *Lord Liverpool* (London, 1984)

Gleig, the Rev. G.R., *Personal Reminiscences of the Duke of Wellington,* edited by Mary E. Gleig (London, 1904)

Hall, Sir John Richard, Bt., *Four Famous Mysteries* (London, 1922)

Hansard. Parliamentary Debates. 1818–1831

Harris, James, First Earl of Malmesbury, *Diaries and Corespondence,* edited by the third Earl (London, 1844)

Harris, James, First Earl of Malmesbury, *Letters* edited by the third Earl (London, 1870)

Herold, J. Christopher, *Bonaparte in Egypt* (London, 1963)

Hinde, Wendy, *George Canning* (London, 1973)

Hobhouse, John Cam, Lord Broughton, *Recollections of a Long Life* (London, 1909)

Jackson, Sir George, *Diaries and letters, 1802–1809,* edited by Lady Jackson (London, 1872)

Jackson, Sir George, *A further Selection from the Diaries and Letters of Sir George Jackson,* edited by Lady Jackson (London, 1873)

Kerry, Earl of, *The First Napoleon. Some Unpublished Documents from the Bowood Papers,* edited by the Earl of Kerry (London, 1925)

Kurtz, Harold, *The Trial of Marshal Ney* (London, 1957)

Laffin, John, *Tommy Atkins* (London, 1966)

Landsheit, Morbert, *The Hussar Sergeant,* (London, 1837)

Lanfrey, P., *The History of Napoleon the First* (London & New York, 1871)

Las Cases, *Mémorial de Sainte-Hélène* (London, 1823)

Lavallette, Count, *Memoirs* (London, 1831)

Lavallette, *The Adventurous Life of Count Lavallette* by Himself (London 1937)

Leveson-Gower, Lord Granville, first Earl Granville, *Private Correspondence, 1781–1821,* edited by Castalia Countess Granville (London, 1916)

Lillie, Lt-Col. Sir J, *Narrative of the Campaigns of the Loyal Lusitanian Legion under Brigadier-General Sir Robert Wilson* (London, 1812)

Longford, Elizabeth, *Wellington* (London, 1969)

Mayne *Narrative of the Campaigns of the Loyal Lusitanian Legion*

Napier, Col. William, *History of the War in the Peninsula and the South of France* (London, 1834–42)

Nicolson, Harold, *The Congress of Vienna* (London, 1946)

Nouvelle Biographie Générale (Paris, 1866)

Oman, Sir Charles, *History of the Peninsular War* (Oxford, 1902–22)

Palmer, Alan, *Alexander I* (London, 1974)

Priestley, J.B., *The Prince of Pleasure* (London, 1969)

Quarterly Review, vol. XIX, 1818

Ridley, Jasper, *Lord Palmerston* (London, 1970)

Russell, Lord John, *Early Correspondence of Lord John Russell,* edited by Rollo Russell (London, 1913)

Ségur, le Général Comte de, *Histoire de Napoléon et de la Grande Armée pendant l'année 1812* (Paris 1825)

Stanhope, John Spencer, *Memoirs of Anna Wilhelmina Pickering together with extracts from the Journals of her Father, John Spencer Stanhope* (London)

Stewart, Sir Charles, Lord Londonderry, *Narrative of the Peninsular War* (London, 1808–13)

Tarle, Eugene, *Napoleon's Invasion of Russia,* translated by G. M. (London, 1942)

Temperley, H. M. V., *Life of Canning* (London, 1905)

Texeira Botelho, J. J., *Historia Popular da Guerra da Peninsula* (Oporto, 1915)

Trevelyan, G. M., *Lord Grey of the Reform Bill* (London, 1920)

Vandal, A., *Napoléon et Alexandre* (Paris, 1891)

Walmsley, Robert, *Peterloo: the case reopened* (Manchester, 1969)

Ward, John William, Earl of Dudley, *Letters to the Bishop of Llandaff* (London, 1840)

Webster, C. K., *The Foreign Policy of Castlereagh, 1815–22* (London, 1925)

Werry, F. P., *Personal Memoirs and Letters* (London, 1861)

White, T. H., *The Age of Scandal* (London, 1950)

Index